Rights to Fair Treatment

A practical study to develop new rights for people seeking health or social care

Ian Bynoe

I??R

INSTITUTE FOR PUBLIC POLICY RESEARCH

Acknowledgements

The Institute for Public Policy Research wishes to thank the Nuffield Foundation for funding this research and each of the organisations for collaborating so fully with the study. Without the interest, co-operation and support of numerous individuals and organisations – staff, service users and local groups – none of the pilot projects could have been contemplated, let alone introduced. We thank you all and hope you find this report does justice to our mutual efforts.

Particularly in its early stages, the project was aided by the valuable suggestions and support of an expert Advisory Group. We are grateful to Terry Bamford, Francine Bates, Jonathan Boyce, Mike Fisher, Denis Galligan, Colin Low and Fidelma Winkler for the time and advice which they so freely gave to us.

The idea for this work was Anna Coote's and her direction, ideas, encouragement and editorial advice have been indispensable. The author also thanks Lucy Delap for her research assistance, particularly with interviews.

The views and proposals published in this document are those of the author. They are not necessarily endorsed by the IPPR, its staff or trustees.

About the author

Ian Bynoe is a part time IPPR Research Fellow specialising in social and human rights. A solicitor who has worked in law centres and in private practice, he was legal director of MIND from 1990-1994. He was the co-author of *Equal Rights for Disabled People* (1991) IPPR and wrote IPPR's report on the future of the Citizen's Charter, *Beyond the Citizen's Charter* (1996). He also provides legal and practice training to local authorities and NHS Trusts on disability, health and social services law.

Contents

Summary

This report describes a new rights-based approach to the provision of public services. It is based on IPPR's collaborative work with four organisations providing health and social care, which aimed to find practical ways of giving service users new "rights" to fair treatment. The following key issues are addressed:

● What is the purpose of rights to fair treatment and how far do they make a difference to service users?

● What obstacles are likely to arise in different service areas and how, if at all, can these be overcome?

● What are the broader implications of a rights-based approach to public services?

Introduction

The work described in this report focuses on fair treatment in the process by which individuals seek and obtain services, rather than with the substantive services or benefits they may eventually receive. Rights to fair treatment are based on principles recognised in the developing common law, in standards of good public administration, and in some specific legislation. They recognise that people should be able to:

● know the criteria by which they are judged eligible for a service

● have their views taken into account in deciding about access or planning provision to meet their needs

● expect that decisions are fair and unbiased

● receive clear reasons for decisions taken about them

● have a decision reviewed if they object to it

● expect redress if rights are not enforced.

Why are rights important now?

Those trying to deliver public services generally have three different and sometimes conflicting objectives:

- To meet needs with finite resources

- To ensure equally appropriate treatment for all, according to need

- To promote individual autonomy and choice

Fair treatment rights offer a means of pursuing these aims and reconciling them as far as possible. They can help to ensure that individuals are fully informed about eligibility criteria and the extent and limits of available services, and that there are fair procedures so that all are treated without bias or prejudice.

More generally, the idea of rights within public services has gained ground with the shift in Welfare State philosophy away from paternalism and towards autonomy, independence and social participation; with the new consumerism manifested in the Citizen's Charter; a new trend towards judicial interventionism; new roles for public audit and inspection; and problems of scarcity and rationing.

The pilot projects
Over two years (1994–6), IPPR worked with four very different organisations to develop and pilot new rights to fair treatment in the following service areas:

- access to community care services in a London borough ("London Borough")

- services for young people leaving local authority care in a city in Northern England ("City Council")

- eye treatment provided by the ophthalmology department of an NHS trust in North-West England ("the Hospital")

- services provided by an out-of-hours GPs' co-operative in South-East England ("the Co-op")

Project One: Community care in a London borough

This focused on access to community care services, in particular: rights to information on eligibility, fair assessment procedures, and information for service users about the outcome of an assessment.

Initial research included consultations with users, carers, front-line staff and managers. It was found that principles of fair treatment were not well established in the borough; such rights and procedures as existed to support fair treatment were not widely known or advertised, nor were they consistently applied. Levels of information to the public about eligibility, services available and reasons for decisions were unacceptably low. Poor levels of administrative support made it more difficult for staff to pursue rigorous paper-based procedures, and communications with clients were mainly verbal and informal. Drawing on this research three pilot projects were set up, in which IPPR worked with London Borough to develop procedures and supporting documentation, to introduce new rights for service users.

Personal Care pilot
This aimed to test the feasibility of giving applicants for personal care clear information about eligibility criteria. It involved issuing a list of criteria, an accompanying leaflet for users and carers, and a written procedure for care management staff. These were drawn up in consultation with senior managers, frontline staff and service users, carers and their advocates. The documents were piloted in 50 assessments and their use was evaluated through questionnaires and interviews with staff, users and carers.

In the development stage, users and carers strongly supported the provision of clear information about eligibility, but few of those interviewed after the pilot assessments said that it had made a difference and some were unaware that anything had changed. For the local carers' organisation it represented an improvement in the borough's practice, but would have a limited effect because it did not help individuals find out about levels of service, only about their basic eligibility. Care managers observed that it helped them clarify reasons for their decisions, but many found the eligibility criteria too vague, incomplete and supplied too late in the assessment process. Senior managers supported the approach and saw it as helping them to allocate finite resources on an equitable basis. Indeed, they introduced the pilot eligibility criteria throughout the borough's service. All staff felt that the information on eligibility could be made more widely available to the public and at an earlier stage in their contact with staff.

Disabled Persons pilot
This aimed to test the effect of proactively advising disabled people of their statutory right to request an assessment for services, such as practical assistance in their home. It involved procedural guidance for participating staff, and a standard letter to identified disabled people accompanied by a standard form for requesting an assessment. The letter and form were sent to individuals who defined themselves as disabled by applying to the borough for a concessionary travel pass.

Managers initially expressed fears about the project generating a high volume of demand. In practice, during the pilot period very few people applied for the relevant travel pass and were therefore sent the letter and form. Of these only one in 10 was prompted to apply for a care assessment. Others were already receiving care or took no action. The pilot demonstrated that managers' fears were unfounded and gave them confidence to consider embarking on a similar scheme in the future.

Care Plan pilot
This aimed to provide written information to people who had been assessed about the results of the process, including reasons for decisions and details of the frequency and level of any services to be provided. It involved standard letters to those refused and offered a service, a Care Plan with a matrix detailing services offered, and a written procedure for care managers.

Pressures from central Government, the Audit Commission and the Social Services Inspectorate encouraged senior managers to embark on the project. Front-line staff were concerned about the administrative burden. Many said it reflected their current practice and merely obliged them to write it down. Some were anxious about the legal consequences of recording their decisions in cases where applicants disagreed. All were concerned about the difficult trade-offs between loose, informal communications which may breed uncertainty and unfairness, and more formal paper-based procedures which may avoid these problems but appear too rigid and daunting.

The pilot ran for 50 assessments and was evaluated through interviews with senior managers, frontline staff, users, carers and advocates. Feedback from the local carers' organisation was highly favourable. Most users and carers appeared not to notice that anything had changed. Staff resented the extra administration and feared the consequences of committing themselves to paper, but appreciated the way in which the procedure clarified the basis on which decisions were made and where responsibility lay. Senior managers signalled their approval by introducing throughout the borough a Care Plan and matrix based on the one piloted.

Lessons from the London Borough pilots

- Introducing fair treatment rights was made easier by the fact that the organisation had a clear command structure and already used procedural guidance to set standards and provide information.

- The professional culture of social work was not obviously amenable to a rights-based approach; managers were reluctant to insist on compliance with highly prescriptive guidance; front line staff habitually communicated with service users informally and verbally.

- There were strong incentives for senior management to move towards a rights-based approach, mainly arising from government-led initiatives to improve procedures and from pressure on resources. Rights-based procedures could help authorities cope with new Community Care Charter requirements, by encouraging better respect for the entitlements of service users, better administrative practice and by encouraging staff to think more carefully about how and why they took decisions.

- Fair treatment rights were more readily appreciated by the local carers' group than by individual users or carers; and more by senior managers than by front-line staff.

- An important advantage of new procedural rights for care managers was that they could clarify the basis on which decisions were taken and indicate where responsibility lay.

- The main danger, from managers' point of view, was that it made it easier for their decisions to be challenged. At a time of reducing budgets and service contraction, this could be particularly difficult. However, managers' fears that providing more information to potential users would lead to escalating demands may be unfounded.

- Administrative systems were woefully inadequate to support a more formal rights-based approach; more administrative support, higher levels of IT and appropriate training would be needed to enable staff to work effectively within a rights-based approach.

- Rights to information about eligibility were of limited use without rights to information about levels and types of services available.

- Many users and potential users, eg. those with learning difficulties and confused older people, would gain few tangible benefits from new rights to information without appropriate help. Full implementation of the 1986 Disabled Persons Act would require local authorities to appoint independent advocates in such circumstances.

• A rights-based approach would founder unless steps were taken to encourage full compliance in every case where it was promised. Partial enforcement of rights undermined the principle of fair treatment.

Project Two: City Council services for Care Leavers

In this project we aimed to design, with social work staff, young people and others, practical changes to City Council's policy and procedures. These would ensure fairer and more open decisions about the planning and provision of help to young people after leaving the authority's care.

During initial research we interviewed young people in care and those who had recently left it, residential and field social workers, foster carers and local organisations. A consistent picture emerged of a service failing to fulfil the expectations of the Children Act 1989: central policy and procedures had not been introduced; planning practice was outdated, inconsistent and hugely varied; forms were inappropriate and counter-productive; financial help was inequitably distributed. Few staff knew what services or assistance care leavers were entitled to. Young people, foster carers and local organisations were in even greater ignorance of what was available.

Financial Assistance pilot

This aimed to introduce a written policy and procedure to determine when care leavers would be entitled to financial assistance under the Children Act 1989. Not only would this help to inform young people of their rights, it would also encourage fairer decision-making and accountability for decisions taken. Draft documents were circulated to staff and local organisations. Local groups – particularly the children's rights service – strongly supported this pilot. However, there was insufficient time to develop it beyond this stage.

15+ pilot

The aim was to adapt the authority's existing documents for statutory reviews of young people in care to the particular needs of those aged 15+, many of whom would soon leave care. We drafted three documents: a new procedure which included an "issues list" and an Action Plan, an

Information Leaflet and Contribution Sheet. The last two documents were produced at a workshop with a group of care leavers and young people in care. An integral part of the new procedure was an offer to the young person of advice and representation from the local children's rights service. After consultation, we tested the documents in statutory reviews chaired by two managers over four months, then interviewed managers, social workers, residential staff and the children's rights service. The contribution sheet and the offer of advocacy appeared to have been positively welcomed and to have encouraged greater participation by the young people. The issues list focused discussions and highlighted the need for advance planning. The Action Plan created problems for those chairing the reviews; copies were not circulated as required by the procedure, which meant they were of little practical use.

Lessons from the City Council pilots

- Important new policy and procedures to implement the Children Act had not been introduced into the service and the rights of care leavers were therefore being ignored or only partly respected.

- The authority's "laissez-faire" approach to professional practice and its decentralised organisation had strongly militated against a rights-based approach to fair treatment and equity in service provision.

- Information on entitlements, though essential to potential claimants, tended to be anecdotal and was not based on departmental policy or any information strategy.

- Basic administrative efficiency and compliance with procedures remained a low priority in the authority, with important forms remaining unchanged despite the Children Act changes in 1991.

- New rights might have been introduced sooner if the authority had been more responsive to what care leavers themselves could tell of their experience during and after leaving care and of their struggle to live independently.

- Support and advocacy for young people in care could play an important role in the review process. A young person's taking up of the offer of independent help depends upon staff encouragement and approval.

Project Three: Eye treatment in a Hospital

In the Hospital we worked with staff in the Ophthalmology Directorate on three projects. These aimed to improve a patient's right to obtain information; to improve respect for patient choice and render decisions on listing for surgery fairer and more open.

Initial investigations showed that the Directorate had no systematic means of determining what were patients' rights and responsibilities, or how patients could be informed of them. Formal procedures were little used and it was therefore difficult to identify administrative standards which patients could expect from the Directorate. There was no comprehensive approach to supplying information to patients, and there were significant variations in listing practice between the different consultants. In the light of these findings we developed three practical projects.

Patient Pathways pilot

With this we aimed to map out and agree a comprehensive and accurate account of what one consultant's patients could expect from the service when treated for a cataract. We would link descriptions of the clinical and administrative stages in the "treatment pathway" with clear references to a patient's right to information, choice and equity. The patient's responsibilities would also be included. After drafting the pathway document we checked its accuracy and relevance by discussing it with two groups of recently treated patients, gaining important feedback. The project ended with the Directorate considering the possibility of developing a Directorate wide pathway. Those involved in the project told us afterwards that it had helped them begin the process of defining the standards of the Directorate's services and testing these against their patients' experiences.

Prompt List pilot

With this pilot we aimed to improve the chances of an anxious or inarticulate patient receiving accurate and comprehensive information when they saw medical or nursing staff for an appointment. Following a survey of patients, a list of questions commonly asked by patients was drafted and sent to those attending a pre-operative assessment inviting them to use this to ask questions of the doctor or nurse. We then surveyed attitudes to the list among those who had received it and those who had not done so. The Prompt List had proved a straightforward and simple change to introduce. Feedback from patients demonstrated its value, particularly to those who were anxious. The Directorate continues to use the List in practice.

Wait-listing pilot

This aimed to improve the patient's experience of waiting for surgical treatment by making listing decisions fairer and more open, and explicitly acknowledging the choices available to patients. In one consultant's practice, wait-listing guidelines were drafted and agreed, patients' views were canvassed by telephone and a new letter and information leaflet was issued to patients at their out-patients' appointment. Shortly after the Wait-listing pilot ended, all the Directorate's consultants adopted the guidelines in their practice and now supply the information letter and leaflet to their patients. The Directorate's Admissions Officer reported a noticeable increase in telephone contact with patients and greater consistency in listing practice. The information leaflet and letter, suitably adapted, are now being introduced in other Directorates in the Hospital.

Lessons from the Hospital pilots

• Each of the projects was judged by hospital staff to have been of positive benefit, with potential for use elsewhere in the Hospital. Procedural rights are clearly relevant to hospital settings.

• Despite this clear progress, the research confirmed how the Directorate's professional culture and organisation could inhibit the development of patients' rights.

• Rights-based approaches depend on commonly accepted standards and collective commitments. Effective communication requires priority to be given to competent and responsive administration in the busy hospital setting.The absence of any Hospital Board policy on key rights for patients meant there was little incentive for the Directorate to give rights a higher priority. The Directorate, like other parts of the NHS, seldom used written procedures and so had not developed any familiarity with this way of working.

• The research also showed the crucial importance, when developing such rights-based work, of involving patients in a continuous process of feedback and consultation to ensure changes are relevant, useful and effective. The Directorate had very little experience of developing such partnerships with patients and no formal structures for encouraging the patient voice to be heard.

• Conventional ideas about clinical freedom hindered the work initially since these tended to favour doctors' independence over the pursuit of commonly agreed standards. The impact of the projects was greatly enhanced by the creation within the Directorate of a new Admissions Officer post. This new member of staff was able to provide detailed information on listing decisions to patients and their relatives. Without this resource available to them, patients' expectations of fair treatment and clear information could well have gone unfulfilled.

Project Four: Out-of-hours services from a GPs' Co-operative

In this project we worked with a co-operative of NHS GPs providing out-of-hours services (telephone advice, home visits and Co-op base consultations). The project focused on the factors which a doctor would regard as relevant when deciding whether or not to visit a patient at home or to invite them to come to the Co-op base to be seen. We aimed to ensure such decisions were fair and open.

We investigated the legal framework for medical decision-making, including recent changes in the GP's contract and the Co-op's intention to reduce home visiting and increase attendances by patients at the base. The Co-op's directors suggested that guidelines on the social factors, if any, relevant to such decisions would be helpful.

The Home Visits pilot
We surveyed the views of participating GPs and found that many believed patients should be seen at the base not at home. The survey showed doctors thought many home visits were made for social reasons, such as the need for transport, rather than for clinical considerations. The Family Health Services Authority convened a meeting, proposing that guidelines be produced for use by the co-ops in its area. The first meeting rejected this suggestion but a second meeting agreed that a pro forma document would be useful. We drafted such a form, together with explanatory notes, but the Co-op's Council declined to pilot them and the project was abandoned.

The Community Health Council and the Family Health Services Authority supported the piloting of the pro forma and believed it would contribute to greater fairness in decisions about home visiting. They both fully accepted that some patients' circumstances required telephone advice or a consultation at the base not a visit from the doctor at home. Despite his earlier support for the project, after seeing the draft documents, the Co-op's Director decided that the approach would be unworkable and ineffective. He accepted that some patients' access to the service would be affected if the majority of patients were to be asked to attend the base, but suggested the problem should be solved by providing a transport service or a carer to those with responsibility for dependants. A paper-based system would not in his view be practicable.

Lessons from the pilot

● The proposed pilot was controversial because it sought to advise GPs what to do and proposed a uniform approach to recording decisions about home visiting. Even if the Co-op had been willing to pilot this, it was difficult to see how rights could be linked to it. Individual GPs working for the Co-op retained their legal and clinical independence and could not be advised or instructed on what was fair or unfair practice, or what factors should or should not be regarded as relevant to their decisions.

● Problems arose because the amendments to the GPs' legal contract were ambiguous and their precise effect uncertain. Doctors received conflicting advice from the British Medical Association and their insurers. Such difficulties could not be resolved by a voluntary paper-based administrative procedure – the law would need to be changed to make policy aims clearer and to define the respective rights and responsibilities of doctors and patients.

● Doctors saw no incentive to introduce the pilot. Many felt that it would make their position worse. In contrast, the Family Health Services Authority considered the pro forma provided as much protection for the doctor as it did for the patient. Doctors might have found the procedure more useful if, in future, home visits were to be more systematically discouraged and if patients complained this was unfair. Financial incentives might have to be linked to completion of documents such as the pro forma for GPs to regard them as being worth the time and trouble.

Conclusions and recommendations

● Rising consumer expectations, increasing inequalities in the availability of public services and failing public confidence in public sector decision-makers all strengthen the case for procedural rights to fair treatment.

● Rights to fair treatment are not just about meeting consumer demands. They help to promote publicly accountable organisations and just dealing between citizens. They may achieve this by improving the flow of information between organisations and individuals, encouraging user participation, and ensuring fair and open decision-making. They may also help to clarify the location of responsibilities within public services and to build public confidence in the way they are run.

- Providers wishing to target resources on those with greatest needs and to ensure that services are delivered equitably may find this approach especially useful.

- The pilots suggested that it would not be difficult to find provider organisations willing to develop feasible projects in similar settings. Procedures do not have to be excessively bureaucratic although high standards of administration are necessary if procedural rights are to be effectively implemented.

- The main barriers to introducing new rights were: inadequately specified services; poor information on criteria and standards; the unfamiliarity of most organisations with the concept of rights; organisational resistance to consistent enforcement; entrenched professional cultures favouring autonomous rather than collective decision-making.

- If the aim is to raise standards of fair treatment in public services, it is recommended that the views of the public are sought to audit practice and develop policy; independent advice and assistance should be available when needed; a new model of partnership should be developed between the provider and service user, based on openness, consistency and a willingness to work collectively.

- Social care organisations are more amenable than health services to the idea of rights for users. They are subject to more intense financial pressures, not bound by the conventions of clinical autonomy, and more exposed to external monitoring and inspection. However, the research suggests that procedural rights are no less important in health than in social care. Both must ensure that services reach only those who really need them and are equitably distributed in ways which can command public confidence.

- Changes anticipated after the election of a new Government in 1997 strengthen the case for introducing new fair treatment rights: these include a revised Patient's Charter and a new Long-Term Care Charter.

● If fair treatment is to be a right, not simply a privilege, it will be necessary to find ways of giving it higher status in health and social care. This may require the introduction of new statutory codes or, where appropriate, the development of a new public service guarantee.

● Implementation of new rights will need vigorous monitoring through bodies such as the Social Services Inspectorate and the Audit Commission and/or ombudsman systems, possibly with extended powers to investigate systemic unfairness or maladministration.

1. Introduction

General aims

This report describes a unique experiment in the development of a new rights-based approach to health and social care. During 1994-1996 IPPR undertook practical research with four organisations in England that provide health services or social care. Two local social services authorities, an NHS Trust and a co-operative of GPs providing out-of-hours medical services each collaborated in the study. In these different settings, we planned how the provider organisation might introduce and pilot new "rights" for service users. By the end of the work, many of our ideas had been thoroughly tested and in two organisations new rights appeared to be permanently established.

The ways in which this research was undertaken – and its results – offer useful insights into developing a rights-based approach to public service. It built on and tested ideas already outlined in theory in IPPR's report *The Welfare of Citizens: Developing new social rights.*[1] Such lessons will be of interest to policy makers, service managers, practitioners and organisations representing users.

Substantive or procedural rights

Given its context, the project was broadly concerned with "social rights". This term can be used to mean one of two types of individual entitlement: a substantive or a procedural one. The first defines an actual benefit or service provided by a public authority. This may be, for example, an income payment to replace wages lost through disability; or an out-of-hours home visit from a GP; or the provision of personal assistance in the home to someone who is disabled. Though the conditions and criteria which qualify someone for such a service or benefit differ greatly, each is an example of a substantive social right.

Procedural rights, on the other hand, focus not on what someone may obtain but how they may do so. These are the focus for our research. Our interest in them acknowledges how often people using services lack personal power, information or appropriate expertise. Such rights are designed to ensure that someone applying for or using a particular benefit or service is treated fairly and justly during that process. They are based on principles recognised in the developing common law, in standards of good public administration and, where they have been expressly introduced, in specific legislation. They can be applied in a great range of situations: to services which are universal as well as those which are selective; to those which are needs-based together with those available without proof of need; and where services are voluntary, such as an operation to remove cataracts, or involuntary, such as psychiatric treatment for a detained patient.

Procedural rights have tangible worth to anyone needing a public service. Without them, services can be denied unfairly, choice restricted, resources inequitably distributed and someone's legitimate grievance ignored. They will have a special importance where entitlement to a service is selective – where there are losers as well as winners – for they can strongly influence the relationship which members of the public have with those who deliver such benefits or services. The following examples illustrate the principles on which procedural rights are based.

Finding out: eligibility

With most benefits or services the onus is upon the public to seek out what may be their entitlement and to apply for it. If people are uninformed as to who is or is not eligible to receive help, access will always be easier for those who are more confident, articulate and skilled in pursuing their rights. Those less able to do this will face an unfair disadvantage. The eligibility principle promotes the idea that those who provide services should take positive steps to publish such information and encourage in the public an accurate understanding of eligibility and the ways in which services can be obtained. A number of "rights" can be linked to the idea and various methods used to introduce them. Some are defined in law. Others are written into guidance, administrative procedures, Codes or Charters. Publishing standards or criteria for the service, producing easy-to-read guides or leaflets about services and how to obtain them, or funding advice and advocacy services are all ways which can be employed to support the principle.

Being heard

Many public services are only allocated to those who have demonstrated their need for them. Even when eligibility has been established, some services must be tailored to a person's particular situation or be designed to meet their stated preferences or choices. For this to happen, individuals must at the very least be consulted about their circumstances and wishes and have their views taken into account. Sometimes, only an approach which secures a person's full participation will guarantee a suitable and effective outcome. Then the person must be drawn fully into the decision-making process. The principle of being heard highlights rights to consultation and participation, acknowledging that unless these are made explicit, some people will face severe disadvantages in ensuring services are responsive and suitable. Where there is no legislation requiring consultation, provider organisations can adopt a range of methods to implement the principle. In their administrative procedures they can acknowledge their duty to consult – and act upon it. They can take positive steps to encourage the public to be aware of the importance of consultation and their role in it, and to assist people wishing to participate in the decision-making process. Documents can be drafted in such a way as to elicit the clear views of those for whom decisions are being taken; positive steps can be taken to provide an advocate, a representative or "friend" for someone wanting support and help in putting across their circumstances and wishes.

Fair decision-making

Fairness has to be an essential objective for those taking decisions about entitlement to benefits and services provided at public expense and according to politically determined priorities. The public has a right to expect that this principle – requiring far more than mere courtesy or sensitivity – will be respected in a variety of ways. Thus, decisions should not be unfairly biased and should not take into account considerations which are irrelevant. By the same token, they should take into account all factors which are relevant to issues of eligibility and in particular any which specifically relate to published rules or standards which set out the parameters for those deciding who is or is not entitled. The principle encourages consistency in approach and equity in outcome. It will be seen to be respected where decision-makers are clearly guided in the matters relevant to their decision, are conscious of the limits of their discretion and are able fully to weigh up all the factors needed to contribute to a fair determination. Practical steps can be taken to "structure" the ways in which discretionary decisions are made, highlighting factors relevant to the decision and, specifically or by implication, showing what considerations will be irrelevant. Guidelines, Codes, protocols or pro forma documentation can all be used for this purpose. There are many examples of such approaches being used.

Finding out: reasons

Discovering the reason or reasons for a decision on entitlement could be fundamental to someone's perception of their treatment and whether or not it has been fair. This will particularly affect anyone whose own view of their needs is not reflected in the decision taken. For example, they may have been refused a service or benefit altogether or offered less than they asked for or told they will have to wait to obtain it. Without knowing the reasons for a decision, individuals will not be able to check their own grounds against any published criteria or standards. It is essential for the decision-maker to provide reasons if someone is to discover faulty decision-making and have any chance of correcting it. Across the range of different public services, practice is patchy and often poor. Often reasons remain secret or are only poorly explained. Many measures can be taken to encourage more open decision-making, in addition to supplying the person affected with a formal written record of the reasons for a decision.

Reviewing refusal

For any decision-making process to be fair it must also provide someone who objects to a decision with a right to have this reviewed. This is the last of our core procedural rights. A review or appeal should ideally be independent of the provider. At the very least, its outcome should include a fresh consideration of the person's entitlement and the possibility of a new decision. This principle is reflected in a range of procedures encountered in public services. Some are highly formal appeal systems, connecting at their summit with the judicial system. Many others are far less formal, relying instead on internal complaints procedures which may lack the essential element of independence. There is now a growing literature on the public services' experience with handling complaints and the essential requirements for an effective and authoritative system.[2]

Guarantees not targets

By their very nature, rights differ from lesser promises or commitments given by those providing public services, such as administrative standards, targets, even guarantees. The distinctions have been fully described and illustrated in IPPR's report *Beyond the Citizen's Charter*.[3] More than best practice is involved when people are provided with "rights". When this term is used it indicates that the obligations in question have been accepted as mandatory: refusing or neglecting to respect them should provide, at least, an opportunity for redress and, at most, some means of enforcement by recourse to independent adjudication.

Throughout the report, this is how we have interpreted the concept of rights and sought to test it in practice. The pilot procedures have been planned and run as though they were providing new rights for the public and for service users. And in our evaluation of their usefulness, we consider what might result if service providers are required to make such provision.

Why rights and why now?

During the research we aimed to take some or all of the above principles and design pilot projects around them, creating new rights for the public and for service users which they had not enjoyed before. From the outset the task was a difficult and complex one. Collaborating with service providers required us to understand their organisations and systems, designing proposals which were achievable and fitted with their own priorities. We had to do so without diluting those robust principles of fair treatment that were the point of the study. The report describes the difficulties which we and our partner organisations experienced in attempting to bridge the gap between theory and practice, as well as our achievements.

The fact that our work was beset with difficulties does not detract from the relevance of this study which, as time passed, increased rather than diminished. From 1994 onwards there was evidence of a growing interest from policy makers and voluntary organisations in finding more room for a rights-based approach to health and social care.[4] Developments which occurred during the research, including the creation by Government of new procedural rights and expectations, confirmed the importance of the questions we were addressing.

Before we describe our work with each partner organisation we will outline the principal factors which have combined to give the idea of rights within public services a higher profile and a harder edge. They are the following:

● human rights and a new language of entitlement

● consumerism and new methods of standard setting

● legal rights and judicial interventionism

● new roles for public audit and inspection

● scarcity and the need to ration

Human rights and a new language of entitlement

Demands for rights to health services or to social care – particularly when these are seen to be at risk – are now often understood or expressed in the language of human rights not simply as social entitlements. To some extent this may reflect public attitudes towards services which are now perceived to be essential to contemporary standards of living.[5] It may also signal a changing emphasis in Welfare State philosophy away from paternalistic notions towards ideas such as rights to autonomy, to independence and to social participation. Drawing on ideas and standards, many now promoted at an international level, rights campaigners and even the authors of Government guidance increasingly refer to social values such as autonomy, participation, choice and dignity in terms of individual human rights requiring respect.[6]

Such thinking increases expectations that services will be available and be reliably and fairly delivered to those who need them, whatever the cost. It fuels dissatisfaction with any unequal distribution of resources and services and inequitable treatment for people with the same or similar needs.

Consumerism and new methods of standard setting
The growth of individual consumerism has obliged health and social care providers to recognise and adapt to "rights" based approaches to delivering their services. Since the 1960s a new and popular philosophy has driven up public expectations of quality and choice in public as well as private sector settings. Public service providers, some faster than others, have had to abandon or adapt traditional attitudes and ways of working to cope with a more critical and demanding public. Consumer organisations, advocating the interests of particular groups of service users and pressing for better standards, have multiplied at a national and local level. Some have been formed from or are controlled by service users themselves.

Government policy has reinforced these trends with its Citizen's Charter initiative in operation since 1991.[7] This programme has required provider organisations to set and publish information on standards and performance usually in service charter documents. Providers have also had to improve how they consult users and how they handle complaints about the service. The published standards we refer to define not only substantive services but also standards of administrative treatment. Fair treatment and procedural rights have therefore acquired a new prominence as a result of this initiative.

Charterism has affected all of the services involved in the research project. Since 1991, a Patient's Charter has set out national minimum guarantees and standards for a range of NHS services. NHS Trusts and GPs are meant to add to these with their own commitments in hospital and practice charters. An administrative Code on Openness in the NHS now offers modest rights to information, monitored by the Health Service Commissioner.[8] Local authority Social Services Departments are also required to publish a local charter for community care services.[9] Some authorities have done this for services to children and young people. In both health and social services, wide-ranging changes have been introduced to the procedures by which complaints are received, investigated and resolved.

New legal rights and judicial interventionism

There are clear examples in recent Government policy of its acceptance that public concerns about fair treatment and respect for rights sometimes justifies the creation of new legal duties and rights. The message from these examples is that law may have a useful role to play in guaranteeing fair treatment and the fulfilment of policy aims.

During the course of this research project, and resulting from long-standing and effective parliamentary campaigns, legislation has introduced important new rights for those receiving community care. Disability groups pressed Government to allow disabled people to receive direct payments from which to purchase care services and personal assistance. From 1 April 1997 the law will have changed to enable this to happen.[10] Carers persuaded Government to support legal changes which, since April 1996, have required assessments by local social services authorities of their needs for community care services not just the needs of the person for whom they provide care.[11]

Earlier, the ways in which local authorities provided for meeting special educational needs was fundamentally reformed. Parents acquired new appeal rights, and a highly detailed statutory Code of Practice was introduced together with legal regulations prescribing in clear terms the procedural duties of schools and local education authorities.[12] There are already signs that these changes are causing providers to have to make greater provision for these needs than under the previous arrangements.[13]

Developments in the courts are also influencing the ways in which social entitlements are framed and delivered, emphasising the importance of fair treatment within administrative systems. There are signs that the courts are now more willing than in the past to review decisions taken by health or social care providers. Social services authorities, particularly, have found themselves the target of recent litigation, most of it directed to challenging the outcome of assessment decisions. In a series of cases following introduction of the Children Act 1989 and the NHS and Community Care Act 1990 the courts have set minimum standards of procedural rights particularly in regard to the thorough and impartial assessment of needs and the provision of choice to service users.[14] Recent litigation on patients' rights has highlighted the role of consent in medical treatment and the protection which this gives to someone who resists a particular form of treatment or is denied adequate information about its possible consequences.[15] Treating the service user fairly was a central argument in each of these examples, with judges establishing legal standards to be recognised and applied by service providers.

New roles for public audit and inspection

The drive for better quality in public services has been accompanied by an ever-increasing emphasis on efficiency and the measurement of operational performance. Inspectorial and public audit bodies have been created or adapted to this task.[16] These developments have affected the ability of providers to publish and deliver clear commitments to the public and to service users.

Within the NHS, the Audit Commission now plays a prominent role in investigating and promoting best practice standards through its national studies and follow up work in individual Trusts and Health Authorities. The Commission and the Social Services Inspectorate together monitor the performance of local social services authorities and have recently begun more rigorous "whole service" inspections of individual authorities.

Changes linked to the Citizen's Charter now require the Audit Commission to define indicators of local authority activity and direct authorities to collect data to demonstrate their performance against each of these indicators.[17] A number of indicators cover social services and each authority is now required to gather data on the scope and level of activity for annual publication in league tables alongside other authorities.[18] NHS Trusts (particularly hospitals) are obliged to gather similar information on their performance against Citizen's Charter indicators and comparative data is published annually.[19]

Changes like these, strongly linked to managerial methods such as Total Quality Management, have been highly controversial and have sometimes missed their targets and distorted outcomes.[20] Nevertheless they have begun to have some positive effects.[21] Service managers, for example, now need to have a far clearer picture of what their services actually comprise (inputs) and what these deliver (outputs). It has encouraged the drawing up and monitoring of written standards of service, in many settings for the first time ever. The Audit Commission's influence, at least in theory, can penetrate far into the managerial systems operating local authority services. Below we show how this influenced even the details of one of the pilot projects we introduced.[22]

Although the Audit Commission has generally resisted defining national minimum standards of service, the Social Services Inspectorate in its reports of inspections has promoted the view that there are core standards for providers to introduce and maintain. For example, the SSI was closely involved in designing and promoting national standards of provision for care leavers – directly relevant to our work in one pilot project.

Scarcity and rationing

There are clearly other reasons prompting more interest in rights and in entitlement – arising when conventional notions of the Welfare State are constantly challenged.[23] This happens both at the level of policy, where there are calls for "fundamental reform", and in the harsh experience of many service users, refused help or required to wait excessive periods before receiving it.

In the long term we may be witnessing a retreat from universal state provision based on citizenship and a new emphasis on notions of individual responsibility, partnership and self-help.[24] Even if core entitlements are to remain guaranteed, flexibility – fewer substantive rights not more of them – could become the defining feature of new welfare arrangements. This will be all the more likely so long as public resources remain limited or actually reduce in proportion to society's growing needs.

Procedural rights may have an essential role to play in guaranteeing fair treatment when services have to be rationed by limiting entitlement or delaying provision.[25] Much of what we describe in the report demonstrates this point. The recent introduction of written criteria for long term care in the NHS also illustrates it.[26] Agreeing such criteria with social services authorities has been a critical step in the NHS's withdrawal from routinely providing nursing care to those with chronic but stable medical conditions. In an unprecedented step, health authorities have now been required publicly to specify who will or will not be able to obtain treatment from their local health service. The innovation signals the contraction and targeting of the service, not its expansion to meet growing demands at public expense. New rights for patients to information and to appeal against the refusal of continuing care to an independent panel[27] will not permit them to reopen questions of policy or resource allocation. However, it will enable them to challenge wrong decisions or failures in procedure; these are important considerations if the public is to regard as fair the ways in which the services are actually delivered.

In social services authorities, which have assumed the main responsibility for community care, eligibility criteria are used for a similar purpose.[28] Ever growing demands for care require more and more priority setting and targeting. As eligibility criteria are made tighter, so the threshold for qualifying for services becomes harder and harder to meet. Fair treatment for the public and service users becomes increasingly important – with the case for clear rights becoming more and more compelling.

These were some of the trends which have shaped the context for our research and given it relevance. How did we set up the project and secure the interest and co-operation of the collaborating organisations?

Methods

Though there were many differences between the collaborating organisations and in the ways in which we worked with them, our approach was along broadly the same lines. Clearly, none of these projects could create new legal rights where none already existed. Any changes that we proposed had to be compatible with existing legal, professional and administrative frameworks within which services were delivered.

To begin with, we therefore analysed the role which procedural rights currently played in the ways that each organisation provided its services. What policies and procedures gave rights to the public and to service users and how did these operate in practice? Next, we suggested how users' rights to fair treatment might be enhanced by introducing new procedures or adapting existing ones. During this process we sought to ensure that our proposals enjoyed the support of those using the service and/or their representatives by careful consultation with user groups and voluntary organisations.

Where the provider agreed to proceed on the basis of our proposals, it then introduced and piloted the new arrangements and, after the pilots ended, IPPR evaluated their effects.

The provider organisations
A number of factors influenced our choice of organisations with which to collaborate on the study. The research concentrated on services providing health or social care. In order to include a range of different services and types of providers we decided that four separate projects should be started, respectively:

● in a local authority providing community care services

- in a local authority providing services to children and young people

- in an NHS Trust providing specialist medical services

- in a GPs' practice or a group of GP practices providing general medical services

For the research to get underway within a reasonable time, IPPR needed to secure early co-operation from each organisation together with a good chance of its agreeing to work on the pilot proposals. To fulfil this practical condition, we selected providers with whom IPPR already had contacts and which had expressed interest in the outline aims of the project. In the case of the GPs' project our initial contact was with the Family Health Services Authority not with GPs themselves.

Thus projects were initiated in each of the following service organisations. It is not necessary for the research for us to identify them and we shall not do so in this report. The organisations were:

- an Outer London Borough Social Services and Housing Department ("London Borough")

- a Metropolitan District Council Social Services Department in a city in Northern England ("City Council")

- an NHS Trust providing a range of hospital and community services to a largely urban area in North West England ("the Hospital")

- a Co-operative Association of NHS General Practitioners providing out-of-hours emergency medical services to their locality, a mixed urban/rural area in South East England ("the Co-op")

The report
The report devotes a chapter to each organisation. We outline the features of each service in which the research took place, analysing the role which procedural rights could serve in guaranteeing fair treatment. Though it was difficult reliably to assess the "demand" from the public for our proposals, we detail the contacts which we made with service users and with their representative organisations and their reactions when our ideas were discussed. Much of each account concentrates on the process of planning and operating the pilot procedures. Drafting and consulting on the proposals was a complex and protracted operation, in some of the settings

requiring opinion research surveying. We analyse and comment on the opportunities and difficulties which we encountered and the lessons which these may have for future policy and practice. Nine separate proposals were formally discussed with our research partners and seven of these were actually piloted, in three out of the four service organisations. Each pilot left impressions on those working with or using them and we conclude our descriptions by summarising the views of public, staff and managers. In the final chapter we draw together our conclusions and recommendations for future policy and practice. We found that each of the proposals required at least one written procedure or guidelines document. In addition, there were new documents to supply to the public or for staff to use in the course of professional practice. The Appendices contain most of the documents which were piloted, and in the case of the Co-op project, documents which were not tested in practice. Many of the procedures written for internal use within the service organisations we judged were too lengthy to include. We have summarised these in the text of the report as well as including a number of extracts.

Key issues

What questions do we attempt to answer in this report? Though modest in its scope and impact, the study raised issues central to any work with procedural rights, especially in services providing health or social care. These services, more than many, have resisted defining relationships with their service users in terms of clear and specific standards, rights and duties. Many would argue there are good reasons for them not to do so. Our research tested this assumption and the thinking which lies behind it. Its principal themes, to which we shall often return, are the following:

Rationale: Do the public and/or service users want new procedural rights? What broad purposes do they serve?

Opportunities and Methods: What opportunities are there for new procedural rights and how can they be introduced in practice? What is their relationship with substantive social rights?

Barriers: What barriers hinder or prevent their effective introduction? How can they be overcome? Do such rights have to be created in law to be at all effective?

Impact: What effects do these rights have when they are created – both for service users and for the provider organisation which adopts them? Can real and lasting transfers of power be identified?

Contrasts: How do social care providers compare with health care providers when having to work with new procedural rights? What do such comparisons suggest for future policy and practice?

Having set the scene and introduced the main themes of the research we can now examine in detail each of the pilot projects.

Endnotes

1   Coote A (Ed.) (1992) *The Welfare of Citizens: Developing new social rights*, IPPR/Rivers Oram Press. See particularly Galligan D's chapter, "Procedural Rights in Social Welfare".

2   See the Citizen's Charter Complaints Task Force (1995) *Putting things right*, HMSO.

3   Bynoe I (1996) *Beyond the Citizen's Charter: New Directions in Social Rights*, IPPR. See, in particular, pp. 33, 88-94, 119-121.

4   See, for example, ACHCEW (1996) *The Patients' Agenda* ACHCEW; King's Fund Centre and NISW (1995) *Community Care Debates: Debate 1, Community Care: A Question of Rights* King's Fund Centre/NISW; Harding T (Ed.) (1996) *Social Services Law: the Case for Reform* National Institute for Social Work.

5   In a MORI poll conducted for the Joseph Rowntree Foundation April-May 1995, 2,141 adults over 18 were asked what they would like to see in a Bill of Rights. 88 per cent, the highest total, proposed the "right to hospital treatment on the NHS within a reasonable time".

6   For example, Department of Health and Department for Education and Employment (1996) *Children's Services Planning: Guidance*, Department of Health and Department for Education and Employment; Department of Health (1990) *Caring for People: Community Care in the Next Decade and Beyond, Policy Guidance* HMSO.

7   Bynoe I (1996) *Beyond the Citizen's Charter*, IPPR; Public Service Committee (1997) *The Citizen's Charter*: Session 1996–97, Third Report, HC 78-I,II, TSO.

8   Quality and Consumers Branch, NHS Executive (1996) *Patient Partnership: Building a Collaborative Strategy*, NHS Executive.

9   Such a requirement had been recommended by the House of Commons Health Committee in 1993. See House of Commons Session 1992-3, Sixth report of the Health Committee, *Community Care: the Way Forward* 482-I HMSO. See Department of Health, (1994) *A Framework for Local Community Care Charters in England* and related guidance to local authorities, LAC (94)24.

10   Community Care (Direct Payments) Act 1996.

11   Carers (Recognition and Services) Act 1995.

12   See Education Act, 1993 and Code of Practice made under this.

13   "Schools squeezed by special needs" The Independent, 1 February 1997.

14   *R -v- Avon County Council, ex parte M* [1994] 2 FCR 259, QBD (community care);

R -v- London Borough of Islington, ex parte Rixon (1996) Times 17 April, QBD (community care); *R -v- Devon County Council ex parte Baker* [1995] 1 All ER 73, CA (community care); *R -v- Tower Hamlets LBC, ex parte Bradford and Re C*, both referred to in Clements L (1997) "Rule of Law" Community Care, 10–16 April (Children Act).

15 *Re C* (Adult: Refusal of Treatment) [1994] 1 WLR 290; *In re MB* (Caesarian section), *The Times*, 18 April 1997.

16 For example, the Social Services Inspectorate, the Audit Commission for England and Wales, the Scottish Accounts Commission and the National Audit Office.

17 Part I, Local Government Act, 1992.

18 Audit Commission (1997) *Local Authority Performance Indicators 1995/96 Volumes 1 and 2*, Audit Commission.

19 See, for England, Department of Health (1996) *The NHS Performance Guide* (available in area guides) NHS Executive.

20 Pfeffer N and Coote A (1991) *Is Quality Good for You?* IPPR; Bynoe I (1996) *op. cit.*

21 The Public Service Select Committee (1997) *op. cit.*

22 The Publication of Information (Standards of Performance) Direction 1995.See p. 46 below.

23 Field F (1995) *Making Welfare Work: Reconstructing Welfare for the Millenium*, Institute of Community Studies; Green D (1993) *Reinventing Civil Society: The Rediscovery of Welfare without Politics*, Institute of Economic Affairs.

24 As seen, for example, in the reduction of income support for mortgage interest payments, proposals for compulsory second (non-state) pensions and insurance for long term care.

25 See particularly, Lenaghan J (1996) *Rationing and Rights in Health Care*, IPPR, and Bynoe I (1996) *op. cit.*

26 Department of Health, (1995) *Responsibilities for Meeting Continuing Health Care Needs*, HSG (95) 8 and LAC (95) 5, Department of Health.

27 Department of Health (1995) *op. cit.*

28 Audit Commission (1996) *Balancing the Care Equation: Progress with Community Care, Community Care Bulletin Number 3*, Audit Commission.

2. London Borough: fair treatment rights and community care

What the Chapter contains

This chapter describes the work undertaken with the Community Care Division of the social services and housing department in an outer London borough (population in 1991: 290,609). It has three main sections. The first briefly sets out the aims of our work with this organisation and its relevance for community care. The second and third sections describe how, in two stages, we planned, introduced and evaluated three pilot projects.

We outline how we gathered information on current procedures, investigated opportunities for new rights for users and negotiated the wording and contents of these new proposals. Our approach is analytical as well as narrative. Problems and opportunities were encountered throughout the project and we comment on these, assessing the impact of the changes for service users and for London Borough.

Project aims

Publicly funded community care services are essential to many hundreds of thousands in our society. Personal help in the home; adaptations to make accommodation more convenient or safe; day-care or temporary respite care: these are a few examples of the practical assistance which such services can represent. They can help to preserve a person's dignity and independence in their own home or fund alternative care in a nursing or residential home. In addition, they can provide much needed relief for hard pressed family carers who would otherwise be unable to cope with the demands of caring.

Since April 1993, local authorities have been legally responsible for assessing someone's need for such services and taking decisions on the level, type and cost of any service to be offered. Such assessment decisions often involve an authority's staff in careful investigations of a person's home circumstances and complex judgements about risk, capacity, choice, cost and resources. The process is little regulated by law: practice and procedures vary enormously between the numerous local authorities responsible.[1]

Community care involves highly rationed services and these are now increasingly means-tested with contributory charges sought from the recipient of services.[2] Determining who is entitled to them is therefore a process fraught with potential for injustice if service users' rights to information and to fair and consistent treatment are ignored or neglected.

Our work with London Borough offered opportunities for creating new rights within this assessment process. As the project developed, our proposals concentrated on improving service users' rights to information. This objective appeared a priority since so little written information was formally and consistently provided by the borough before, during and after staff completed their assessment.

Our research with this organisation therefore tested possible changes designed to guarantee the public and service users information when they needed it and the impact these changes would have on assessment practice and user experience.

First Stage: planning

Aims and methods

During this initial stage we investigated the contribution then being made by procedures to the assessment work of staff in the Community Care Division. We envisaged that the pilot(s) proposed for the practical research would involve some modification of existing procedures or the introduction of new ones. We also sought users' and carers' perceptions of how the Division worked and their reactions to the prospect of new rights. To gather this initial material we used the following methods:

- observations of staff at work

- examining London Borough's written procedures and assessment documentation

- preparing an interim report and discussing this with senior staff

- listening to service users/carers and their local representative organisations

- and conducting a questionnaire survey of care management staff

Observations of staff at work
The researcher spent a number of days with staff at one area office in the borough. He observed work on the reception desk; accompanied a care manager on her visiting and interviewing clients during the conduct of assessment work; joined duty staff for a session dealing with telephone and personal callers and attended a meeting of the allocations panel determining decisions on the funding of placements in residential or nursing home care. Interviews were also held with the Area Service manager and with the Assistant Director responsible for community care.

Documents and procedures
We obtained and read the documents published for care management staff and for the public on assessment for community care. These comprised a range of public information leaflets widely available in the borough; an internal unpublished manual of services for the elderly; four separate unpublished procedures relevant to the assessment process; and the standard forms and pro formas employed by staff for recording information, noting decisions and ordering services in the course of individual casework.

The Interim Report
Early into this planning stage, we wrote an interim report setting out preliminary findings as to current practice and how it might be improved to strengthen users' rights. We suggested some principles to influence the development of new procedures, and proposed to senior managers a number of subject areas for more detailed investigation and development. The report was discussed with senior staff and agreed as the basis for future work. Its key findings are summarised below. We obtained approval to further our work on three of the four procedural rights outlined in the report, namely:

● the right to clearer information on entitlement to services

● the right to fairer procedures on assessment for services

● the right to clearer information, fairly presented, at the conclusion of an assessment

Contacts with service users and carers
We contacted relevant representative local organisations in the area to obtain their perspective on the authority's work – particularly its approach to service users' rights – and on the aims of the research project. With their

help, we convened three user/carer focus groups and listened to their experience of seeking and using London Borough's services. These groups – and to a lesser extent the local organisations – provided us with feedback on the pilots during the second stage of the project.

The questionnaire survey of care management staff

Before we could start any detailed drafting of procedures we needed a clearer picture of managerial and staff attitudes to current procedures and to their role in work with the public and with service users.

It was important to discover from front line staff themselves some reliable impressions of how they saw their work and how it could be affected by procedures and ideas of procedural rights. A questionnaire survey was therefore drafted and circulated for staff to complete anonymously and return to the researcher. Questions sought detailed replies on a range of practice points: these included, for example, the criteria which staff used when assessing for personal care; how often reasons for decisions were given in writing; how often a written care plan was supplied to a client. Fifty-nine out of one hundred and twenty staff returned these survey forms.

First Stage: findings

What did this first planning stage tell us about assessment in London Borough? Care Management had been introduced during 1992, prior to full implementation of the NHS and Community Care Act 1990. In other words, a specialised system of procedures and personnel was in place available to investigate a person's need for community care services and decide whether or not the borough should provide or purchase this for them. Staff had some experience of working in this way before legal changes required them to do so. Procedures and documents had also been printed and were in use or had been piloted prior to the borough's assuming its new legal responsibilities in April 1993. We summarise below what these contain.

The assessment process in London Borough

How will a member of the public have their needs for community care assessed by the borough's staff? This could, for example, be an elderly person in hospital and awaiting discharge at risk of ill health or injury if help at home is not arranged for them, or a physically disabled adult needing adaptations to their house or a person with alcohol dependency problems needing time in a residential treatment centre.

Someone who contacts a local area office, and whose problem cannot be handled on reception, is likely to be referred first to the duty staff who will speak to them, provide information and advice, and even conduct a straightforward assessment of needs. If the person's problem is more complex a care manager or, in some situations, a social services officer will be "allocated" to assess their circumstances. We shall in future use the description care manager to refer to both of these officers. A care manager could make contact within days if the needs are urgent and the assessment is judged a priority. For requests or referrals given less preference, the person may have to wait from days to weeks before being seen.

If a person is in hospital and awaiting discharge to home or into care, a hospital based care manager will handle the assessment, called in to help by clinical staff. Someone whose needs might require specialist assessment, for example, due to their severe and/or enduring mental health problems or severe physical or learning disability, will usually be referred to specialised teams.

All requests for help or referrals which are accepted attract some type of assessment, even if this is simple and straightforward. Decisions on more costly or scarce services, for example, personal care at home, a referral to a day centre, respite care or a placement in a nursing or residential home result in a more complex and time-consuming process.

This is directed, at least in theory, to investigating a person's full range of needs before any decision is taken on the service(s) which they might require, and, more important, whether this should be purchased or provided by London Borough. A care manager may want to see the person being assessed more than once; will want to speak to any carer(s) or relatives; may have to seek medical views from the person's GP and may have to refer the case to superiors for them to approve decisions taken and authorise expenditure on the services needed.

Such assessment activity suggests that a heavily procedural regime may be required to govern the contacts which care management staff have with the public and with carers and service users. Though someone assessed by staff in London Borough would not necessarily be aware of this, staff were provided with a range of procedural materials. In particular, there were:

- written criteria on eligibility for many services

- at least four procedures on a range of matters relating to assessment

- extensive standard documentation for use during the process of assessment and care planning

Written criteria on eligibility for services

Eligibility criteria are the means by which social services departments can influence individual assessments made by their staff. They represent a way of controlling or "structuring" the exercise of discretionary power vested in care management staff. In 1994, there was already an acceptance in London Borough of the need to define eligibility for services. For one major group needing help from the department – "elderly people" – an internal manual had been produced and circulated to assessment staff on the services available to them and how these could be accessed. One example from this manual sets out criteria for personal care services as shown in Box 2.1.

Box 2.1: Criteria for Personal Care from "Manual of Services for Elderly People"

Service provided:

1. Assistance with personal care tasks such as washing, dressing, toileting, continence care, bathing, shaving, hair care etc.

2. Assistance with daily living activities such as getting out of bed, putting to bed, making hot drinks, preparing food, feeding, supervision of medication.

3. Participation in a defined and agreed programme of rehabilitation.

4. Monitoring of safety of those at risk due to severe physical or mental frailty.

5. Support to informal carers who carry out the above functions to enable them to continue caring.

6. Domestic tasks if in conjunction with any of the above.

The service can be provided between the hours of 7.00am and 9.00pm, up to seven days per week, depending on the availability of resources.

Criteria for eligibility:

1. Have a degree of mental or physical infirmity/disability which would otherwise make their admission to residential care likely.

2. Have been recently discharged from hospital and do not require medical/nursing care.

3. Require domestic services as part of a rehabilitation process based on an agreed care plan.

London Borough's eligibility criteria: limitations
We identified a number of limitations in the way eligibility criteria were being used in London Borough.

First, as a general rule, these were not available to the public at all. For example, though London Borough issued an information leaflet for the public on personal care, this did not contain details of criteria and there was no procedure in operation which required them to be supplied to people during the assessment process, even if they had been refused personal care. The only written criteria actually made public at this time were for residential and nursing home placements. They were to be found in the Borough's Community Care Plan, prepared jointly with the local Health Authority and NHS Trust:[3] most people would know nothing about this document and were even less likely to have seen it.

Secondly, London Borough's practice did not reflect a close and consistent adherence to clear and published criteria across the full range of assessed services. The following observations illustrate this.

Only in respect of one customer group – elderly people – had a concerted effort been made to formulate comprehensive guidance to staff on eligibility. Furthermore, the status of the manual which contained this seemed uncertain. Some of the criteria mentioned in it were more detailed than those which had been published in the borough's Community Care Plan (eg Residential Care – Permanent). It was not clear to us which criteria should be used by Care Managers.

Some written criteria were also incomplete with additional and unpublished criteria being employed by staff in order to determine eligibility. Thus, the researcher was informed that a person assessed to need hot "Meals on Wheels" and appearing to be eligible for this service (according to the Manual criteria and the published leaflet) would not be entitled to have the service if living in sheltered accommodation. Care managers did not seem sure why this should be so.

Eligibility criteria: voluntary sector views
Consultation with voluntary organisations revealed two conflicting impressions. Most regarded the borough's eligibility criteria as unclear and, where written, not used with rigour. This was supported by a parallel observation that assessments on similar facts could lead to different outcomes. It was thought that this might result from a poor understanding and application of the criteria. This view was particularly applied to personal

care, where the level of service offered could vary considerably and, in our respondents' opinion, for no apparent reason. Others outside the department commented that the introduction of eligibility criteria had led to the service becoming more inflexible and rigid than in the past – perhaps a reflection on the more restricted service now available, particularly for domestic help in the home.

Eligibility criteria: staff views

Our early conclusions were further reinforced by evidence of staff attitudes to eligibility criteria, elicited by the questionnaire survey. We asked respondents to describe the criteria which they applied when deciding someone needed personal care. Despite the guidance given in the Manual (see Box 2.1 above) the replies which we received did not refer to any single set of criteria nor to any ready source of guidance, nor clearly matched the requirements of the guidance. The responses included the following:

The person, due to physical or mental frailty, would need help with all or some personal care tasks; also to support the carer in all aspects of caring. The aim should be to help the customer achieve as high a standard of living as possible in their own home.

If only need is meal preparation or bathing, I would not introduce personal care. In all cases – only if there is no relative who is willing/able to do tasks.

Could they afford to go private for help if necessary?

Inconsistency in use of criteria

Before conducting the survey and in discussion with our user/carer groups we had identified problems with assessment and provision of personal care at weekends or on Bank Holidays. The accounts which we heard in the groups suggested that some assessments would result in a service at weekends or on Bank Holidays whilst for others, in similar circumstances, there would be no service.

Since consistency appeared an important test of the significance of any formal criteria we asked staff how they assessed whether or not a person needed personal care at weekends or on bank holidays. A number of replies confirmed our fears that different considerations might apply, there being no strict adherence to the standard criteria:

I feel this decision is often resource led.

Whether there are relatives/friends to take over on weekends.

Ability to pay for private agency help.

Staff support for clearer eligibility criteria

We asked whether care management staff would welcome a clearer definition by London Borough of its eligibility criteria for personal care. Out of fifty nine respondents, 56 per cent agreed; 34 per cent disagreed and 10 per cent gave no answer at all. Respondents were asked to give reasons for their answer. The following statements illustrate the views of those wanting greater clarity.

Make borderline cases easier to assess.

To avoid variability in provision of services by care managers and service managers.

I like to have clear written criteria for all services to avoid conflict with service users and carers. It makes for more consistency.

Managers should take more responsibility for determining eligibility.

The following replies illustrated the contrary view:

This can lead to inflexibility in assessment.

No, because each customer is assessed individually.

London Borough's procedural guidance and assessment documentation

Care management staff in London Borough were already familiar with using procedural guidance and standardised assessment documentation. A number of procedure documents had been issued giving guidance on the various stages of assessment, on the care manager's role and authority and those of others involved in the process. We saw:

- a "Referral and Assessment Process", with an annexe giving additional guidance on detailed assessments

- a protocol governing the purchasing power delegated to each level of care management staff

- a recording policy, governing the recording of facts and judgements in case files

●   a procedure for responding to service complaints and suggestions

Assessment procedures: limitations for disabled people
Early into the research we saw the potential for a procedure enhancing the statutory rights of disabled people to request a formal assessment of their need for services.

London Borough's documents did not provide staff with clear guidance on the position of disabled persons, nor on these particular rights. Thus, care managers were not informed of the authority's obligation to provide a full Disabled Persons Act 1986 assessment for a person found to be a "disabled person" during any care management assessment.[4]

The effect of this lack of guidance was seen in the survey replies. We asked staff to give a definition of a "disabled person" for the purposes of the Community Care Act, and in particular asked if this included someone with mental health problems. We also asked them to detail the additional rights which such a person has during the course of an assessment. Although most respondents replied to this question, none referred specifically to the legal definition which is the source of the definition and which includes someone with a mental disorder. Neither were there signs that staff were aware of the disabled person's statutory right to request an assessment of their need for services under the Chronically Sick and Disabled Persons Act 1970.

Forms… and more forms
Extensive documentation had been produced and was in use by care managers in the course of their needs assessment and for ordering services from the borough's in-house staff or from the private sector. This comprised standard letter formats, checklists, report forms for others, such as a person's GP, service user or main carer, to complete and return, and a financial means assessment form.

Despite this, we quickly learned from service users and from carers that one essential stage in the process was often ignored in practice. This was the provision of detailed information on the results of an assessment in a written form which could be retained by the service user and carer (if any), the document commonly termed a "Care Plan".

London Borough's missing Care Plan
A pro forma Care Plan had been produced in London Borough and piloted during 1992. This included space for describing the overall objectives of the individual's Care Plan; needs which had been identified and the services

requested to match those needs. In one section, the care manager was required to detail unmet need giving the reason for this. Attached to the plan was a simple timetable listing the nature, frequency and cost of various services.

Although piloted and still to be found in area offices, we were informed that the form's use had been discontinued by the Assistant Director before April 1993 in view of advice the authority had received from the Department of Health.[5] This drew attention to possible legal consequences if an authority recorded an individual's unmet needs for services – a step which London Borough's form would have required. No replacement form had been introduced as a substitute.

Users and carers told us that they were frustrated by this absence of any uniform documents recording the outcome of an assessment, disclosing reasons for the care manager's decisions and specifying the services actually provided. Admittedly, in some cases care managers would write with details of services or would supply a copy of their order. But the views we heard suggested that, in many situations, neither document would be given. This was reinforced in further results from the staff survey.

Assessment procedures and documentation: staff views
Staff were asked how they informed customers of the reasons for their decisions. Out of the fifty-nine respondents, forty-five stated that verbal means were their chief or only means of doing so. Eight mentioned telephone or writing as their main method, whilst six replies were blank. Of the overall total, only twenty three replies mentioned the use of writing.

For those staff who said they sometimes gave reasons in writing, they were asked if they ever supplied a copy Care Plan or service order. In 65 per cent of cases the answer was either sometimes, rarely or never.

We asked staff what would prevent them from sending or supplying more written communications. Responses included the following:

Time.

Lack of WP support.

Culture of verbal communication.

Most customers would appear to prefer a verbal explanation. Some might not read (or be able to read) written communications. Could provoke anxiety.

In the past, management have advised us not to put in writing that we cannot meet someone's needs if we are not able to meet them. This was due to the legal implications of a case in Hereford.

Nothing really prevents – no need to supply information if the assessment is straightforward. Plans are left for the customers to read.

Certain information is confidential and restricted.

If I felt they would use this information wrongly.

Despite their views on the difficulty of providing information, a large majority of respondents (68 per cent) believed that all service users would benefit from having a written record of the outcome of their assessment. A further 9 per cent felt that *some* would benefit. An even higher majority (83 per cent) believed that others (carers, GPs, district nurses etc.) would benefit from such a change.

Finally, staff were asked if they would tell a customer if they had assessed them as needing a service but one would not be provided to the extent required or at all. A majority of respondents (51 per cent) said they would always do this and a significant proportion (17 per cent) said they would often do so. However, these answers need to be put in context. Other replies showed that most communication with customers was verbal. Customers might therefore have heard the care manager's opinion on their needs but would have no formal record of this.

Administrative support to care managers

For complex procedures to be consistently and accurately used, good standards of administration are generally required. Administrative support will be needed in order for this to be achieved, particularly in busy office environments demanding a high turnover of work.

In London Borough, limited administrative support was available to care management staff for the typing of letters, taking of messages etc. Staff told us that there was sometimes delay in getting letters typed. This probably encouraged the use of more informal means of communication (verbal, telephone). What was particularly noticeable was the minimal assistance given to staff from Information Technology. A central customer database could be accessed on VDU screens in offices but screen pages could not be printed at all, nor were staff provided with word processing facilities with dedicated care management software.

First Stage planning: conclusions and outcomes
By the end of this first stage, we had gathered some clear impressions of assessment in London Borough and some useful material for detailed work on the pilot projects. Some key observations had emerged from our early contacts with staff, service users and carers in the borough:

- London Borough was already using paper based procedures and standard documents extensively to conduct assessments for community care services.

- Though some basic leaflets for the public were available, there was little information to explain the detailed process of assessment and what people could expect from it. It was assumed that explanations would be mainly verbal and informal.

- There had been little attempt to explain to the public who was or was not entitled to services, such as personal care, although written eligibility criteria had been issued to staff.

- Where it had been issued, London Borough's guidance to practitioners was often treated as permissive rather than mandatory; this may explain why practice varied significantly between different members of staff.

- Relationships with service users and carers were often linked to particular staff and were generally informal, with communications mainly verbal, not in writing.

- It had not been difficult to suggest to London Borough many ideas to pilot in practice, nor had there been any resistance to further work on three of the four areas proposed.

- The only barrier we encountered was some initial lack of enthusiasm for the idea of procedural rights among London Borough's managers, service users, carers and some local organisations. Procedural rights, evidently, can appear abstruse and off-putting.

It is not surprising that the benefits of this approach can seem only marginal until practical changes are proposed. The second stage of the research required us to draft procedures for London Borough to pilot in their service and is the focus for the next section.

Second Stage: three pilot projects

Aims and methods

The aim of the second stage was to draft detailed pilot procedures to provide new entitlements for people involved in London Borough's community care assessment process. The procedures planned to increase the information supplied by staff during and after the assessment. If London Borough agreed to introduce the procedures, these would be piloted in practice and we then intended to gather initial impressions on them from staff and service users involved.

We negotiated agreement with London Borough through a highly collaborative drafting process. The researcher produced early drafts for discussion with senior managers. Initial work started on five ideas. Three of these were developed sufficiently for piloting. When final drafts were ready these were circulated for consideration and feedback from care management staff and from the user and carer groups convened during the first stage. The three projects that were introduced and evaluated were:

- a Personal Care Pilot Project

- a Disabled Persons Project

- a Care Plan Project

We next describe each of these, outlining the problems which were encountered, the outcomes of each project and our conclusions.

The Personal Care Pilot Project

London Borough's limited use of eligibility criteria for personal care provided an opportunity to test some generic criteria for this service. It also offered a chance of informing those being assessed of the nature and importance of the criteria. With these twin aims in mind we drafted three documents:

- a list of criteria

- an information leaflet to accompany the list

- a procedure for care management staff

The Eligibility Criteria

A copy of this document is reproduced in Appendix A below.[6] The criteria reflected and built upon what we had discovered of the approach being taken at the time by London Borough's care managers. Thus these firstly defined who was to be regarded as in need of personal care. Then they outlined the types of assistance which were included in the definition of personal care. Then, at some length, the criteria defined six factors needing to be considered by care managers and positively identified before a service could be ordered by the borough. Lastly, the document reminded those applying the criteria of the need for service users to be advised of their obligation to make a financial contribution to the service, if assessed as liable to pay this.

The Information Leaflet

The pilot attempted to structure the discretionary decision of care managers and to render them more accountable for their assessment of needs. We hoped that this would be achieved by making the grounds for their decision explicit.

The information leaflet (reproduced in Appendix A[7]) explained the process so that individual applicants and carers given it could understand how the care manager might use the criteria in making decisions. It also summarised who ought to get a service – paraphrasing the criteria – and what someone should do if they disagreed with the decision of the care manager.

The Procedure

The procedure offered detailed guidance on how and when staff should use the new documents. It reminded care managers of the dangers of subjectivity in assessing risk and need, and stressed the importance of helping individuals to understand how the criteria applied to their own circumstances.

Care managers were told the criteria could be used in three ways: as a reference, when deciding what information was needed to complete the assessment; as information for those being assessed, their relatives, friends or advocates; and as an aid to explaining their assessment decision and the reasons for it. The procedure's final version required care management staff to hand to each person assessed for personal care a copy of the criteria and the leaflet at the time of their interview with them.

Finalising the documents

During consultation on the draft documents we obtained reactions to them, and suggestions, from three different perspectives: senior managers, front-line staff, and service users/carers and their advocates.

With senior managers there was considerable interest in the project and in the eligibility criteria which the researcher had drafted. Indeed, the work achieved an entirely unplanned and unpredicted momentum of its own. Shortly after discussions over the first draft, and after minor modifications, the Assistant Director submitted the criteria to the Social Services and Housing Committee and had these approved and introduced throughout the whole of the authority's area as the guidance on eligibility for personal care.

Managers were open about their reasons for doing this. We were informed that the Department was encountering severe problems with overspending on personal care due to unforeseen demand for this service. Divisional managers felt that formal adoption of the modified criteria drafted by IPPR for the pilot project would help to control spending on personal care.

We were surprised at the ease with which our draft was adopted and introduced in practice and even more so that it was perceived by managers as a potential rationing mechanism. We framed the criteria broadly so as to permit care managers a high degree of discretion in assessing need and in ordering a service funded by London Borough. With the phrases and words of the criteria expressed so broadly, we even felt that refusal of a service might be harder to justify than before.

Furthermore, in spite of the evident interest in using the criteria for cost containment, we understand that they were not formally costed by the Department against expected demand or in the light of past spending patterns.[8]

Front-line staff reactions

Front-line staff had more predictable reactions to the prospect of using the procedure to give more information to those they assessed. Comments ranged from a perception that it was useful and reflected current practice, to a view that it would require a degree of "sophistry" for care managers to use it.

Some staff feared that it would be publicised, that it would have to be explained to customers, and that there would be a need to interpret it. There was a concern that some of the terms used in the criteria were woolly or vague, for example, "safe home environment" or "safe and hygienic standards". They preferred to link eligibility to conditions such as the receipt of specified disability benefits such as attendance allowance.

There was a widely held view among staff that the criteria were too wide for the resources available to care managers to fund the services needed. (So much for managers' perception that the criteria would act as a rationing mechanism!) Whether or not a person got a service would continue to depend on the availability of resources not on the wording of the criteria. There was insufficient time available to explore in more depth this significant criticism of the criteria. Our scope for doing so was, in any event, limited by the adoption and use of the criteria throughout the service.

User and carer perspectives
Consultation meetings were held with the user/carer focus groups convened earlier during the investigation stage. All supported the piloting of the procedure with most interest for it being expressed by the carers' group. Participants judged the wording of the criteria to be clear and useful.

They strongly recommended that these be supplied to the person being assessed at the same time as the explanatory leaflet was given to them. The first draft procedure did not require this and we modified it as a result. They also considered it essential that the information be sent in advance of an assessment starting and that the leaflet should refer to the right to complain. We incorporated the second suggestion into the final draft leaflet. The first idea could not be adopted: according to London Borough this would encourage the view that assessment was about ordering a pre-determined set of services, not assessing a person's needs and finding the best way to meet them – an underlying aim of the new Community Care policy.

The draft documentation was circulated to the local organisations contacted during the first stage of this research. Only one organisation responded to this consultation, a local carers' advocacy organisation funded by London Borough. It supported the pilot on eligibility criteria describing all the proposals as representing "…clear steps forward in addressing the confusion and uncertainty many people currently feel about Social Service procedures."

Outcomes and evaluation
The pilot commenced during the autumn of 1995 and, as agreed with London Borough, ended when fifty assessments had been undertaken in accordance with the new procedure. The low number was for practical reasons. We wished to maintain staff co-operation with the project and had only a short time within which to complete the study.

Feedback was obtained in a number of ways. After staff had used the procedure they completed a short questionnaire. The completed forms provided us with some initial impressions. A group of supervisory staff was convened to give their views on the pilot followed by a meeting with a larger group of care managers and social services officers. All customers involved in the pilot were sent a letter asking if they would agree to be interviewed about the experience and permit us to examine their file at the department's area office. Eighteen responded confirming their agreement to our inspecting their file and contacting them. Seventeen files were examined and fourteen interviews took place.

Our evaluation of the pilot concentrates on the following questions:

● Feasibility: was the procedure practicable?

● Impact: did the procedure affect outcomes?

● Rationale: did the procedure fulfil its aims?

Feasibility of procedure
According to the staff who piloted the procedure, complying with it did not present any significant practical problems. The feedback group told us this and it was confirmed in questionnaire answers. Some stated that a little more time had been needed to explain the criteria and there was a general impression that assessment was more complex when the customer's capacity to understand the documents was affected by dementia or memory loss. Also, when people were in crisis, there was not the time to sit down with the client and discuss the criteria with them.

Staff asserted that the criteria and information sheet summarised details they would have planned to provide to the client verbally in any event. They added that their recording of any information or decision had not changed as a result of the procedure. This was borne out by their file records. When we examined the files we could find only one reference to the written criteria – in the case of a person refused a service.

Despite these assertions, we cannot be sure that the procedure was fully and properly used on every occasion when it should have been. We state this because of what we heard from service users and carers. When we interviewed them we discovered that the procedure and documents had made little or no impact at all. Repeatedly, they told us they did not recollect receiving the written criteria and the information sheet. Some we interviewed were confused and forgetful and their recollection may be unreliable. Others were very sure that no documents had been given to them. We even received this response from the client and from her daughter in the case where a service had been refused and the borough's officer recalled how the criteria had been referred to specifically by her when explaining the reason for her decision!

Reasons for conflicting impressions
The conflict between staff and service user impressions may have been encouraged by the very high proportion of assessments leading to services being ordered, as much as by any omission to provide the documents. Care managers reported that in 49 out of the 50 cases in the pilot, the customer obtained a service. It may be fair to assume that if the customer obtained from the assessment what they wanted and expected, then there was little reason to be interested in standard "paperwork". Care managers told us the customer just wanted the service set up quickly, observing that by the time an allocated officer came to interview the client, many already assumed that they would be obtaining a service. Indeed, they noted that clients were now more interested in the details of their individual Care Plan than they had ever been in the pilot documents.

Impact of procedure
Did the procedure have any impact on the care manager's assessment of needs and decision on personal care services? The statistic revealing a service provided in 98 per cent of assessments is important though, on its own, is inconclusive, though not simply because the sample was so small.

Care managers told us that it could reflect the filtering which occurs earlier in the process of referral and allocation. By the time a person's circumstances come to the notice of a care manager or social services officer allocated to assess their need for community care, prior contact with the department – or delay in allocation – may have filtered out those requests which would not be likely to attract a service or were only marginal.

No effect on outcomes
Care managers felt that using the procedure had not altered the outcome of the assessment though they admitted that the criteria were worded so generally that most referrals could be brought within its terms. Questionnaire replies confirmed this impression. In the one case where a service had been refused, the social services officer did not say that her decision had been affected by the procedure but felt the procedure was useful and practicable. It had helped her to explain her decision more clearly.

Staff felt this to be the main benefit of the procedure. They were conscious that so much of what they may have told the person assessed would not be remembered and a note left in the home would provide a useful record of this. In the one case where the wording of the criteria was crucial, the officer reported that she felt the documents backed her up in her decision enabling her to explain it in "black and white".

Staff acknowledged that they were much more accountable than in the past and that the public was aware of this. All agreed that it would be easier to "say no" on the basis of the criteria document and welcomed the fact that their publication now showed that London Borough seemed prepared to provide information to back them up when they had to do so.

Rationale of the procedure
Despite these impressions, it might be wrong to conclude that the procedure fulfilled its main purpose: that of giving to the public clear and useful information on entitlement. We base this observation on the following weaknesses of the procedure:

- the criteria were too vague

- the criteria were incomplete

- the criteria were supplied too late in the process

Vague information
Staff repeated what they had said of the draft criteria: these were too vague to use in deciding on eligibility. Because of this, they felt that the document would have left the client with the impression that assessing need was still very much up to the care manager. Staff observed that if Council Members and senior managers expected them to work more closely to criteria then they would have to be drawn more tightly than those used in the pilot.

Incomplete information
We were also told that the pilot procedure was limited because it did not enable the client to see how much of a service someone might receive if they were assessed as eligible to it. The criteria made no mention of resources nor the source of the service and these were key factors in determining the amount of the service provided to someone.

To one team member, open criteria such as these could also permit wide variation between different care managers. This could range from a 20 to 30 minute service ordered by one team compared with one, for the same person, for 90 minutes ordered by a different team which considered the person less able to cope.

Delayed information

In general, staff felt that the procedure supplied information to the public too late during the process of assessment. That a service was offered in 49 out of 50 cases, suggested to them that the information supplied would not be of value to most of those receiving it, especially if it could not answer crucial questions about the level and frequency of services.

The staff group felt that information on eligibility ought to be provided to the client at an earlier stage in the assessment process and be published and be more widely available throughout the borough. It was suggested that details could be sent when it was confirmed that an allocated care manager would visit to assess the person's needs. This was the suggestion made to us earlier by the carers' group. Against this, it was observed that such a practice would bias assessment towards being "service-led" not "needs-led".

Service users' and carers' views

Since most of the service users and carers we interviewed could not recollect seeing any documents, we could hardly raise with them issues of vague or incomplete information and the best time to receive information. We did meet one carer who had been totally surprised to learn that the borough would provide her with help in caring for her mother. She had always believed that it was her duty – and the authority's expectation – that she would have to continue providing all the care her mother needed. Assessment had been triggered by her mother's discharge from hospital. She had not learned of her mother's eligibility for a service from the pilot documents but directly from the care manager. She did not recall receiving any such papers at all.

When we listened to the concerns which users and carers had about the services they were getting or wished to get, it was noticeable that basic eligibility was simply not mentioned – it was a non-issue. Where they were not entirely content with the arrangements set up by the care manager, users complained of the discontinuity of personal care staff (a problem particularly associated with weekend care from private agencies); their incompetence; poor administration in the area office; and the level of service provided. They did not mention eligibility, because, it seemed, they did not need to. (Had we talked to would-be users we might have heard very different opinions.)

Carers' organisation views

We sought the views of the principal local advocacy organisation on the impact and usefulness of the project. Its representative was sceptical about the claims made for this procedure, though welcomed the progress which it represented in terms of better practice. Her observations may help to explain its limited impact.

She commented that the criteria could not help an individual to work out how much of a service she or he would get. The language was so broad and inclusive that it simply could not be used as a measure. For the public it therefore did not of itself address the problem which they faced in needing to be able to judge if they were obtaining the right level of service, not merely questions of eligibility.

> *I know that's not what eligibility means, but alongside eligibility you should have some less broad means of deciding how much of a service you get. That would be quite difficult to arrive at. You particularly see variability in level of service not so much in eligibility. Eligibility is something in [the public's] minds rather more exactly measurable than what you might see as being broad entitlement in theory to a service. If a person is told that they may be eligible for something then they would probably like to have a fairly clear indication of how much of it they are going to get. After all, if you are eligible for disability living allowance you get something like £46.00 per week. If you are eligible for a home care service that may cover an entire spectrum between half an hour three times a week and three visits of one and a half hours per day.*

She felt that care managers might also find the criteria of limited use when trying to explain the differences in their assessments and the levels of service arranged for them.

> *Care managers would not have found it a tool with which to answer questions. I think people do perceive differences in the way they are being treated. Therefore, there needs to be some kind of good, solid reason for explaining that. Just to say that everybody's circumstances are different doesn't quite fit the bill.*

She recognised that London Borough had not formerly had any published eligibility criteria and so they needed to take this initial step of introducing them. However, she urged that their limitations also be recognised. Someone might read published criteria for domestic help, for example, and believe they were entitled to it. Domestic help in the borough amounted to just one and a half hours per fortnight and, in her view, this was something the public should be entitled to learn about beforehand, before an assessment after which they might feel aggrieved to obtain so little help.

Senior managers' conclusions

We put these points to senior managers and asked for comment. They had introduced throughout London Borough the same criteria prior to the pilot starting. They judged that the wording accurately reflected the scope of the service currently provided to customers, though they acknowledged that the level of service provided would depend on additional factors which could include a consideration of the resources available to the authority.

Rationing comes into deciding on the amount of assistance the person needs. This depends on other supports, on the physical environment, age of the carer etc. We cannot say that if we are going to assist [a customer] then [that customer] will get an hour's assistance. Someone might get half an hour and someone else might get two hours. That's where the judgement comes in. Its affected by how much resource we have.

Both managers interviewed believed that it would be very difficult to develop the criteria so that they would be able to tell someone being assessed how much of the service they would actually receive. The criteria needed to be drawn so as to be neither too restrictive nor too open.

If you tighten them up and make them more explicit then care managers will complain, because it has rendered the whole thing mechanistic – social work "by numbers". [If you]... set them as too broad they criticise us for not being specific enough and not being explicit enough.

They accepted that the outcome of the pilot suggested the need for the earlier supply of information on eligibility, for example, in a leaflet widely available to the public listing and explaining the criteria.

Discussion and researcher's conclusions

To publish a document which unambiguously defines criteria determining a person's eligibility for a particular service or benefit seems the very epitome of a procedural right. The impact of taking such a step could be significant if the current allocation of services does not match the public commitments made in the criteria. If the behaviour of decision-takers does not change to bring decisions into line with public policy, they may be held to account for their failure.

Not surprisingly, then, carers and service users supported a pilot which aimed to put into the hands of the person assessed a list of the factors which were to influence the judgement of the care manager conducting an assessment.

Politicians also seem keen on the idea. In its election manifesto, the new Labour Government said it would publish a Charter listing national eligibility criteria for long term continuing care. By this means, so it argued, equity could be guaranteed throughout the country.

Audit Commission guidance on criteria
According to the Audit Commission, the purpose of eligibility criteria is to show the limits to which authorities can provide help.[9] Once approved and published these should therefore influence an authority's decisions on providing or arranging services to someone whose needs are assessed in accordance with them and are found to qualify the person for assistance. The Commission advises authorities to draft criteria carefully so as to ensure that they will not cause the authority to incur expenditure in excess of the amount available for this purpose.

Such a sophisticated use of criteria assumes, firstly, that the authority is allowed to take into account the level of its resources in fixing its criteria and that the concept of "need" for a service is a relative not an absolute one. Secondly, this view supposes that the social services authority will be able to predict levels of demand and their likely costs, using the wording of possible criteria as the basis for their projections.

The Gloucestershire Case
Regarding the first assumption, a recent decision of the House of Lords in the Gloucestershire Case[10] has now clarified the role and lawfulness of eligibility criteria framed with regard to available resources. Faced with having to reduce its budget, Gloucestershire restricted its criteria with the result that for many hundreds of service users their care or assistance was reduced or removed altogether.

One service user challenged the lawfulness of the decision, arguing that the authority was not permitted to take into account its available resources in setting its criteria. Need for community care, it was said, was an absolute concept which could not be concealed behind the published policy of a cash strapped council. The House of Lords has now rejected this argument, firmly re-establishing the role and legitimacy of eligibility criteria in the allocation of community care services.

The challenge of criteria

What remains is the second assumption, namely, that authorities will have the competence and resources to use criteria in a sophisticated way, and will carefully match thresholds of need defined in their wording with resources available. If social services authorities are able to accomplish this then criteria can, indeed, represent the authority's published policy on entitlement – until, that is, the authority has to change the criteria to introduce a further reduction in service!

Our study provides a number of valuable insights into whether this might be achieved and, if so, how this would affect current and potential users.

London Borough seemed far from yet being able to work in this highly focused way, although its agreement to experiment with published criteria suggested a willingness to try. We were struck by the speed with which the Borough accepted our draft criteria, slightly modified them and then introduced them throughout the service. What motivated the Borough was not primarily a desire to create new rights for service users, but more a need to contain expenditure on personal care, though it was not apparent that the criteria had been costed. As care managers noted, the criteria were very widely drawn and could be made to fit "most referrals". It is impossible to reconcile these conflicting interpretations of the same document and its potential impact. Perhaps the omission of bathing from the list of personal care tasks (pilot criteria) was conclusive, as far as managers were concerned?

Despite the prominence given to using criteria by the Department of Health and the Audit Commission, there are no guidelines as to how these should be worded; whether or not they are published varies considerably across the country. London Borough's situation is probably typical of many authorities with little or no experience of using criteria rigorously.

Slack use of criteria

The Borough had issued some limited written criteria to its staff (in the Manual for Elderly Persons) but neither these, nor the fuller IPPR pilot criteria, seemed to be acknowledged as the main or exclusive source of guidance for the care manager. Yet the inclusion or exclusion of a particular type of help, eg bathing or domestic cleaning, could be highly influential.

Furthermore, neither set of criteria could be used to calculate the level or frequency of service which were needed and doubts were expressed that it would be possible to draft criteria which could deal with this. It was precisely in relation to this point that we had been told care managers' practice varied considerably. In their enthusiasm for published criteria to be provided, perhaps the carers we listened to failed to appreciate this fundamental weakness in the document they welcomed.

Social work by numbers?

Managers admitted to us their reluctance to insist on compliance with highly prescriptive professional guidance. They regarded their staff as universally unwilling to work under such direction. There may be some truth in this but the research study provided solid evidence of care managers wanting to have clearer guidance on questions of eligibility. It will be recalled that staff told us they welcomed this for the collective and managerial support this lent to their personal judgements about need and entitlement.

Without clear criteria to determine how much service someone in need should receive, staff had to resort to other sources of guidance or authority, some of which would be highly influenced by resources available. The study suggests that until criteria can be drawn up which will determine eligibility and, for those eligible, the quantity or level of service they will receive, then the helpfulness of criteria in London Borough may remain limited. Managers stated that the personal criteria developed during the pilot would remain in operation for the time being throughout the Borough. However, the practice of supplying a copy of these to people when they are assessed would not be repeated.

Nevertheless, the criteria may be useful as a means of providing the public with a more accurate picture of who will nor will not be broadly accepted for the borough's services. All were agreed that people needed information about the criteria earlier in the process and many suggested details could be included into a leaflet specifically written for this purpose.

Criteria and refusal of service

Two observations remain. In the study sample, nearly every customer received a service. For them the question of eligibility was a non-issue. If the pilot had run for long enough to gather a reasonable sample of customers refused personal care we might have found the criteria taking on a greater significance both with those who were disappointed and with staff. Then the case for continuing the practice might have had merit. One practical suggestion would be to provide the criteria to anyone who is refused as part of the "reasons" for the decision.

Secondly, did the staff actually comply with the procedure? We realise the documents were unimaginatively presented (they were prepared with very limited resources) but it was still remarkable that these made so little impact on those allegedly supplied with them. The feedback we received strongly suggests that not all those entitled to the documents received them, though we would not be surprised if sometimes they were mislaid, disposed of or forgotten immediately given their relative unimportance.

If a practice like that required in the pilot was ever to be introduced as a clear procedural right, some means would have to be used to encourage compliance in each and every case. Otherwise, we fear that the practice may depend on professional preference not on respect for the clearly accepted rights of the person being assessed. If public service providers, such as local authorities, were able to formally guarantee aspects of their service, including procedures such as this one, then it would be easier for managers, staff and the public to distinguish between what the authority had committed itself to do and what was still just a good practice target or aspiration.

The Disabled Persons Project

Setting up the Disabled Persons Project required us to work in a similar pattern. The "disabled person's" statutory right to request an assessment is not found in other community care legislation and is a clear procedural right which could be enhanced by an approach designed to inform those entitled to it. Having identified this aim we designed a procedure to test what would happen if London Borough clearly and openly acknowledged the statutory right by writing to an identifiable group of disabled customers who might need and be entitled to services.

The project had three elements:

- a procedure to inform participating staff what they should do and when

- a standard letter to be sent by London Borough to customers involved in the pilot

- a standard application form, accompanying the letter to be used by any customer wishing to claim their statutory right to an assessment

Though the procedure itself is not found in Appendix A, due to its length, the standard letter and application are reproduced there.[11]

The procedure
The group we invited to apply for an assessment were defined in the

following way. London Borough invited persons prepared to define themselves as "disabled" to apply for a concessionary Travel Pass permitting free or cheap travel on public transport in the borough. In order to obtain this, a person also had to be registrable (though not to be actually registered) on the borough's register of disabled persons.

The procedure provided that, whenever London Borough approved a person's application for a travel pass on the basis of their disability this person would be sent, unsolicited, the standard letter together with a copy application form.

The letter would be signed by a care manager, would explain the nature of the person's right to ask for an assessment and the type of services which might be provided. It was initially envisaged (in a first draft) that the letter would also include reference to a local voluntary organisation which could provide a source of independent advice and assistance.

With this pilot we were keen to see the effect of acknowledging very openly the existence of rights which are specifically defined in law but which usually remain hidden if not secret. Would London Borough agree to such a measure in spite of potential resource implications of the unforeseen demand it might encourage?

Consultation with the authority
By their own managers' admission, this was a highly unusual project for London Borough to undertake given its potential resource implications. The services linked to the assessment right included practical assistance in the home ie "personal care"; adaptations to housing to render it safer or more convenient; holidays; transport; and the provision of a TV or telephone. Furthermore, litigation proceeding in the High Court and the Court of Appeal before and during the pilot, suggested that once the authority accepted a person needed any such service, it might be obliged in law to provide it, regardless of the amount of resources at its disposal.[12]

We did not encounter any difficulty in agreeing the contents of the documents which were straightforward. Apart from some drafting amendments these were quickly approved. Negotiations mainly concerned how the project could be controlled, if its resource implications became unacceptable. Managers openly expressed their fear that the procedure might raise demand to an extent current resources could not meet. This was the reason for their insisting on limiting the scope of the project.

Furthermore, both Divisional management and those actually in charge of staff running the pilot sought an assurance from the researcher that the pilot could be discontinued if it led to demands which could not be met within budgets available. In the circumstances, we were obliged to give such an assurance. Given what occurred in practice, it is well worth noting this highly cautious approach. Legal advice on the effect of the pilot was not apparently sought by senior managers at any stage.

Consultation with voluntary organisations
Apart from the general support from one organisation which we have already mentioned, we received no specific feedback from any local organisation responsible for advising disabled people of their rights or representing their interests to the borough or the public. The researcher was conscious of the potential need for someone receiving the standard letter and form to obtain advice on their contents and importance. He therefore proposed to a local disability organisation that their details and telephone number appear on the letter, but due to operational pressures at the time, it could not agree to this request.

Consultation with service users/carers
The disabled persons' group consulted earlier in the research were interested in the project and supported its aims. They were surprised to learn of the group being targeted by the pilot since they believed such people could not be said to be a priority. Once they understood that an aim of the pilot was to test out this very assumption, they supported it more enthusiastically. The carers' group also approved of the aims of the pilot and the documentation intended to be used.

Outcomes and evaluation
The project ran from the start of October 1995 until the end of March 1996. We realised that the numbers of customers sent the letter and application form would be low. Indeed, we were only able to undertake the project on this assumption given management's concerns about its possible resources implications.

In the event, the pilot achieved little due to the very small numbers of customers who were contacted in accordance with the procedure. The area office piloting it reported that only ten travel passes were newly approved during the pilot period and thus attracted the required action. One person applied for an assessment as a result. Two were already known to the department and were receiving services following an assessment. In the remaining seven cases, the customer did not apply for an assessment.

In the Adult Disability Team, which also piloted the procedure, all newly approved travel passes were granted to customers already known to the borough with allocated care management staff. They were therefore already being offered or were undergoing an assessment. In one remaining case, contact with a care manager had ended a mere eight weeks prior to their pass being approved and, in view of this, the team felt it inappropriate to use the procedure.

In order to contact people who received the letter and form, we asked care managers to write to each of the customers who were invited to apply for an assessment asking them if they would agree to be interviewed and/or to permit us to examine London Borough's file about them. None wrote to us supplying this permission and we were therefore unable to contact any customers involved in the pilot to discover their views on it and why they reacted as they did.

Reactions from senior managers

Managers were surprised at the low take up of the offer of assessment even among the few customers affected by the pilot. This demonstrated to them "the difference between expectation and reality". They had insisted on a limited scope for the project because of their need to protect resources. One stated: "I put all sorts of limits on this, thinking that we would be spent out of house and home".

They admitted they had found attractive the fact that the project was highly controllable. Indeed, even the limited results from the pilot gave them enough confidence to consider embarking on a similar scheme in the future. They said that they would not now be so frightened to do so.

Discussion and conclusions

It is ironic that the most innovative of the three projects should have been the least successful. No-one was telling London Borough that it should improve access to its assessment services nor remind customers of their statutory rights – least of all local organisations of disabled people themselves. Yet, the pilot sought to do just that in a straightforward and easy to use way. Given its meagre impact we are left with intriguing speculation and little more.

Now that the House of Lords, in the Gloucestershire Case, has permitted social services authorities to have regard to available resources when assessing a person's need for services under the Chronically Sick and Disabled Persons Act 1970, there is far less reason for caution.

The Care Plan Project

The aim of the third pilot was to supply information in standard documents at the conclusion of an assessment telling the person assessed (and others, if any, involved) some essential results of the process. Its effect would be to increase the accountability of care management staff (and thus the borough) for their assessment decisions by requiring these to be far more formally recorded and more open. The documents would give reasons for care managers' decisions and would detail the frequency and level of any services to be provided by London Borough. They would also indicate where needs were accepted but would not be met by a current service from the authority.

Documentation

We drafted the following documents for use with the project. All except the procedure itself are reproduced in Appendix A:[13]

- a standard letter to those refused any service

- a standard letter to those offered a service

- a Care Plan for those offered a service

- a separate Matrix to accompany the Care Plan with details of services offered (level, frequency, charges etc.)

- a detailed written procedure for care managers

This was the most complex and challenging of the three pilot projects. The procedure document was itself long (8 pages) and complicated. It summarised the purpose of the procedure, set out when the letters and plan should be used and how, providing guidance on customising the letters and completing the various sections of the Care Plan.

We were conscious that the length and complexity of the procedure might cause operational difficulties for hard pressed care management staff with limited administrative support. To secure their co-operation we limited the pilot to fifty completed assessments across the area staff team.

External pressures on London Borough

Two developments occurred during the time we were planning for this project which raised its importance for London Borough, exerting strong pressure on the authority to agree to run the pilot. The Department of

Health issued guidance to social services authorities, requiring each of them to draft, consult upon and publish by April 1996 a local Community Care Charter.[14] This included the need for authorities to provide service customers with a Care Plan detailing the services which they would obtain following assessment.

The Audit Commission had also published new performance indicators for community care services, to be introduced from April 1996. To obtain the performance data required, local social services authorities would need to generate a written Care Plan at the conclusion of each assessment. Just prior to the finalisation of the pilot Care Plan we were asked by London Borough to modify it so that it would comply with these Audit Commission requirements.

Managers also informed us that the Social Services Inspectorate was pressing the authority to introduce some form of Care Plan document into its care management practice.

Staff views on project
Acknowledging the potential difficulty staff would have in complying with this new procedure, we fully consulted them on it. Service managers were concerned with the wording of the draft letters, regarding them as somewhat official and daunting. Some staff, it was felt, would have difficulty using them. They were concerned about the amount of paperwork required and the length of the Care Plan document for staff judged to be already swamped in forms.

Front-line staff were apprehensive about the legal consequences of giving information to the person they had assessed, where their decision would not meet the person's wishes or expectations. They reckoned that expenditure was now being more strictly controlled and sensed that this would lead to many of the assessment letters and Care Plans revealing needs for services which would not be met. They anticipated the pilot resulting in more complaints and appeals. Nevertheless, they welcomed the wording of the draft letter and how it sought to explain the reason why a service might be refused or limited.

Many care managers stated that the procedure, letters and Care Plan reflected their current practice. The difference, they perceived, lay in the fact that now they were going to have to write it down. Some felt this was good practice which had to be introduced. Others felt that the procedure would cause administrative chaos and that it was essential for administrative staff to guarantee to care managers the support which they would need in order to work to the new requirements.

Service users' and carers' views

We discussed the pilot with our three groups of service users and carers. There was general agreement with the idea and with the style and contents of the documentation. Carers were most positive about the new procedure though they felt that some of the wording of the draft letters was cold, impersonal and contained too much jargon. As a result we softened the language and suggested care managers personalise their letters.

Local organisation's views

Only one organisation provided views on this pilot project. As with our other work, there was strong support for the idea in principle. However, it expressed the fear that the project "may founder under the weight of its own administration". There were echoes of the reactions of staff in the view that "...Care Managers will have to be sufficiently resourced in terms of equipment or secretarial support if they are to cope with individual letters to each customer after a comprehensive assessment." In addition, there was a concern that the extra time and trouble involved might lead to a reduction in the number of comprehensive assessments undertaken by staff.

Operation and Evaluation

The pilot was run until a total of fifty assessments had been completed. All area office staff participated and undertook from one to four assessments under the procedure. Feedback was obtained in a number of ways. A group of senior staff was convened to give their views on the pilot, followed by a meeting with a larger group of care managers and social services officers. All customers involved in the pilot were sent a letter asking if they would agree to be interviewed about the experience and permit us to examine their file at the department's area office. Sixteen responded confirming their agreement to our inspecting their file and contacting them. Fifteen files were examined and ten interviews took place.

As with the eligibility criteria, we shall evaluate the pilot procedure in relation to the following questions:

- Feasibility: was the procedure practicable?

- Impact: what was its effect on assessment outcomes?

- Rationale: did the pilot procedure fulfil its aims?

Feasibility

Nothing in the feedback we received from staff suggested that the procedure had been impossible to implement. Reactions tended to focus on additional administrative burdens and the rigidity of the standard letters, the need to streamline other procedures and forms to avoid duplication and the care needed in composing documents which would be seen and read by others.

Staff said they had taken longer on many assessments due to the additional documents which had to be completed and the time required to return to the client to explain the form and to obtain a signature to it.

Some said they had needed to devote more care to recording details on the Care Plan form since the document would be disclosed to the client and could be seen by others, such as friends or family members. This particularly related to aspects of medical diagnosis or history which might need to be kept confidential.

A number of staff had encountered problems with the draft standard letters, observing that they were too long, inappropriately worded for those with whom the worker had already established a relationship and too formal. This aspect of the procedure was considered too inflexible.

Many regarded the new procedure, though practicable, to add to their case administration without customers benefiting. They stated that because they had devoted more time to these assessments, other work had been delayed.

From the accounts of service users and carers and examination of their files a different perspective emerged. This suggested that some staff clearly struggled with the new practice expected from them. Some forms we read were poorly completed with signatures missing, sections unwritten and sometimes conflicting information when the Plan was compared with the service matrix.

There can be no doubt that some of the information required on the Plan was complex and it could be contentious. Staff would have to explain its contents before asking the customer to sign if the person was not going to be confused by the whole process. Often this would have to be done in a face-to-face interview. Contact by post or the telephone would not suffice. Staff were therefore correct to observe that the new procedure would add to the time and complexity of their assessment.

London Borough's Community Care Charter

In assessing the practicability of the pilot we must acknowledge its impact on the borough's mainstream practice. Unlike the other procedures, the Care Plan project left a lasting impression and only shortly after it ended. From 1 April 1996, and with only minor modifications, the Care Plan and Matrix documents were introduced for use throughout the whole borough. Care managers were directed to employ these documents for each and every assessment which led to a service being ordered or arranged by London Borough. Furthermore, customers were to be provided with the document whether or not they asked for one.

Impact

We asked the staff group whether or not they believed the new procedure had made any impact on the outcomes of their assessments. The fairly universal response was that the new procedure merely formalised what they already did and that there was no impact on outcomes – despite their earlier assertions that it would lead to more refusals of service. Given the limitations of the study we could not explore this further.

Rationale

Did the procedure fulfil its aim of supplying the public with better information on the outcome of an assessment? Staff reported significant variations in the public's responses to the documentation. For example, in one care manager's experience when clients had been refused a service, despite being assessed to need one, they had positively appreciated receiving a record of the care manager's opinion. The group accepted that there was a proportion of their customers, receiving a service, who would welcome the documentation and want a copy of the Care Plan if this was offered to them. Its advantage was that the customer was able to mull its contents over after the care manager had left. This was particularly important where there was a carer involved.

On the other hand, other clients, particularly those too confused to read and understand the document were not interested, though staff recognised that a carer or friend might have appreciated seeing it.

Collective responsibility for decisions

When considering the draft procedure earlier, staff had welcomed it for the new emphasis it gave to the borough's collective responsibility for the decisions care managers were having to take. This effect was identified by one care manager who commented on her experience of using the pilot as follows:

Advantage was being able to make clear that decisions in an assessment were as a result of specific procedures, laid down by a higher authority, rather than the client feeling I had made a personal decision. I feel this is very important for them to understand.

Service users and carers

If the aim of the procedure was to give service users new rights to information, what did they tell us which helps to judge if this happened? We heard echoes of many of these earlier points when we interviewed a small number of service users and carers after reading their files at London Borough's area office. Some stated that they had not received the form. Others said they had but that it had meant nothing to them – the assessment was obvious, the service a simple one and they could not understand the significance of the documents. Alternatively, the Care Plan had been introduced into an existing and productive relationship which worked well on the basis of informal communications and meetings. Minor modifications to service scope or level were not perceived to need confirmation in this way.

In contrast, one carer, though entirely happy with his mother's assessment and the service provided, felt the Care Plan was especially useful for others, especially the carer. He had not expected to be given the Care Plan and Matrix. He was pleased to receive it saying, "Its like a commitment". He felt it would be easy for someone providing personal care to go in and do half of what they were supposed to do. The Care Plan and Matrix, in his view, helped to prevent this happening. It would be especially important for a vulnerable person living alone. Such considered and positive comments were exceptional amongst the feedback which we obtained.

Service users had received the standard letters in many instances. No-one we interviewed regarded the letters as important or particularly useful. The file records showed that the letters and Care Plan had sometimes had to be sent at the conclusion of a protracted assessment where there were many contacts. Timing appeared crucial to its relevance and being sent at this point seemed to reduce its usefulness.

We expected the information in the documents to be most useful to someone who was unhappy with the decision it recorded. This was not its effect in the case of one service user whose needs were reassessed resulting in a reduction of service to her. The customer felt conned by the new system, particularly when she had been asked to sign the Care Plan. She had done, now regretted doing so, and felt the new documents were peculiar and unhelpful. In her situation, they had not empowered her at all.

Carers' organisation: its conclusions

Alongside these very mixed results were positive reactions from the local carers' advocacy organisation, suggesting that these new rights might take time to become effective. Its representative believed that this pilot had been very relevant and worth undertaking.

It is quite noticeable for a number of years that although the rhetoric was about a written Care Plan neither I nor my colleagues saw very many of them. I think that a lot of the times actually having written down the information about what was agreed and what you cannot have helps to clarify. So often people are not really sure what they may have talked about unless it is written down. I think this is an important step forward.

In her view, it means that the customer has got accurate information about the reasons for their assessment and the services which they may receive as a result of it. If they wished to ask for another decision or to make a complaint then they would have a solid foundation from which to do so. She felt it probably also helped people to keep aware of their situation and to clarify who is providing or not providing a service to them. To her, procedural rights were "...all about knowing things; about things being out in the open; about reasons being made public". If these principles were ignored then the chances of the public benefiting could be much reduced.

If you don't for a start have your rights set out in a way you can understand and then you don't have written down what somebody has decided about your personal ability to use these rights you're wading through a bowl of cold porridge. And people are confused, still very confused about what they are entitled to. Anything which simplifies and shines light on the things to which people are entitled in an accessible way – that can only improve the position.

There might have been problems with the complexity of the procedure but assessment was rightly regarded as a complex activity. She could understand how greater accountability and openness as to the reasons for decisions could create difficulties for care management staff, used to taking the flak for decisions which might not be their responsibility.

Once you give reasons for your decision you are deliberately putting yourself in a position of being vulnerable because you are giving somebody the tools with which to challenge that decision. So actually giving reasons is quite a brave thing to do.

In her view, such a step needed careful training to ensure that staff feel properly supported in giving those reasons and that they understand with their hearts as well as their minds that "...having their reasons challenged is not a dreadful thing, it is one of the inevitabilities of openness". At the same time, it could require care managers to recognise the vulnerability of customers and their need, on occasions, for independent advice and advocacy.

She did not feel that any of the pilot procedures were too rigid or formalistic. However, there were important distinctions to be drawn between those getting the service and those who felt they were not. In general, the former favoured an informal, friendly relationship with the care manager. On the other hand, people who are not getting a service are often frustrated by informality, for example if it prevents their being able to ascribe decisions to a named person. Having to talk to people over the phone who decline to put what they know in writing just adds to their frustration because they are already dissatisfied with the service they are (or are not) receiving. She summarised the case for greater formality thus:

> *If you are trying to assist somebody to achieve some kind of change in their circumstances... it is always tremendously helpful to have written down who else has been involved, what they are doing, what they are responsible for. Because a lot of the people you are going to try to help do not themselves necessarily have a clue. You have to do a lot of detective work.*

Senior management's conclusions

Next we summarise the views of senior managers on the aims of the procedure and whether or not they considered these were met. To them, this pilot had been one of their greatest priorities though it was clear from what they told us that there were more reasons for this than the creation of new rights for service users.

As we have already stated, there were certainly external factors forcing such changes on to their authority's agenda. The Social Services Inspectorate applied significant pressure on the authority to ensure that it introduced a Care Plan and its new Community Care Charter offered everyone who received a service a copy of their Care Plan. The Audit Commission's new performance indicators also made it essential for London Borough to have such a document. They acknowledged to us that the current Care Plan document had been introduced on 1 April 1996 due to these external pressures.

They also saw the pilot as helping to raise standards of assessment practice. They had anticipated having some problems with staff adjusting to the demands of the pilot. They feared that it would be regarded as just another piece of paper and a bureaucratic demand thrust upon care managers. But to senior managers it reflected a standard of good practice that had "a price worth paying."

> *It brings an open way of working; a structured way of working. It takes people through a process whereby you actually have to think systematically about how you are going to try and assess and then meet someone's needs. It takes people through a process that I am keen for them to go through rather than just be like a knee jerk reaction – 'I like Mrs Jones because she makes nice tea'. It gave a much needed sense of structure... we actually say to people, 'This is what we think are your needs, and this is what we intend to do about them'. It is not something that should have any more point to it than that.*

We should observe at this point that one Practice Manager told us that some of his team's recording had become more succinct and direct due to the need to complete the Care Plan.

Senior managers saw a third objective for the procedure. They were conscious that some of their staff did not always take responsibility for their assessment decisions. In their view, the Care Plan documentation therefore helped to link the care manager's assessment and decision on services with London Borough, the organisation.

As to the main aim of the procedure – to provide information to service users – they recognised that it was not a document which customers would necessarily find of use at once. It was like an "insurance policy" which they might have to turn to later on.

Given the reactions which we had received from service users, particularly those with established relationships with the Department, we asked if there was an important contrast here. Managers felt the documents were relevant both to short and long term relationships between London Borough and its customers. Their experience told them that it was often impossible to predict when contact was first made with a customer how long that contact might last or how complex the care package might be. They therefore saw the need to continue to require a Care Plan wherever a service was provided or arranged. However, it might be necessary to refine the lengthy and complex document currently in use to make it shorter and more simple for use with straightforward assessments. There had also been complaints that the procedure was unduly bureaucratic and required staff to duplicate records which they were already expected to complete elsewhere. They planned to re-examine existing documentation to eliminate the causes of these concerns.

Discussion and researcher's conclusions

The culture and style of working which we discovered in London Borough were not such that the adoption into practice of a written Care Plan would ever be easy. Care managers with modest administrative support and virtually no assistance from IT tended to communicate with service users, carers and other third parties in an informal, often verbal way. This may have suited the type of relationship they would prefer to develop and maintain with service users, one stressing their personal responsibility for ensuring that arrangements worked to the customer's satisfaction rather than the corporate responsibility of London Borough.

Requiring care management staff to complete, have approved and supply a copy of a written Care Plan would therefore have represented a major shift away from this manner of working and would be seen as involving extra time, trouble and disruption. Thus we were not surprised at staff's lack of enthusiasm for piloting the new document nor at the difficulties which they encountered when they did so. To hand to someone a precise written specification of your professional judgement on needs and services must have appeared daunting for many of London Borough's staff. We found it very hard to accept the account we heard that this was equivalent to current practice, simply "written down".

Carers and users in the groups we convened were strongly in favour of these documents. The local advocacy organisation thought they were crucial. The feedback from those who were actually given the forms hardly reflected these views. A number of reasons could explain this lack of impact. The forms may have been given following a review when satisfactory services changed little or not at all; they could have been filled in so poorly as to be of little use to the recipient; the person who received the documents may not have been able to read or understand them.

Although the assessment section of the document is fairly complex and the public's reactions to its contents will vary depending on a range of personal factors, if staff do not complete the document accurately and helpfully, its potential will be lost and service users will be further confused not empowered.

Training needs

Staff will need training to equip them with the skills and confidence to make the most of the document. The ability to write up professional file notes is not the same as that needed to describe succinctly and "on the record" the reasons for a judgement about a person's need for services and the Borough's possibly limited response to meeting this.

Promoting a rights culture

What is also likely to be needed is professional development and training on the rationale for these types of policies and practices, in effect on London Borough's Community Care Charter, from which service users and carers now derive their "rights" to information and to a care plan if a service is provided following assessment. We sensed a strongly held view – almost a prejudice – among many care managers that "paperwork" was at best a chore and at worst an irrelevance of no benefit to service users. In part, this may represent an understandable reluctance from social care professionals to become pen-pushing bureaucrats. Paper based communication can also be rigid, impersonal and ineffective. The letters we drafted for use following assessments did not appear to have assisted anyone and other ways may need to be found formally to convey the "reasons" which they contained.

However, such thinking will constantly hinder the effectiveness of any rights which depend on good standards of administration, recording and written and verbal communication. Many procedural rights depend on all of these. If a procedure is introduced to provide rights for all, this will require 100 per cent compliance, not merely a response when articulate "consumers" make a fuss or press for good practice. What this means for staff and how they will be assisted in accomplishing the new levels of practice needs to be spelled out to ensure the new policy gains constructive support, not resigned compliance. The observations on guaranteeing procedures which we made above in relation to the eligibility criteria apply here with as much force. Later, we suggest how a new form of public service guarantee may be needed to encourage higher standards of practice and greater respect for users' rights.[15]

There are reciprocal responsibilities resting on the organisation and those managing it. Staff can reasonably expect their employer also to provide the administrative support needed to meet new levels of expectation. The virtual absence of assistance from IT in London Borough was striking. Without it, we expect staff may struggle for a long time to meet the demands of the Community Care Charter.

Advocacy for those unable to use their rights
The views from carers and from the advocacy organisation suggest that those without assistance and especially those with limited understanding will have great difficulty in using the information supplied and gaining tangible benefits from the disclosure. Yet, as one family carer observed, such service users will be the most vulnerable in the circumstances. In public policy terms, this strengthens the argument for full implementation of the Disabled Persons (Services, Consultation and Representation) Act 1986 so that local authorities, like London Borough, are required to appoint an independent advocate to represent the interests of those unable to do so themselves.

Conclusions and lessons

Feedback
What had been the project's objectives and had these been met? Why had London Borough collaborated with us on the study? Senior managers in the division considered that the collaboration had been a productive one but they clearly saw it as helping to raise standards of practice as much as providing rights to service users or the public.

They accepted that there were problems with variable practice in the department which contributed to some inequitable allocation of services. One reason for this, they judged, was the mismatch of professional approaches, represented on the one hand by the new care management role and, on the other, by conventional social work practice. As a result, staff gave insufficient priority to administration in their thinking and in their practice.

> *If you start talking about rights, accurate assessment, accurate recording and so on and have this overlay – I am working with this person's emotional difficulties – you start to have a torn individual.*

The research introduced methods which sought to resolve some of this conflict.

Senior managers were conscious that the research had focused on rights to information. They recognised the problems which arose because the department was not clear about the services which they provided and who was entitled to them. Developments, such as the research pilot, which brought more clarity were useful and necessary but, in their experience, they also proved to be a double edged sword from the political and managerial point of view.

Political costs of new rights to information
They said that if the public became better informed about their entitlements, then people would complain when a service was reduced or eliminated.

Clarity for us is vital. But in terms of actually then making people shut up and go away and only worry about themselves, it has done exactly the opposite. Protest groups, three years ago, were not dreamed of. They are there because people actually now see what they think they should have and see it disappearing over the horizon.

These observations were also developed in relation to the Audit Commission's encouragement of clear and comprehensive eligibility criteria. They drew attention to the political price to pay for greater openness at a time of reducing budgets and service contraction.

The thing that the Audit Commission has been driving us towards is clear eligibility. If you do not have the resources then you ratchet them up so it is very clear who is not going to get a service. Well, it will be a miracle if our house work service survives another year. Fifteen hundred elderly people without their floors being hoovered!

They judged that their work with IPPR had had an impact on the ways in which senior managers approached these issues. They felt that it had influenced the culture of the division, at least at a senior level, and in particular the approach which they had adopted when drafting and introducing the Community Care Charter. It had also prepared them for coping with the new Audit Commission performance indicators for community care. They believed that it had encouraged a recognition, even from those in London Borough who might be resistant to change, of the need "...to think about what they were doing and why".

Reasons for progress in London Borough
Senior managers commented that, in their view, the project had made progress because they had been permitted to select, from the options given to them, the subjects for the pilots. "We were allowed to participate in exactly what the priority was", one manager stated. This choice, they believed, enabled them to identify those areas of work which were priorities for the department and from which it would obtain the greatest benefit. However, without IPPR's assistance they would not have had within their department the skills and resources needed to co-ordinate and "drive" the project work. An external research institute had combined clarity and independence of

thought with single-mindedness and applied these to the department's activities – qualities generally lacking in social services departments.

Carers' advocacy organisation
The local voluntary organisation most closely interested in the research considered the study had addressed central problems faced by anyone seeking a community care service from London Borough. Its representative summarised these challenges as the availability of information on services and the approachability of the authority. Information was improving but could still be much better. She believed it was still difficult for people who had not been in touch with social services to make the first contact with the department. Approaching the authority for help still had associations which were stigmatising to some people and when their initial contact with the department's staff was a negative one this could leave an indelible impression on the person and their future relationship with London Borough.

Conclusions and lessons
The project as a whole worked relatively smoothly in London Borough for some clearly identifiable reasons. While care managers have a degree of professional freedom in practice and in decision-making, their employer can direct each of them to work to minimum standards and their scope for independent operation is limited. Local authority departments are managed in traditionally hierarchical ways and this facilitates authoritative standard setting from the centre. Furthermore, the area of activity in which the pilot projects were established was already one where procedural guidance was used to set standards and provide information. Staff could not argue that procedural rights would introduce a new bureaucracy where none was seen before.

What also gave the work a fair wind were the increasing external pressures on the authority to implement public policy aims using the types of methods we were proposing to London Borough. The authority had a vested interest in collaborating with the study and there were tangible gains for it if it did so. One has to observe, though, that there was little pressure for these types of changes being exerted on the authority from independent users' and carers' organisations in its locality. There may be a number of reasons for this. It may reflect their concern for other priorities, particularly the future of the borough's substantive services. The lack of systematic and rigorous consultation with users and carers could account for it. It may also be explained by low expectations of administrative openness and consistency which users and carers may have.

Impact on London Borough
The research led London Borough to introduce two new procedures which had an immediate effect on its services, will both continue, at least in some form, and which may help to contribute to longer term changes in the organisation. Although we cannot measure the impact of the procedures on individual outcomes, we can offer some broad conclusions on the projects.

Local social services authorities are now expected to have clear policies on eligibility for services.[16] Our work on the personal care criteria and their introduction throughout the authority showed how these might be developed. The pilot built on this basic expectation by demonstrating how staff could use the criteria in an open way with people being assessed for services to help to show how they made their decisions and why.

As part of its Community Care Charter an authority such as London Borough is also required to provide service users with a written record of services arranged for them – a fundamental procedural right. The Care Plan documents we piloted with London Borough fulfilled this basic obligation. It extended earlier practice in the borough on disclosure (the discontinued first Care Plan) and tested the administrative capacity of the organisation.

The Disabled Persons Project had little or no impact on the borough, except for the fresh perspective it gave to senior managers on measures designed to improve the public's access to assessment and, through this, to services. Increasingly, local authorities must provide information on entitlement to those who are intended to benefit from it despite the obvious disincentives which they may have for doing so. Sometimes they are placed under a specific legal duty to do so.[17] The Disabled Persons Pilot showed there may be ways of managing this without fears about effects on resources being justified.

Lessons: accept the rationale of fair treatment rights
Each of the pilot projects offered new ways of providing information fairly and effectively. The role for changes like these will become more not less important in the future. Authorities such as London Borough will have to accept the rationale for them, adapting to the distinctive ways of working which they require and giving prominence in policy and practice to meeting new standards of fairness, reliability and consistency.

Guarantee high standards of administration
The pilots showed the need for a disciplined and rigorous approach to administrative practice. For the borough to approve and publish eligibility

criteria, even to the modest extent required by the Personal Care pilot, suggests to the public that the authority accepts an obligation to comply with these criteria, showing a willingness to be accountable to them if it does not. To require individual written plans which record assessed needs, planned care and needs remaining unmet increases the authority's responsibility to be clear about what it guarantees to provide and what it merely hopes to offer.

The research demonstrated just how important high standards of public administration are to a "rights based" approach to assessment. If these do not have much priority within the organisation then fair treatment rights may well be ignored or indifferently respected.

A strategic plan for Charter rights
As we were concluding the research, London Borough's Community Care Charter was published and distributed to staff for them to comply with it. We discovered during this research a range of barriers to introducing new rights: administrative overload, resistance to "paperwork", poor compliance when using procedures. In view of these, to introduce a change as far-reaching as the Charter may demand an approach altogether more strategic and planned than the one which was adopted.

A Departmental Action Plan may be needed explaining the philosophy behind the Charter, the new standards which staff must meet to comply with it and innovations which will help them to do so. The parts of the Plan which set out fair treatment standards could be written like a code of practice. Built into the Plan would be a timetable for evaluating its impact and procedures for ensuring users and carers could describe their experiences and express relevant views on the Charter's impact.

Improve administrative support to staff
From what we learned in London Borough, innovative investment in IT and other administrative support is essential if new bureaucratic burdens of supplying individuals with full information is not to produce its own distortions, costs and disincentives.

Audit impact of changes
London Borough should evaluate the impact of its Community Care Charter, and carefully audit the effect of using its new Care Plan, to judge whether more direction is now required to ensure full compliance. It must assess how staff are coping with these complex documents and whether or not users' and carers' rights are being fully respected. Are service users also

obtaining clear and useful information from the Care Plan, and has its introduction affected outcomes at all? Service users who are alone and unable to cope with written information may have gained little from the practice. The borough may have to consider new measures to help them to do so in the future such as the provision of an independent advocate or friend.

The authority should also research the impact of the personal care criteria and whether or not they have affected care managers' assessment decisions. Senior managers believed the IPPR criteria to be narrow enough to contain expenditure. Front line staff judged them to be far too vague to do this and said they would have to resort to rationing the level of service not eligibility for it in order to keep within budget. Both views cannot be correct, unless the authority is fully funding all needs for services for everyone within the criteria – an improbable assumption in view of all that we heard.

Front line staff: impact and lessons
The pilot projects assisted staff who were already inclined to use such ways of working during their assessments and who welcomed new opportunities for openness. It clearly challenged some care managers who found paper-based work difficult or viewed it as distracting.

The message from the research is that any rights based approach to assessment will always depend to some extent on collective policy, formal records of decisions and on written communication. If there is resistance to using these skilfully and accurately then respect for rights is likely to suffer.

Fair treatment not consumerism
The priority for training and staff development should be to increase staff confidence in working in these ways, to the higher standards of accountability which they introduce and within the overall philosophy on which they are based. For rights like these – to guaranteed fair treatment – derive not from any narrow perception of the public's rights as consumers but from their citizenship itself. To be effective and respected, the rights do not therefore have to depend on service users actively recognising and "claiming" their rights. If this was the case, staff would only have to provide information to those who deliberately asked for it or those who they judged would use it profitably.

Service users and carers: impact and lessons
What has been the impact on service users and on carers? Are there any lessons for them? On the basis of the small samples of service users to

whom we listened, and feedback from care managers, two of the three pilot projects had little significant impact upon them during and after the assessment process. In the Disabled Persons pilot, none of those involved agreed to be interviewed. Such results suggest a low level of demand for the measures which were piloted, in fairly stark contrast to the enthusiasm of carers and users consulted before the projects were introduced.

The role of independent advice

Those with experience of problems, or with expert knowledge of acting as advocate and therefore able to compare practice across the borough, had needed no convincing of the usefulness of changes. What this may reveal is that the documents and procedures will achieve little on their own in situations where what is needed is the added intervention of an independent adviser or informal advocate.

It is very possible that, in the same way that care managers were heard to complain of bureaucracy and paperwork, service users and carers would have precisely the same reaction and would find it hard to have a positive attitude towards documents and procedures appearing impersonal and complex. The picture is not entirely clear and further research is needed to clarify what is going on. A Senior Care manager involved with the Personal Care Project observed that customers appeared to be far more interested in their written individual care plan now that everyone had to be provided with one than they had been in the standard leaflet listing the criteria given to them during the pilot.

Bias towards information rights

The problem arises because of a bias found with many procedural rights. Although guaranteeing fair treatment amounts to more than merely responding to individual consumerism, it does lean towards ensuring a person receives information, assuming that they will then be able to act on that information. Anyone who is unable to understand, interpret or challenge information will therefore operate at a disadvantage if they cannot obtain assistance or support in interpreting and using the information. The obvious lesson here is the crucial importance of ensuring the public and service users have access to expert, independent and effective advisers and advocates. For those lacking capacity to seek or act on such advice, it is essential for their interests to be protected by the formal appointment of an independent representative, as was envisaged under the Disabled Persons (Services, Consultation and Representation) Act 1986.

Despite these observations, it is possible to overstate the principle that users will need to be aware of their rights in order that these can be effective. With measures to increase openness and accountability, active user engagement with their rights may not be needed at all. The existence of published criteria may influence the fairness of a care manager's assessment decision, whether or not a person can read and understand a leaflet listing them. Similarly, the requirement to disclose the reasons for an assessment on a written care plan may improve the quality and consistency of a care manager's decisions, whether or not service users actually read the plans she writes.

For local policy purposes, it will be important to distinguish between these and recognise when vulnerable service users need assistance in order to pursue their rights effectively.

The public: impact and lessons

The public, as would-be users and as local citizens, were not formally involved in any of the work which we undertook with London Borough and we cannot say it had any impact on them at all. However, what the authority learned in the course of the research may encourage it to be clearer with the public about what it offers and to whom. In time, London Borough's standard information on services may give more precise details of the threshold for eligibility, even some idea about the level of service a person might expect to receive given a range of commonly experienced needs.

Endnotes

1 Audit Commission (1996) *Balancing the Care Equation: Progress with Community Care*, Community Care Bulletin No. 3 HMSO; Association of Metropolitan Authorities and the Association of County Councils (1995) *Who gets Community Care: A Survey of Community Care Eligibility Criteria*, AMA.

2 National Consumer Council (1995) *Charging consumers for social services* NCC.

3 Under s. 46 National Health Service and Community Care Act, 1990.

4 Under s. 47 National Health Service and Community Care Act, 1990.

5 Social Services Inspectorate (1992) CI (92)34, Implementing Caring for People: Assessment.

6 See p. 181.

7 See p. 183.

8 Managers informed us that at the same time as the criteria were introduced a maximum limit on weekly spending on personal care was also introduced which had a significant impact.

9 Audit Commission (1994) *Taking Stock: Progress with Community Care*, Community Care Bulletin No. 2, HMSO.

10 *R -v- Gloucestershire County Council and Secretary of State for Health ex parte Barry* (1997) The Times 21 March, HL.

11 See pages 185 and 186.

12 This refers to the Gloucestershire Case, note 10 above.

13 See pp.187–196.

14 See Department of Health (1995) A Framework for Local Community Care Charters in England and LAC (94)24.

15 See p.175 below.

16 Audit Commission (1994) *op. cit.* and Audit Commission (1996) *op. cit.*

17 For example, under the Children Act, 1989; see s.24 and Schedule 2.

3. City Council: fair treatment rights for care leavers

What the Chapter contains

In this chapter we describe the work which we undertook with the Social Services Department of City Council, a Metropolitan District Council in Northern England (population: 275,000 approx.). It falls into four sections. First, we outline the aims of our project and its relevance to the broad purpose of the research. Next follows a description of the first stage of our work – initial investigations and planning prior to designing the new pilot procedures. In the third section we tell how we designed two such procedures and introduced one of them into trial practice. We conclude the chapter with our overall conclusions and lessons.

Project Aims

Young people who leave local authority care[1] in their middle to later teenage years often face severe disadvantage and difficulty when trying to establish stable and independent lives.[2] A number of reasons may cause or aggravate these problems. For a start, the care leaver is forced to leave home on average some years earlier than the person who has not been in care. Most do so between the ages of 16 and 18 years whilst only a third of those not in care leave home before their 19th birthday.[3] The factors which led to their being in care may also disrupt or inhibit their emotional or educational development. The young person's race or cultural background, any disability which they have or the absence of any formal substitute family will further increase their disadvantages. Widespread youth unemployment, recent reductions in social security entitlements for those under 25 years old and in the availability of public housing further threaten the care leaver's opportunities when starting out on their adult life.

Faced with these circumstances, many care leavers discover that independence for them will mean homelessness,[4] poverty, poor health, limited educational opportunities and vulnerability to crime.[5] For some, there will also be an added risk of exploitation, loneliness and problems with relationships and their sexuality.

There is now a well recognised connection between the degree of risk that a care leaver will face such problems and the adequacy of their preparation for independence from the authority.[6] Young people having to cope alone need a good grounding in the practical skills and information required when on their own. Where resources from other agencies or services are required – such as for health or education – plans may have to be carefully and rigorously co-ordinated. Reliable and continuing personal contact and support will often need to be offered to the young person to help them manage new emotional and practical challenges. Financial assistance may be needed to help to establish and furnish a home, continue in education and training or retain contact with family and friends, particularly former foster carers. Here would appear to be a system where rights to fair and adequate assistance are of fundamental importance.

Despite growing acceptance of the importance of after-care planning and the benefit this can give to outcomes, recent studies continue to confirm widely varying provision of resources – in terms of policy, staffing, accommodation and finance – which local authorities commit to the needs of their care leavers.[7] A geographical lottery, not any fair system of rights, seems to determine the opportunities given to young people having to survive in such circumstances.

The Children Act, 1989: new law and policy guidance
When child care law was fundamentally reformed by the Children Act 1989, this situation was acknowledged and the opportunity was used to attempt to raise the low baseline in local funding priorities and in social work practice. Thus in 1991, when important parts of that Act came into force, a set of new duties and powers for local authorities was introduced. These were intended to influence how social services departments provided both for young people in their care and those who had recently left it. To complement them, new regulations and guidance from the Department of Health sought to raise standards of practice and provision across the country.

The new duties stressed the need for consultation with all parties affected, for long term planning and for information, ensuring that any young person who needed this received "advice and befriending" after leaving care and until they were 21 years old. These were consistent with the new philosophy found in the Act, which highlighted concepts such as partnership, participation and openness. An authority's power to provide assistance, particularly financial assistance, was also defined.

Fair treatment principles and care leavers
The 1989 changes have not provided care leavers with any new enforceable personal legal rights. However, they have raised expectations that authorities will act fairly when assessing needs and meeting them. Care leavers and those who represent their interests will therefore expect greater accountability from practitioners and from authorities for their decisions. In these circumstances, fresh approaches will be required if young people in care and beyond it are to be treated fairly and authorities are to deliver on their new commitments.

Fair treatment principles are highly relevant when this new deal is planned and introduced. Local authorities must now ensure that those entitled to decent preparation and after-care are provided with these when they are judged to need them. Such judgements will need to be made within an equitable and open system of decision-making. Taking our model of procedural rights as a starting point, how could these be applied to any new strategy for care leavers? A fair system would be built around at least the following core rights:

- *"Eligibility" information*: a care leaver should be able to discover what assistance she or he is entitled to receive after leaving care and how to obtain it.

- *The right to participate*: a care leaver should be able to take part in the process by which their plans for leaving care are decided, if necessary being provided with independent assistance when doing so.

- *Fairness and consistency in decision-making*: decisions on plans and provision for care leavers should be consistent with policy and decisions in similar cases, take account of all relevant factors and not be arbitrary.

- *"Reasons" information*: a care leaver affected by decisions taken about them, should be able to learn the reasons for these.

- *Complaints and Review*: a care leaver affected by decisions taken about them, should have access to a speedy, independent and effective review system providing the means to challenge any significant decision with which s/he disagrees.

Our research with City Council explored new initiatives to test out these principles and rights. Social work practitioners are already familiar with working to procedures and we quickly discovered considerable potential for linking each of these principles to practical procedural rights. The Department of Health's extensive Children Act Guidance itself and the experience of local authorities already developing practice in this field, suggested possible ideas. These included published policy documents setting out criteria for action and entitlement; new procedures for planning services linked to the statutory review system; information leaflets and the provision of advocacy and advice for the young person leaving care. After our initial investigations, two particular ideas were developed into pilot projects. Next we describe why these were chosen and how they were planned.

First Stage: planning

Aims and methods
During the first stage of our work we aimed to investigate the ways in which services were organised in City Council and to propose options for further development and piloting.

To investigate the situation fully in order to consider and report on options we:

● researched the relevant legal and policy background to the planning and provision of services for care leavers

● obtained and considered City Council's documents and published policies on care leavers

● prepared an interim report containing our preliminary findings and proposing recommendations for pilot projects in the authority

● listened to Social Services staff and managers describe current practice and its limitations

● listened to voluntary organisations describe their perceptions of City Council's services for care leavers

● listened to young people in care and those who have recently left care describe their preparations for independent living

● listened to foster carers describe their relationship with City Council and the limitations of current practice and provision

We had hoped to survey the current practice and attitudes of City Council's field social workers using a questionnaire in the same way as we successfully elicited views in London Borough. However, senior managers would not agree to this, believing that it would add to the practical demands on staff in the department and might adversely affect morale.

Initial observations and interviews

IPPR's researcher spent two weeks meeting managers and staff working in various parts of City Council's Social Services Department, in local voluntary organisations providing family support and in homeless persons' accommodation provided by the Housing Department.

After it was agreed that the research would focus on the position of care leavers, we conducted a number of more structured consultations with national and local voluntary organisations concerned with the rights and welfare of children in care. With the assistance of a local voluntary organisation providing advice, assistance and advocacy for young people in care we convened a meeting of young people, some of whom were still in care but within sight of leaving it, and some of whom had already left formal care.

City Council staff responsible for fostering convened a meeting of foster carers who told us of their impressions of social work practice and its weaknesses. We also spent time in separate meetings with residential and field social workers obtaining their perspectives on current arrangements for planning and providing after-care.

City Council's documentation

Given that City Council had not yet developed new policy and procedures to reflect its obligations to care leavers, there were few documents to consider when planning our projects. City Council was one of the social services authorities piloting for the Department of Health the use of annual Children's Services Plans setting out the authority's policy, strategy and targets. The council's intentions in relation to care leavers were covered in a section of this document, setting out a candid assessment of its failings in this area of provision. Future objectives, including the creation of a discrete service for care leavers, were outlined in the 1994/95 Plan.

Statutory review forms and notes

We obtained and considered a number of practice documents in current use. These included the forms and guidance notes used when the circumstances of a child or young person in care were formally reviewed in a meeting chaired by a social work manager – termed a statutory review. The documents were written in 1987 and had not been modified to take account of the changes resulting from implementation of the Children Act in 1991 or the regulations made under it. Separate forms were available for completion by the various participants in the review. These were the means by which the field social worker responsible conveyed background information to those attending the meeting and the young person, parent and foster carer, if any, made a written contribution setting out their views and wishes. On another form in the series the review chair would record the decisions of the meeting for circulation to participants.

Written guidance on expenditure for care leavers
Guidance to staff on authorising expenditure was given in an "Allocation of Functions" document, again unchanged since before the Children Act came into force. This set out the circumstances in which financial assistance could be made to a young person who had left the care of the authority.

Interim Report
After our initial observations and investigations had been completed and the focus for our research had become clear a detailed interim report was delivered to senior managers in City Council. Our reasons for concentrating on care leavers were these:

● City Council had not developed any new policies or procedures to comply with its Children Act duties and there were therefore many ideas we could experiment with.

● There was support from appropriate voluntary organisations for the research to focus on care leavers.

● Care leavers offered a clearly defined group of potential service recipients for whom new "rights" could be relatively easily introduced and piloted.

Next we shall set out our findings on the legal and policy framework for after-care and the features of the service, such as it was, provided to its care leavers by City Council.

Findings: the legal framework for care leavers' rights
Section 24 Children Act, 1989 imposes on a local social services authority such as City Council a number of defined duties which are designed to improve after-care. The provisions can be summarised thus:

- Where a child or young person is being looked after by the authority then it has a duty to advise, assist and befriend the child or young person with a view to promoting his or her welfare when they cease to be looked after.

- The authority has a duty to advise and befriend a person under 21 years who, at any time after s/he was 16 years of age, was looked after by the authority.

- For this last duty to apply, the person must be in need of such help, not able to obtain it from anyone looking after them and must ask the authority for the help.

- The authority is given a power – not a duty – to provide assistance to the person who has left care. This may, exceptionally, be financial, and may be offered subject to conditions such as repayment (though not this if the person is on social security).

- The authority may assist the person by paying towards living expenses associated with employment or education and training, and by making a grant towards expenses of education and training.

The Children Act introduced a number of additional duties to complement these specific provisions.

- Every local authority must establish a procedure for considering any representations (including a complaint) made to them "by a person qualifying for advice and assistance about the discharge of their functions... in relation to him".

- Every local authority must publish information about its services under s.24 and, where appropriate, comparable services which others provide. It must take "such steps as are reasonably practicable to ensure that those who might benefit from the services receive the information relevant to them".[8]

As well as these duties relating to care leavers, the 1989 Act also established some general obligations which are relevant to the research. Thus, an authority is required to consult a child or young person in its care, their parents, if any, and others, where appropriate, whose wishes and feelings must be taken into account and given due consideration before any decision is taken which affects such a person's welfare or plans.[9]

An authority is also required to establish and conduct a system of regular reviews of the child or young person in care's situation and of its plans for their future care.[10] The law specifies a number of matters which each Review has to encompass. One of these concerns after-care since every Review must consider:

> 8. *Whether arrangements need to be made for the time when the child will no longer be looked after or provided with accommodation by the responsible authority.*[11]

Findings: policy and practice guidance

Extensive, well-written guidance to local authorities and social work practitioners has been issued by the Department of Health. This clarifies the meaning and effect of many of the Act's provisions and requires local authorities to issue various local policy and procedure documents and to publish information for those intended to benefit from the authority's service.

This guidance:

- amplifies the meaning of "after-care". It is to include "...advice, general help and moral support, financial assistance in exceptional circumstances and specific financial assistance in connection with employment, education or training";[12]

- requires the careful formal assessment, with the young person, their parents (if appropriate) and other agencies involved, of after-care needs and the planning of services;

- obliges local authorities to formulate and publish a clear written statement of its philosophy and practice on the preparation of young people for leaving care and the provision of after-care support, particularly the criteria it will use for the giving of financial or other assistance to a young person;

- requires local authorities to provide an "easy to read guide to its services for young people when they leave care... informed by the views of young people who are being, or have been cared for, and their parents and foster parents";

- requires each local authority to nominate a "designated officer" within the Social Services department to be responsible for the statement and guide; and

- describes necessary elements of good practice in the planning, delivery and regular monitoring of aftercare, and the co-operation which other agencies (housing, probation, social security etc.) will need to render in order for effective services to be available.

What impact had this law and guidance had upon City Council's approach to providing for care leavers' needs? Next, we outline the key characteristics of the service which we saw in operation.

Children's services in City Council: some general observations
Both from background documents we read and during our many interviews we learned of the severe pressures on City Council's service and the limitations which this placed on its scope and effectiveness. Due to budget reductions, the social work department had been contracting since 1987 and some staff had been made redundant. Social needs in the city were increasing due to economic recession. Fears of children being abused were particularly acutely felt. Severe poverty affected a significant proportion of the city's population and its children.

These pressures had consequences for children's services in City Council. We were told that a proportion of children subject to child protection procedures and placed on the "at risk" register did not have any social worker personally allocated to them. The same situation affected a number of children or young people in local authority accommodation. It was acknowledged that the needs of care leavers, amongst many groups with a claim on the authority's diminishing resources, had not been given priority.

Even during our short period of contact with it, we obtained a strong impression of the culture, style and organisation of the department. It had a distinct reputation for community social work. This was reflected in the generic practice which had existed until very recently and in the local autonomy given to area offices and to individual social work practitioners.

This had encouraged many variations in practice and approach which had been tolerated by senior managers for many years. There was diversity in practice and different degrees of compliance with centrally ordained procedures. When interviewed, one senior manager told us that he had recently discovered there were eleven different versions of a standardised child protection form. Though common child protection procedures had been introduced throughout the department the 1994 report of the Area Child Protection Committee reported a failure to use the CP1 form on all occasions when this was necessary and that for 35 per cent of children on the "at risk" register, their cases were not being reviewed at the appropriate interval.

In addition to these contrasts, area offices had varying budgets and staff resources which led them to respond differently to those seeking help. Some of those we interviewed described the areas as each having their own distinct ethos: the consequences for care leavers are detailed below. We were told that the department was not one that was directed or led by senior managers responsible for policy at the centre. Certainly, our investigations of practice regarding care leavers appeared to confirm this description. One practitioner described a "deeply rooted resistance to a corporate approach".

Although these observations accurately portrayed the service as it was in 1994, major changes were planned and about to be implemented. By January 1995, management structures in children's services had been reconfigured in a fundamental way, the aim of these being to achieve more effective policy implementation and to rein in the autonomy of area offices. One of the intended practice changes, we learned, was to introduce a "child planning" system for children and young people in the care of the authority based on the Dartington model promoted by the Department of Health.[13]

After-care for care leavers
In 1994, City Council had no clearly developed service at all for care leavers. It had only just begun to acknowledge the need for new policy and for resources to be channelled into a discrete and responsive after-care service. No specialised procedures had been introduced to aid the care leaver's preparation for independent living; no information strategy had been designed to inform young people, parents, foster carers and staff of the department's approach and how it would be operate in practice; prior to 1995, it was not even clear as to who was the designated officer required by the Government's guidance; lastly, there was no explicit policy in City Council explaining what assistance, particularly financial help, would be available to any care leaver and how this might be obtained. Indeed, we were given reasons for doubting that managers even knew what budget actually existed for s.24 expenditure by the authority.

City Council's Children's Services Plan conceded that much needed to be done to improve aftercare to comply with the legal and policy expectations created by the 1989 Act. Although the housing department's policy meant that homeless 16–17 year olds could be accommodated in council housing, the Plan stated that "[m]any of these tenancies fail, however, because of a lack of integration between housing and support services and a lack of direct practical help...". Examples such as this caused the Plan to conclude:

[City Council] is also characterised by a lack of consistency in practice by field and residential staff. Support to individual young people depends on the commitment of the individual worker, residential unit or foster carer rather than agreed policy and consistently applied practice. This is so in terms of financial, social and educational support with huge variations in the quality of service.

Social workers we interviewed confirmed this was the situation. One stated:

What does s.24 amount to? Basically, duty [ie limited help from the duty social worker] and a bit of financial assistance. The idea of advising, assisting and befriending is not something we can actually do. We do not have the resources to do that. We do not have the resources to deal with those who are being looked after and those on the at risk register.

Some graphic observations from those who had once been in City Council's care reinforced this impression. One person could still recall what it felt like to be forced into independence with little warning and less preparation:

I was tret like an article of food in the shop which was past its sell-by date and was taken off the shelf and just discarded.

The detailed comments of all those we interviewed confirmed a picture of absent or failing policy and procedure and the impact which this had on the service.

Planning and preparation
The statutory review system was governed by a series of forms and a set of guidance notes dating from 1987 which had not been adapted at all to take account of the important changes made by the Children Act. The guidance notes did refer to the need to be aware of "critical points in the life of a child in care including preparation for leaving care". However, nothing in the procedure or forms required staff to conduct reviews concerning a child facing this situation in any different way. Without any specific focus on after-care planning being triggered by age or some other event, staff told us that "they tended to drift into it".

The form used in the review process to obtain the young person's written views and plans was the same for all children whatever their age. It was universally criticised for inappropriate language for use with teenagers and for poor presentation. Most of those we interviewed doubted that young people could take this form seriously. They feared that they would therefore be put off the review system as a whole and fail to engage with it. Someone still in care appeared to confirm this when he told us that he:

> ...*got sick of the forms. One of the questions – I always put a funny answer to this one. Name, address, telephone number, sex. What do you do after you come back from school? How easy it is to make friends? What do you want from this meeting? I always used to leave that blank.*

What was unsuitable about the Contribution Sheet? The first question was worded: "Play and activities: What sort of things do you like to do in your spare time?" A field social worker commented to us on the self-evident difficulties she had when using such a document in the case of a pregnant teenage girl in care about to become a mother.

Foster carers and a local voluntary organisation highlighted the consequences of poor preparation for reviews. This was particularly noted where the plan was for a placement for which funding was required, where this was applied for and assumed to be forthcoming. When the money did not come through no alternative plan was in place and a hiatus could result. In one case described to us, foster carers had to continue to provide a home for a young person for a period without payment until other arrangements could be organised.

Residential staff observed that planning was sometimes inflexible. They also felt the need for a procedure which would unravel all the unmet needs for training and preparation for independence. A checklist of questions, tasks and skills was suggested. Foster carers also mentioned to us that administration for some reviews was poor. Written reports of decisions taken were circulated after unacceptable delays or not at all.

A local voluntary organisation often heard complaints or observations from young people that planning was left too late so decisions were rushed, the young person was left with a *fait accompli* and made to feel guilty if they did not agree to what was put to them. In any event, there were often restrictions on their choice and staff were reluctant to allow a young person the freedom to change their mind. In its view, some care leavers also found the formal meeting process a daunting one and often felt overwhelmed by it. For this age group it believed that the reviewing process should provide a place where plans for the "transfer of power and responsibility" could be discussed and set up. Instead of this, many reviews continued to reflect traditional and paternalistic ways of working.

Financial assistance to care leavers

Our investigations and interviews uncovered wide-ranging uncertainty as to the criteria for financial assistance and the process for obtaining it. It was accepted that there was available a leaving care grant usually up to a maximum of £450.00. Apart from this, one voluntary organisation likened predicting the availability of assistance from City Council to tossing a coin. Even the leaving care grant, staff informed us, had been known in one case to stretch to £950.00 or be limited in another to £200.00.

Field social workers did not appear to know precisely where the budget for s. 24 was held and their description of how money was distributed revealed a totally discretionary system with many variations, some of these plainly inequitable. They gave us the impression of a hit and miss system which could be unfair for a number of reasons. Some staff would know how to use it and others would not. Some staff would try harder than others and benefit clients by their imagination and persistence. Lastly, those taking decisions on eligibility would do so without reference to any explicit criteria. Mistaken assumptions could be made; important factors ignored or the decision depend entirely on the state of the budget.

Residential social workers and foster carers highlighted examples of apparent inconsistency and unfairness. The former described two care leavers with identical needs, one of whom had obtained a weekly top-up payment from an area team whilst the other had been refused a payment from another area office and for no apparent reason. A foster carer mentioned how her request for £15.00 to pay for a pair of spectacles for a 15 year old girl fostered with her was refused by a social worker from one office. During the next month, another social worker from a different office then took out a boy in her foster care on two occasions, visiting a local Pizza Hut to buy the boy a meal. The foster carer could see neither logic nor justice in these two contradictory approaches to financing assistance.

With others in the group, this carer felt the need to be compensated for the financial costs of providing continuing help to young people she had formerly cared for. Expenses on transport, meals, telephone calls, holidays and shopping could be incurred if contact was to be maintained with a care leaver and support offered to him or her when it was needed. None of the foster carers were clear as to whether or not City Council would agree to reimburse them for such expenditure if asked to do so. Neither were they clear as to any assistance which might be available to a care leaver. They were sure that assistance could not cover clothing or hobbies. They doubted it could ever pay for books. It was not clear in what circumstances and according to what criteria a foster placement would continue to be financed under s.24 beyond a young person's 18th birthday when they would have left care.

Information

The absence of clear and comprehensive information on eligibility meant that knowledge of what it would cover could be simply anecdotal with some staff aware that s.24 expenditure could be used imaginatively. Residential staff in the one City Council facility – a hostel – able to provide some preparation for independence described the many items of expenditure which they had successfully funded: clothing, sport, driving lessons and driving licenses, hobbies, travel, education, holiday activities, exam fees, books and stationary. Lack of information might also be suppressing uptake. One social worker drew our attention to the numbers of leaving care grants which he believed were not claimed for those needing them. He estimated that 20 per cent of the total who could be eligible received no grant.

The local voluntary organisation commented on the complete absence of information in the department and outside it on entitlement to financial assistance to pay for expenses such as these. Young people were simply not told about the opportunities and staff did not know either. There was no leaflet produced and given to care leavers. Although there were a number of voluntary sector leaflets which were available and sometimes imaginative social workers would provide these there was no expectation from City Council that they would or should do so.

Scope for procedural rights projects

After completing these initial investigations we proposed to the authority further work on two specific projects arising from what we had discovered. These comprised:

●   producing guidelines for claiming s.24 financial assistance

●   modifying the Statutory Review procedure for those in care who had reached their 15th birthday

More interest was shown in the former idea, partly because the department had nothing equivalent to such a policy document and the need for this was clear and obvious. As to the 15+ review, at first managers were hesitant about our modifying the review system whilst long term arrangements for child planning were being actively considered.[14] However, they did not object to our designing a pilot project around each of these ideas and in the next main section we describe how we did this.

Second Stage: pilot projects

Aims and context
In our work on the two projects, we intended to design, in consultation with staff, young people and others affected, some practical changes to the way in which after-care was planned and provided so as to render the system fairer and more open.

All those who realised what was required to establish an adequate service for care leavers would acknowledge the scale of the changes required in City Council and the time it might take to implement them. Resources – new or already committed to other expenditure – would need to be freed for new services to be established, with City Council social workers and voluntary sector staff working in new ways and towards different objectives.

As each of the pilots were being designed, discussed and in the case of one of them, introduced, the pace of change increased in City Council. So much so that by late 1996, when we came to interview staff in connection with that pilot, the core elements of a specialised after care service had been created. It was expected to be fully operational by April 1997. Later, we shall comment on the impact which these developments had on the scope and usefulness of our research and the attitudes of senior managers towards it.

Guidelines on financial assistance

The aim of this project was to produce a written policy incorporating both eligibility criteria for making decisions on s.24 financial assistance and a process for doing so. Our earlier investigations had revealed examples of apparent unfairness and the consequences of there being no single source of information for staff and care leavers. We hoped to design the new document so that both of these problems could be avoided. In the event, and due to the timescale which it would have required, City Council did not agree to our developing the pilot beyond a draft stage. We cannot therefore offer any conclusions about the potential impact of the document nor evaluate its usefulness in meeting these aims.

Our draft addressed the following questions:

- what does the Children Act and the Guidance issued under it expect City Council to do?

- who is entitled to ask the authority for financial assistance and when can they do so?

- what needs can be covered by financial assistance from City Council?

- how is an application for assistance made; who decides it and how are those affected informed of the reasons?

- how are care leavers to be informed of the contents and effect of the policy and procedure document?

The final document was to include two appendices – an information sheet for care leavers, and an application and decision form for use by those applying for and deciding on assistance. We reproduce, in an extract found in Appendix B,[15] the two central sections of the draft dealing with eligibility for assistance.

After explaining the legal provisions governing the authority's powers to provide assistance, the guidelines summarised Department of Health Guidance. This argues for a presumption that assistance will be provided when it was needed.

The eligibility criteria sought to capture in words the concepts which might be relevant to an assessment of need. Given City Council's circumstances the criteria included a clear reference to the relevance of resources and their availability in determining decisions on eligibility. Our list of possible expenses offered illustrations of needs which might be covered where the basic criteria were also found to apply. We envisaged that this would be an important source of consistent information and would form the basis for the leaflet for care leavers.

We circulated the draft guidelines to voluntary organisations and to senior managers in City Council. Local organisations were more keen on this pilot project than on the 15+ review for the substantial improvements in fair treatment rights which they perceived it providing. City Council's managers did not disagree, nor did they deny the need for new policy. However, the timescale which they predicted would be needed for the pilot fitted neither

IPPR's overall timetable nor its available resources. Accordingly, we did not pursue the idea.

Given the limited work which we undertook on these draft guidelines we are clearly unable to evaluate them. We did ask City Council's manager responsible for after-care whether or not she considered they would prove of use to the authority in the future. What she felt the department needed was a budget – possibly increased – for which there was a "coherent set of standards". These should be based on an assessment of needs rather than on the concept of simple entitlement. She judged IPPR's draft criteria would be very important when City Council came to finalise its policy in this area.

The 15+ Review procedure

The aim of this project was to take the existing guidelines on the conduct of statutory reviews and rework them to create a distinctive yet recognisable system for reviewing the needs of the 15+ age group. The idea was modelled on practice already introduced in a number of other social services authorities and on suggestions we had gathered from those we had interviewed. We undertook the work in the following stages:

● draft new supplementary procedure

● consult City Council staff, voluntary organisations and foster carers on contents of draft

● write new contribution sheet and information leaflet in conjunction with young people's group

● pilot the procedure and documents

● interview those involved in pilot reviews

Additional practice guidelines
The draft guidelines explicitly emphasised the importance of planning for after-care and the steps needing to be taken to prepare those about to leave care for independent living. They set out the aims of a 15+ review and the contribution which it could make to forward planning. Taking up a suggestion from residential staff, we drafted an "issues list" which determined additional agenda items for consideration in the 15+ review.[16] After those present in the Review had estimated the likely time when the young person

would no longer be in care, they had to predict the probable needs and ascertain the wishes of the person in relation to each of the issues, how each of these might be met, plus timescale, the resource implications and the name of an individual with direct responsibility for implementation.

If any work was to be done in the following six months then the Review had to decide who would have direct responsibility for doing this or co-ordinating the efforts of others. Further detailed guidance was given for each of the issues mentioned on the list, including accommodation, education, income, financial assistance, emotional development and relationships, race and culture.

The second half of the guidelines covered procedural aspects of the 15+ review. Thus the young person's right to seek independent advice and advocacy was explained together with the Children Act consultation duties.

Under the new system, a social worker preparing for a 15+ review would employ new documentation when seeking the written contribution of the young person in care. Instead of completing the standard form, a young person would be asked to fill in a new questionnaire sheet and be supplied with an information leaflet explaining the nature and purpose of the review meeting. Both of these documents are reproduced in Appendix B below.[17]

One of the local organisations which we consulted on the wording of the draft guidelines proposed to us that it offer an advocacy service for young people involved in the pilot reviews. The suggestion was incorporated into the document. It was agreed that an introductory letter from the organisation offering this assistance would be supplied to the young person with their Contribution Sheet and Information Leaflet.

The role of the Chairperson was described and their obligation to ensure that the procedure was complied with, especially a consideration of the topics on the issues list. If the Review meeting decided that after-care planning and/or preparation needed to start or to continue then a further document would be completed by the Chairperson and copied to participants in the Review. This was an Action Plan designed to detail identified needs, agreed responses, defined tasks and the personnel responsible for undertaking them. This document is reproduced in Appendix B below.[18]

The final substantive section of the guidelines dealt with disagreements. It stressed the need for anyone affected by a Review meeting decision with which they disagreed to be informed of their right to use City Council's complaints and representations procedure to have the decision reconsidered, being supplied if necessary with the council's own explanatory leaflet about this procedure.

Consultation on the guidelines
First drafts of the procedure were sent for comment to all social work staff, foster carers and voluntary sector staff whom we had interviewed and revised accordingly.

Contribution sheet and information leaflet
From what we had heard in interviews, it was essential for the revised documents, intended for young people themselves, to be clear, relevant and accessible to teenagers. Possibly the only way to achieve this would be to draft the documents with a group of young people in care or who had recently left it. In conjunction with the local children's rights service we therefore ran a day workshop with just such a group.

First, young people familiar with the review process told us how they would explain what went on to those with no experience of such meetings. This material went into the information leaflet. Next, they listed the types of questions and phraseology which would elicit information, opinions and plans relevant to the 15+ review. These ideas were used in the Contribution Sheet. Drafts were prepared in the light of the workshop's conclusions and submitted to participants for comment and agreement. Subject to minor amendment these were approved for use in connection with the pilot procedure.

The pilot in operation
Despite the earlier co-operation which we had obtained from City Council, during the crucial design stage for both pilots senior management showed few signs of genuine interest in the research projects and in the methods which we were proposing to their department. This was brought home to us particularly when we discovered, as we were drafting the 15+ procedure, that a working group had been established to implement key changes to the reviewing system. We were not informed of the group's existence nor did it seem to be aware of ours. This impression of ambivalence was acknowledged by managers when we interviewed them at the conclusion of the project. Below, we include some of the comments which explain it.

However, we did obtain agreement to run the 15+ review procedure for a number of months. Two children's services team managers were identified who would be willing to apply the new system, together with the new documentation, in the statutory reviews falling to be chaired by them during the pilot period. Together, we estimated that about twenty pilot reviews might therefore take place under the new arrangements.

The period lasted from late January until the end of March 1996. In the event only nine reviews took place during this time for young people 15 years and over. One team manager chaired five under the new procedure and in these cases the young person was assisted by the local children's rights service. The other team manager chaired four reviews and in none of these was the young person independently assisted.

Evaluation

To obtain their impressions on the effects of working with the modified procedure we asked the team managers to forward to each participant who had taken part a standard letter and reply form indicating their agreement to be interviewed. We asked the children's rights service to write to each of the young people they had assisted with the same objective. Interviews were then held with each of the team managers and the children's rights service. Some of the social workers and care staff involved agreed to be interviewed. No replies were received from the young people assisted by the rights service. Two replies were received from young people involved in the other reviews but for practical reasons they could not be interviewed.

Feasibility of 15+ procedure

The first elements of the pilot were the information sheet explaining the purpose of the review and the new Contribution Sheet. We were told that both these documents were supplied to the young person either by residential care staff or by the social worker responsible for preparing documents for the review. Social work staff did not say there had been any practical difficulties in complying with the new requirement, nor in completing the new Contribution Sheet. There were no complaints about the additional paperwork, which in the case of one set of reviews appeared to have been written with the assistance of the home's staff. The team manager said that fully completed contribution sheets were available for each of these reviews. In the other series of reviews, practice varied with one social worker failing to use the new sheet at all and the advocate telling us that on two occasions when he met the young person he was assisting, the sheet had not been completed at all.

The second element in the new procedure was the offer of independent advice and assistance from the children's rights service. Five of the young people living in one of the homes wished to use the service and did so. None of the four young people in the other home decided to use the service. Again, without having access to those young people we can only speculate as to their reason or reasons for not making contact with the service. Neither the team manager chairing the reviews nor the children's rights service itself were surprised to discover this. Both were sure that young people would only seek outside assistance if positively encouraged to do so by the residential staff looking after them. The chairperson considered the home to be "an extremely supportive and nurturing place". She felt that staff there would not feel the need for independent assistance and would not push it with young people facing a review.

On those occasions when the children's rights service was asked to help, its staff complained that sometimes they had been contacted at short notice and consequently had little time in which to prepare for the meeting and develop a trusting and valued relationship with the young person involved. Apart from this, helping with the small number of reviews where their role was actively promoted to young people did not present them with significant practical problems.

In relation to those reviews where the children's rights service was present the chairperson reported no difficulties due to its attendance. On the contrary, she was sure that it facilitated the accurate expression of the young person's views and helped them to engage better with the process. She valued their independence in the meeting.

The third and fourth elements of the procedure were the "issues list" and the matrix Action Plan. With these we need to consider two issues concerning practicability. Firstly, the independent chairpersons, who had to employ the issues list and complete the plan, were relatively happy when working with the former. It had not presented major problems such as lengthening meetings excessively or making them impossibly formal and rigid save in relation to one point. The issues list required the meeting to agree an estimated date when the young person was likely to leave care. One team manager was not prepared to ask the meeting to do this where the young person was only 15 years old and leaving was not being actively considered. She felt it was "profoundly wrong" to look a long way ahead and threaten to disrupt the person's emotional security by selecting an arbitrary date. Both chairs mentioned the difficulty which the meetings experienced in having to consider agenda items – religion, for example, or health – about which no-one present could think of anything to discuss. However, they accepted that this was a useful and necessary discipline.

Practical problems arose with using, completing and distributing the matrix Action Plan. It had proved impossible for the chairpersons to chair the meetings and at the same time fill in the complex Plan so that a finished copy could be discussed with and agreed by all participants before the end of the review. One said it was simply not workable within the current type of review. Both chairpersons felt this would be the best use for the Plan which they agreed was a helpful record of the meeting's decisions. If a document such as this one was to be retained and used in the future then they suggested that a preliminary version be drafted and circulated prior to the meeting by the social worker, as part of their preparatory work. In addition, they considered it essential that review chairpersons be provided with clerical support in the meeting so that full and accurate minutes could be taken and the Plan finalised before the meeting ended.

We had intended a copy Plan to be sent with the chairperson's report to each participant within a short time of the review being held. This did not happen in any of the pilot reviews. We interviewed the children's rights service some five months after they attended five reviews and they had not received one of the copy Plans. We interviewed residential care workers some three months later still and they had not been sent any copy Plan.

We asked each team manager to explain how this could have happened. Distribution, we were informed, was the responsibility not of the chairperson but of others in the department and they had acknowledged there had been delays. One said:

> *The reviews were very late in being with us, very late in being countersigned by the assistant manager, and then very late in being distributed.*

That these Plans were not fully circulated as required seems to have been due to administrative failure and the low priority given to the task by those responsible for it. In addition, the reported difficulty when completing the Action Plan during the meeting cannot have encouraged its early circulation.

Impact

In assessing the impact of the modified procedure we focused on three potential effects it might have had, identified in advance of its being piloted:

- raised expectations: did the planning process unfairly raise expectations which could not be met from current resources?

● content of reviews: did the documents prompt consideration of topics which would otherwise have been ignored or remained unexpressed?

● young person's attitude/behaviour: did the 15+ procedure enable the young person to take part fully in the reviews?

No-one reported to us that expectations had been raised beyond the level at which they could be met. We were told that this probably reflected a very low level of expectations about the capacity of a review to secure major or dramatic changes.

Content of discussions
Whilst one residential care worker felt that the procedure simplified the discussions, a social worker thought it made no perceptible difference and the other social worker could not remember the meeting. None of these felt that the 15+ review caused new issues or questions to be raised.

One of the team manager chairs, on the other hand, was quite struck with the combined effect of the guidelines and documents, particularly the contribution sheet:

Questions came not from the matrix but from the Contribution Sheet. For example, the final questions such as number 18: "Anything else you want to tell?" I don't think young persons get asked this much in reviews. We got sensible responses to that as though they had thought about it. "At what age would you like to leave care?" Those were questions which got them thinking. Those questions wouldn't have been asked in that way in a review. We would have checked out that was happening, but to ask the young person whether they were being helped. It added another dimension to it, really, which was their perception of the process.

Continuing her observations on the effect of the procedure she said that:

It broadened our discussion. Because the questions were so directly phrased: "What do you think?" "What do you want?" "What are your plans?" "What would you like to see?" It became less of the young person having to wait for a plan to be made. Some of them don't want to think. It became more in the ownership of the young person.

Commenting on the issues list and Action Plan, she welcomed the fact that separate subjects such as financial assistance and practical advice were singled out, saying this was helpful. In one of the reviews she had chaired the young person's needs required co-ordinated planning across a number of services and over a very long term. She had found the required structure for their discussions helped to start the planning process efficiently.

In the absence of views from young people we must look to their advocates for an independent view on this. The children's rights service was sure that, although reviews were similar to previous ones, the new procedure had structured the discussion and direction of the meeting in a useful way:

> *I felt all of [the reviews] were skewed and not straightforward, but it was good that there was that structure there that had to be followed through, because otherwise there was a feeling that they might have got completely overwhelmed by other things going on.*

The meeting "had a sort of backbone to it which was helpful". This person also reported that the young person who they assisted had raised a question after discussing it with him beforehand. Without an advocate present it is likely he would not have been prepared to do this:

> *There was one who said things he would not have said otherwise. I had been through it beforehand. He asked me "Do you think its worth asking about the possibility of a foster placement because I keep getting told its not worth asking?" So I said, "Lets go for it, because that's what the meeting is for". And he did and it was looked at. And they said: "You've never mentioned that before. We'll go into it". It was recorded.*

The same advocate said he raised an aspect of planning which appeared to have been ignored by the social worker responsible for two teenage brothers about to start independent living. This revealed the social worker's total ignorance of s. 24 Children Act 1989 and of the possibility of financial assistance to continue the level of income which they had received in residential accommodation. When he raised the need to continue payments of a weekly cash sum and provision of a bus pass under s.24 it was agreed that this would be investigated.

Attitude and behaviour of young person

Without access to the views of the young people themselves we do not know the extent to which the information sheet was useful and had any impact on them. We were told that nearly all of those involved in the pilot were probably familiar with the procedure having had reviews in the past.

We received a consistent impression of the value and usefulness of the Contribution Sheet, where this had been completed by the young person.

In their comments, review participants often contrasted this form with the 1987 version. One chair referred to the "nonsense" of the 1987 form and how using this encouraged a young person to think that it was not worth talking to her. She compared it to the pilot Contribution Sheet. The following comments are a selection of those she and her colleague chair fed back to us:

The form that we used this time was filled in well. People had taken time to fill it in. They felt that the contribution was therefore more valid. There is a purpose in the paper being completed.

Compared to the old sheet, which was very much aimed at younger children and was so universally despised by young people, I think this treated them better. It was much more age appropriate and it asked their opinions and it elicited their feelings and their hopes in a way that the old sheet did not. So they came with a more positive attitude.

They would still grumble about having to fill in a form and be at their review but it was not such an incongruous form as the previous one. They were OK with it. It was tangible. We got more serious answers, that was my impression. There was more thought put into the responses. There wasn't so much messing about. Some of the questions on the other forms just invited a silly response. An open door to winding someone up. The way the Contribution Form addressed the young person as someone whose views were valid went a very long way to having them there as a working member of that meeting.

The young people had been better prepared for them. They knew what to expect and they had prepared what they wanted to say in a better way. None of the young people said, "To hell with this, I'm leaving", or did not turn up.

The children's rights service was more sceptical of the impact of the procedure on the young person's perception of the review. They felt that the person would not feel very connected with the process anyway and did not sense that this was greatly changed in the reviews which they attended. One of the advocates noted "Definitely, a feeling of disconnectedness". However, the same person acknowledged that:

[The two young people] were both there and that possibly is because I was there. I encouraged them to take part and that their views would get across. That might have given them a wee bit of incentive.

Rationale

Did the procedure deliver the rights which were claimed for it? Three distinct fair treatment rights were incorporated into the new procedure. These were the participation right; the fair decision-making right; and accountability rights associated with the recording and giving of reasons for decisions. We shall now examine these in turn.

One of the social workers whom we interviewed reminded us of the difficulties which young people in care might have in engaging with the statutory review system and in the making of plans. His observations served to confirm our belief that the rights we had piloted were valuable and necessary.

The vast majority of children and young people in care, he told us, were from a working class background and would find it difficult to put their rights and views forward. The situation of many would also be associated with dysfunctional family relationships, with poverty and delinquency. They did not see much of the future planned out for them and tended to be "myopic", with low self-esteem and poor communication skills.

One of the independent chairpersons was clear as to the aim of the pilot in encouraging more effective participation. It was:

....to empower young people to have a voice and to feel that they were central to the review, not the social worker or the documents. That their wishes and their views were central and they were being given the offer of outside support.

With so few pilot reviews and without hearing from the young people involved we can only speculate as to whether or not this aim was fulfilled and, if so, which element of the 15+ review may have been most significant in securing the right. Was it the Contribution Sheet, or the presence of an advocate or the issues list agenda? From the feedback which we received, it appeared that the new arrangements may have encouraged more effective participation for some young people. However, the benefit may have amounted simply to encouraging the person to attend the meeting and little more.

The comments of the children's rights service reminded us of the young persons' profile we included at the start of this section and the need to hesitate before concluding that measures like these would naturally "empower" young people. One of its staff remarked:

I think its a whole cultural thing where the young person does not feel very connected with the process anyway, does not feel it has to do with them. I don't know how much was particular to these young people. They all seemed to be like young people who did not like writing very much or who were, may be, not good at writing and sitting down and discussing serious things. I did get the impression that the key workers had tried in some cases to engage them and had not been successful and maybe thought that we would do it better.

However, even this realistic insight contains the suggestion that advocacy was an element of primary importance to the 15+ procedure, particularly where the young person's relationship with their carers might have been poor or unproductive. The children's rights service acknowledged as much when they gave the following assessment of their usefulness:

When you are an advocate sometimes you sit through a review and at the end of it you feel that I didn't really do much. Maybe you said two sentences and you tended to sit and listen mainly because you found that the person you were representing was very, very articulate and very able to say what they thought. But at the end of the day the person will say to you they talked because they knew that there was somebody there for them. It was just the fact that you were there that they did talk. If you had not been at the review and they had been asked their opinion, they might have just went "I'm not bothered". 'Cos we've seen people go "I'm not bothered". But you see them outside and they are bothered. They just feel completely isolated because they are surrounded by these people who they are used to seeing making decisions about them.

Another aim of the 15+ review procedure was to require the meeting to have regard to a set of prescribed factors, even if some of them would only be considered briefly. This was designed to encourage a fairer outcome from the planning discussions and decisions resulting from them. Most participants observed that the structure intended for the meeting could be recognised. However, in order to discover if this right had been truly provided by these means the procedure would have to have been significantly more extensively piloted and evaluated.

The third principal aim of the 15+ procedure was to provide independent scrutiny of discussions and decisions taken in the review, rendering those involved more accountable for delivering on the plans decided there. One of the social workers we interviewed saw the concept of accountability as crucial as far as the young person in care was concerned:

If it became a regular procedure it would raise the stakes of accountability and I have no problem with that. The problem with this concept of "corporate caring" is that it comes down to ownership. Often with relationships between different aspects of care – fieldwork, residential – there is not necessarily any general agreement about who does what and often things are left unspecified. If the child is at home then obviously there is one carer, there is less scope for slippage. When you have got a number of people who can take that role, things can get lost. We require a system which causes us to negotiate specifically who does what rather than just leave it to be lost.

The children's rights service regarded accountability as crucial. It informed us that an independent inspector of residential homes had reported to them that 50 per cent of the children and young people who she had seen in City Council's homes did not have any plan. The limitations on the research meant that we could not investigate what happened at the review meeting immediately following the one which piloted the new procedure. This might have indicated whether or not accountability had been raised by the issues list and the Action Plan.

The independent chairpersons both commented favourably on the fresh focus which the procedure gave to the planning purpose of the reviews and to the responsibilities of participating professionals. Advocates from the children's rights service also felt that the procedure helped to ensure that some matters were raised which might have been lost.

However, the Action Plan was not circulated promptly to those expected to use it to remind themselves of decisions taken or to follow-up those assigned tasks on the Plan. In these circumstances, one has to conclude that its value in improving accountability was seriously weakened. We should emphasise that the young people themselves did not appear to have been sent a copy of the Action Plan. The children's rights service voiced their frustration at this failure with these comments:

I wanted to ensure that I did the follow up to ensure that things which were agreed were actually put into operation. I have never had records of the meeting. You cannot even do the follow-up work which you would automatically expect to do. You have built a relationship with [the young person] and it is very unsatisfactory the way that relationship is ended, which annoys me most about it. You want some way of winding down a relationship with a young person and we haven't been able to do that.

That was part of the point of us being involved... we would chase things up if what was agreed did not happen. Also, for people who were leaving care if they came unstuck from their social worker or previous carer, they could come back to us.

The children's rights service could not comprehend how anyone could have neglected to copy and distribute the record of decisions in the course of a pilot project. Its staff were clear in their estimation of the importance of the paperwork and the consequences of ignoring or neglecting it:

The thing with this procedure is that the paperwork is very important because that is what's agreed. It is the actual written agreement. They will say that the work is being done anyway, which is true, but it's not the point. The point is how can you change things procedurally. How can you do that without the paperwork existing?

The staff can always say "There's no plans. Well, this is what we're doing and this is right". And there's nothing which you can actually look to, "This is what you said, so what you are doing isn't right because you are not following it". It means you can just make it up as you go along.

The contrasting perspective of one of the chairpersons is revealing. She said she was surprised when the children's rights service wrote to her asking for copies of the Action Plans. She had not regarded the review meetings as planning meetings as such. She observed:

The plans should be in place and my reviewing merely validates those plans. They should not make a difference to them. Occasionally we say "Six months ago we decided this. Why has that not happened? Or, what's the barrier to prevent that happening?" But it is not really where the plans are made. But it was clearly very important. Something I had certainly underrated.

What of the future? One chairperson said she would certainly want to take the Contribution Sheet forward without modification and also the offer of advocacy, even after the Department introduced the "Looking After Children" documentation and procedures. In her view the matrix Action Plan needed more work on it before it would be viable, but she regarded it as workable. Her colleague chairperson expressed almost identical views.

Conclusions and lessons

City Council
The research project raised important questions about how new policy is introduced within a large social services authority serving an area with pronounced levels of unmet need. Finding answers to them should concern

us. Policy was needed to implement changes in law and practice intended to increase and protect the rights of children and young people in care and beyond it. The pilot tested how such rights might be introduced. Why had City Council been so slow to deliver on the procedural rights provided by the Children Act and does it's experience offer lessons for this authority and for others?

We suggest that the following factors might provide some of the answers to this question:

- a professional culture resistant to corporate policy and procedure

- an uncommitted and overstretched senior management

- a reluctance to introduce policy until a new service was in place

- cuts in service demoralising the organisation

- low priority given by City Council to administration and paperwork

- exclusion of the service user voice in policy and practice development

For any rights-based approach to be viable and effective within the authority's after-care service each of these factors will, where practicable, have to be addressed.

Resistant professional culture

Many of those we interviewed described a distinctive professional culture in the department. We judged it an improbable environment for the successful introduction of clear and consistent standards of practice and eligibility since practice did not link up to a central source of direction and authority. Thus senior managers referred to "total laissez-faire". They went on to describe the department in the following terms:

> *This is not an organisation where procedures tied to systems and standards is a major feature of organisational life. That will explain something of why the research was never embedded into organisational life. Because it is not part of the culture of this place. When you have a laissez-faire attitude you don't have tight policy and procedures tying you down. We have never overcome that "you make it up as you go along" in a way.*

One of the social workers we interviewed, who had experienced work in another authority, said this of his area team:

Different areas are given considerable discretion and autonomy and ways of operating. Procedures and ways of operating are very loose. There has been a lack of direction and leadership. There has not been a history of co-ordination and collaboration. Given areas have done it their own way. The idea of "This is what we do as an authority" is not used.

As we found with other projects undertaken during this research, it is essential for the professional working culture to be receptive and attuned to the ways of working which a rights-based approach demands. Corporate direction and the management of minimum practice standards will have to replace laissez-faire and it will need to work within a culture which understands and appreciates values of consistency and equity and new ways of working, such as the involvement of independent advocacy.

These lessons were already recognised by City Council and steps were beginning to be taken to change outmoded approaches to practice and organisation. We understand that the statutory reviewing function is now mainly the responsibility of a central reviewing officer able to maintain and monitor standards of reviews and their effectiveness. A modified "Looking After Children" planning system is being introduced throughout the authority and all staff trained in using it. This will also break down variations in practice and reduce the unfairness which can result from it. More can and should be done and will be if City Council introduces corporate policy on eligibility for s. 24 assistance.

The role of senior management
Current managers, understandably, regarded the commitment and will of senior managers to be crucial to the success of introducing new rights for care leavers. What was needed was "putting stuffing into the word rights". This had been done with the new changes in community care. The policy had to have high status with managers agreeing to match delivery with the aim. They added:

Unless it is seen as a clear departmental responsibility with the right backing it won't happen or it won't happen consistently or it will happen in pockets, which is what has happened over the last thirty five years.

Such an approach had not been reflected in the past as far as the Children Act was concerned. One manager we interviewed attributed this to a "fairly serious dysfunction" between responsible managers which prevented the development of new policy and provision for care leavers. We were told that "the work was attempted but there was no way of integrating it with practice because of the person leading it".

Why had their own approach to the pilot projects lacked enthusiasm? Mostly, they said, it was due to bad timing. The detailed research started in earnest as they both took up new posts and sought to achieve a fundamental reconfiguration of children's services. Management resources were overstretched and priorities had to be chosen. They could not treat the research as a priority when IPPR needed this to happen. One acknowledged:

I suspect the reason why [the research] fell between stools is that from a service point of view, we were faced with quite a massive problem of reconfiguring services across the board – all services. That's what we were involved in. In terms of the timing, it was bad because we could not at the same time focus on young people or children's rights issues as such... We were going to have difficulty fitting it in. On the other hand, we did not want to kick it out. From a philosophical and professional point of view we wanted to try and keep it happening in [City Council].

Service first, rights follow

If our research was judged to be badly timed, when would it be well-timed? The pilot work did not prosper since managers were reluctant to formulate and publish clear standards of eligibility and procedure until the new after-care service was designed, in place and operating. As one manager commented, "Who is interested in procedures if there is no service?" The success of an initiative can depend on its ability to deliver services to meet new expectations from staff and service users. Without this, new policy and procedures could be demoralising and ineffective.

Nine years of budget cuts

We have already mentioned the dispiriting impact of years of budget cuts on City Council's hard pressed social services department. This would have undoubtedly discouraged innovation and expansion of the service to meet the new expectations of the Children Act, however well argued was the case for this outside or within the authority. The after-care service which City Council has recently introduced and is operating has been funded from the redirection of spending already devoted to children's services.

Administration and paperwork

There would appear to be weaknesses in City Council's capacity to prioritise administration and paper based procedures and to treat them with the seriousness which others expect – and their own commitments promise. It would have costed next to nothing to replace the discredited young person's Contribution Sheet when prompted to do so by the Children Act changes in 1991 and the clear guidance issued under that Act. Instead the department persisted in using the old document despite what appears to have been universal disapproval and clear evidence of its counter-productive effects.

This reflects an organisation which has not yet grasped the importance of high standards of administration and the need to fashion bureaucracy so that it is responsive. We saw a similar reluctance to take paperwork seriously when the Action Plans produced as part of the pilot reviews were not circulated to participants as intended by the procedure. Many procedural rights depend on reliable and effective written communications. For a rights-based approach truly to affect the way City Council or any similar organisation works, greater priority will need to be given to this function and the resources which it may require.

Service user participation in policy
A residential care worker interviewed early in the research reflected on the reason why City Council had not moved earlier to introduce new rights for care leavers. What was lacking, he maintained, was any means by which young people still in care and who had recently left care could have access to policy makers at the highest level in the department. There was no way in which the service user's voice could be heard effectively by those who needed to hear it. Information about their needs and the crucial importance of new policy to comply with the 1989 Act had not gone far enough up the management ladder.

From what we saw of the authority, we consider this insight an accurate one. City Council maintained links with voluntary sector organisations broadly advocating improvements to services for care leavers. They had done so for many years without success, producing high quality proposals, well-researched options and so forth. Some of these received funding from the Council. Such formal channels, however, seemed for many years unable to affect the policy void though the inclusion of commitments in the Children's Services Plan hinted that change might soon be promoted.

A programme might have emerged earlier if policy makers at the highest level of the authority had listened to young people describe their experience of the system and encouraged their active participation in improving standards of planning and fairness. We hope that the new after-care service has this dimension incorporated into it to provide a constant feedback on its responsiveness and relevance to young people.

We saw how working with service users could have a powerful influence in the workshop which was run to design the information leaflet and

Contribution Sheet. Here we saw the energy, imagination and expertise of young people knowing the system. These should be harnessed in similar ways by the authority and there are signs that this may have begun. The children's rights service compared this to the recent participation of young people from the service in the training of City Council's staff. Thus, one worker commented:

> *What you [the researcher] said about how you found young people got to the centre of things very quickly...got to the heart of the matter and to issues which affected them. That alone sums up the whole ethos of involving young people effectively in partnership with decision-makers. At the end of the day, their views can be used to develop procedures, different pieces of the way that the local authority behaves. It seems to me like common sense. We have done it with the authority since. Very positive.*

Voluntary sector and service users

Our experience in designing two procedures and piloting one of them showed us the essential role which voluntary organisations can play in work of this kind. One organisation had expert knowledge of both City Council's procedures and the practice introduced by other authorities. We relied upon this when choosing the topics for the pilot projects and drafting the written procedures. This body championed the research project to the authority, when interest in it wavered or disappeared. Another organisation, the children's rights service, was crucial to our consultation with young people and to the participative workshop we ran on the Contribution Sheet. Its advocacy role in the reviews showed us how dry procedural rights could come to life when personal advice and assistance could also be available.

Many of the ideas we incorporated into the research therefore came from these organisations. The independent ethos and advocacy culture which they promote have close affinities with the idea of rights and with respect for the interests and preferences of service users over and above professional or provider interests.

The research suggests an increased role for voluntary organisations in the design and administration of services and co-ordination of assistance, and in the provision of information, advice and, on occasions, representation. For a rights culture to be effective, such help must at least be available. If City Council's new service is to be built around this philosophy then the role for the voluntary sector must greatly expand. For similar developments to prosper elsewhere, the same lesson would need to be applied.

Endnotes

1 Only a small proportion of children or young people will be technically "in care". Since the Children Act 1989 was introduced the appropriate term to use is either "accommodated" or "looked after". However, the expressions "in care" and "care leaver" are still commonly used and provide useful shorthand for the more complex legal definitions.

2 Biehal N *et al* (1995) *Moving On: Young people and Leaving Care Schemes*, HMSO, London.

3 Beihal N *et al* (1992) *Prepared for Living? A Survey of Young People Leaving the Care of Three Local Authorities*, Leaving Care Research Project, Leeds University.

4 Kirby P (1994) *A Word from the Street: Young people who leave care and become homeless*, Community Care, London.

5 Home Office data suggests that more than a quarter of prisoners (26 per cent) had at some time before the age of 16 been taken into local authority care. See Home Affairs Committee (1993) *Juvenile Offenders* Sixth Report House of Commons Session 1992–93, HMSO paragraphs 28 & 32.

6 Biehal N *et al* (1995) *op cit.*

7 Social Services Inspectorate (1997) *When leaving home is also leaving care*, Department of Health, London; Audit Commission (1996) *Misspent Youth: Young People and Crime*, Audit Commission, paragraph 131.

8 Paragraph (2)(b) of Schedule 2, Children Act, 1989.

9 ss.61 and 64 Children Act, 1989.

10 s.26 (1) and (2) Children Act, 1989 and the Review of Children's Cases Regulations 1991 (S.I. 1991 No. 895).

11 Regulation 5 and Schedule 2, the Review of Children's Cases Regulations, 1991.

12 The Children Act, 1989 Guidance Volume 2, paragraph 2.32.

13 A Working Party on this subject had reported on the options for the department in June 1994. The findings of the Department of Health research are found in Ward H (1995) *Looking After Children: Research into Practice*, HMSO, London.

14 See p.74 above.

15 See pp.206–209.

16 See p.197.

17 See pp.198–204.

18 See p.205.

4 The Hospital: fair treatment rights and specialist medical services

What the Chapter contains

In this chapter we describe our work with the Ophthalmology Directorate of a District General Hospital in North West England. The chapter has four main sections. Firstly, we outline the project's aims and their importance for hospital based care; next we describe how we planned for the pilot projects, by investigating the organisation of services in the Directorate and the options for practical research. In the third section we report in detail on the three projects which were developed, evaluating each of these in the light of our aims. Lastly, we set out the lessons from the research.

Project aims

What rights do patients have when they need medical care? The NHS provides hundreds of thousands of treatments every year yet citizens are not entitled to treatment because they have any legally enforceable right to it. To get access to what the service offers and at the standard they expect, they must constantly rely on the decisions of others. Neither are hospitals subject to the sort of systematic inspection now considered essential in other settings, nor has the Patient's Charter or changes to hospital complaints procedures fundamentally altered that imbalance of power which still characterises health care provider/patient relationships.

Principles of fair treatment

In such circumstances, principles and practices which encourage or guarantee fair treatment take on a crucial significance. They help to ensure that services of high quality reach those who need them in ways which respect their individuality and dignity. At the same time they reinforce the objective that public services should first respond to those with the greatest needs. These principles may be self-evident, but it is still worth repeating them before we show how we applied them to the Hospital's eye treatment services. By "fair treatment" we mean the following principal expectations:

- a patient should have access to diagnostic and treatment services on the basis of a principle of equity, ie without any unfair bias or discrimination influencing either basic access to them or the speed at which they are offered

- a patient should have a right to participate in decisions taken about their treatment, not simply by passively consenting to this, but by expressing treatment preferences and exercising choice, as far as possible and practicable

- a patient should be given reasons for the decisions which others take about them, with reasons for important decisions being clearly recorded, referring to any agreed policies or criteria, if taken in reliance on these

- a patient should be free to make representations and/or to complain about their treatment, obtaining speedy, effective and sensitive redress when their grievance or criticism is justified

- a patient should be given information and, where necessary assistance in interpreting or understanding it, to enable them to use fully all their rights

Potential for procedural rights
Such ideas present a daunting challenge for the complex and ever changing environment of the NHS. Yet if they are ignored or neglected the consequences for patients can be serious. Patients may be unfairly refused treatment or have this delayed improperly; may have their choice of treatment restricted or excluded altogether; may be unable to find out why something has gone wrong, or to obtain an explanation, apology or redress.

Applied in practice they may require the creation or monitoring of referral procedures; or guidelines to govern the manner in which decisions are taken on wait-listing, particularly where priority is given for social reasons, such as the impact of disability on employment, caring responsibilities or coping alone.

Fair treatment principles highlight the need for changes to equip patients fully to participate as partners in their treatment and in decisions concerning choice of treatment, consent and how they will manage their illness or disability after discharge. These expectations are also central to the sensitive and effective planning of discharge from hospital, particularly for those unable to care for themselves at home.

Lastly, the NHS will need robust, speedy and responsive complaints and representations procedures. Recent changes to these, particularly extending the role of the Health Ombudsman, have given a welcome prominence to the need for fair treatment across the full range of NHS activity, clinical as well as administrative – according to recent reports of the Ombudsman, still very necessary.[1]

The Patient's Charter highlights many of these points though offers little guidance on how health service providers are expected to meet the new commitments. IPPR's research sought to investigate the implications of applying these ideas in practice.

First contacts with the Hospital
When we invited the Hospital to collaborate on the research project, we had no pre-conceived plans for working in any specific area of its medical or hospital services. A procedural rights approach was potentially relevant to a range of different activities or specialities. Elective surgery, though, since it usually involves straightforward and planned procedures, was likely to be most relevant to our aims.

The Medical Director suggested that the Ophthalmology Directorate might offer a suitable setting for the project. It was relatively small, self-contained and undertook mainly elective treatments. When we approached them, its Clinical Director and Ward Sister agreed.

First Stage: planning

Aims and methods
The aim of this first stage of our work was to investigate the ways in which out-patient and in-patient services were organised in the Directorate. We needed to discover what were the options for new rights and what might be the priorities for change. To do this, our methods were as follows:

- observations and interviews with staff

- obtaining and considering Directorate documents and written procedures

- making contact with former patients, with the local social services authority and with the Community Health Council

- preparing an interim report containing our findings and recommendations for pilot projects in the Directorate

Observations and interviews
Early into the research, the author spent two weeks in observations and interviews at the hospital and in making contacts outside it with key local organisations and authorities. As well as speaking to medical, nursing and administrative staff, he interviewed over the telephone a number of patients who had recently been seen or treated in the Directorate.

Documents and procedures
The administration of hospital medicine involves a moderate use of documentation within the hospital and in communications with patients. We obtained copies of the standard letters sent to patients, the pre-operative assessment documents and treatment information leaflets produced by the Directorate and supplied to patients. Procedures such as these did not appear to have been produced except for the planning of discharge from hospital and for dealing with complaints.

Contacts with patients and outside organisations
In the course of our early planning, we discussed the aims of the research and received views on current practice from a number of organisations outside the hospital. Although the local Community Health Council did not have any special interest in or knowledge of the Directorate's services, it supported the aims of the study, as did the local voluntary organisation for people who are blind or partially sighted. Staff in the latter group had assisted the hospital in improving information on general surgical procedures for blind patients.

We also met with the specialist officer in the local social services authority responsible for services to those with visual impairments to obtain his impressions of the service and how patients' rights might be improved.

After observing the service in action, we contacted by telephone 15 patients who had recently been treated as in-patients in the Directorate. We sought from them their views on their experience relevant to our investigation.

The Interim Report
When our initial research was completed, we presented to the Hospital's Medical Director and to Directorate staff an Interim Report on the project. This set out our initial findings, suggested ways in which procedural rights could be introduced or enhanced within the Directorate's service and proposed how we might take forward this work.

The report had been written at speed and after limited observations. When discussed with senior clinical staff some of its findings were questioned, though mainly on points of detail. The Medical Director, however, was sure that the report provided a solid foundation and some useful insights for further work and all the consultants were persuaded to agree to the next stage. By this time four of the many proposals mentioned in the report were agreed to be priorities. These were:

- to develop a written treatment pathway or pathways describing what a patient could expect when being treated. Into this description would be inserted, at the appropriate points, references to a patient's rights and responsibilities

- to develop a list of standard but common questions in relation to a routine treatment (eg cataract removal) and supply these in an easy-to-read form to the patient before a consultation to help "prompt" requests for relevant information

- to develop wait-listing guidelines for staff and use these to inform patients of their rights and responsibilities

- to review and revise all written communications with patients for readability and improve or replace any which were hard or impossible to read

In addition, it was agreed that work would proceed on the basis that the Hospital would apply to the Health Authority for additional funds to cover the employment of a part-time project nurse to help run the pilot projects.

Before describing our work on the pilot projects, we summarise the key points from the interim report's findings and conclusions.

Findings: facilities, treatments and organisation
The Directorate provides diagnosis and treatment services for patients with eye conditions referred by their GP, by Accident and Emergency staff or by other Consultants in the Hospital Trust. The "Eye Ward" offers surgical and other treatment on a day-case or inpatient basis and is situated on the Trust's principal District General Hospital site. Ophthalmic outpatients' facilities are provided in premises close to the Ward and at another hospital in a neighbouring town.

Conditions commonly seen and, where appropriate, treated in the Directorate include cataracts, glaucoma, macular degeneration, childhood squints, tear duct problems and conditions associated with chronic diabetes. The great majority of treatments are for age related cataract removal. Most surgical treatment is provided on an elective basis.

During 1994 the Directorate was in transition. Plans were about to be implemented to increase substantially the proportion of patients having their operation on a day basis without being admitted to hospital as an inpatient.

Staffing and management
At the time of our first visit, there were four consultant posts, with one of these filled by a locum consultant. One of the consultant surgeons was Clinical Director. The Directorate's senior nurse – known as Care Manager – was responsible for nursing management except for that provided in the operating theatres. In 1994, the hospital's central Medical Records Department managed admissions administration and listing and there were no dedicated personnel solely responsible for the Directorate's lists. (By the time planning for the pilot projects got under way, a Directorate Admissions Officer had been appointed and had moved into the Eye Ward to administer wait-listing and admissions for all its patients).

Management of the Directorate was effected through a variety of groups, often involving the Business Manager, Care Manager, Clinical Director and other senior staff in the Directorate and hospital. A Clinical Audit Group monitored and developed medical and nursing practice.

Findings: access to services
The Directorate was a very busy department with a high level of activity throughout all of its various services. Out-patients' clinics thronged with patients and those accompanying them. The Laser Clinic – to which all patients seemed to be called at the same time – also appeared frenetic. Nine operating theatre lists of six patients per list brought a steady flow of patients through the Ward for day or inpatient surgery.

A patient comes into contact with the Directorate in one or more of the following settings:

- *Accident and Emergency Department*: patients on urgent referral or self-referral will be seen here by junior medical staff and if urgent treatment is required will be transferred to the Eye Ward.

- *Out-patients' Clinic*: patients referred by their GP (or another of the Hospital's consultants) will be seen here by a consultant or junior doctor for initial examination, diagnosis and listing for treatment, general review of their condition or post-operative review.

- *Laser Clinic*: at this out-patient treatment clinic patients receive laser treatment for a variety of conditions.

- *Pre-operative Clinic*: some days before their operation patients are called for a pre-operative assessment usually undertaken by junior medical and nursing staff. At this time, amongst other things, it is decided if the patient is fit for the operation, and, if so, whether they will be admitted as an in-patient or on a day basis and whether they will have a general or a local anaesthetic.

- *Admission and surgical treatment*: if the pre-operative assessment confirms the person's fitness for surgery the person is then admitted as an in-patient or on a day basis and surgery is performed. Following treatment, the patient's condition is assessed and, if appropriate, the patient is discharged home to return to hospital later for review.

- *Aftercare*: day surgical patients return to hospital the day after their operation for assessment and treatment. All patients have to return to hospital in due course after their operation for review. The District Nursing service provides nursing in the community and the local social services department will provide for any social care needs which a discharged patient requires during their recovery.

- *Low Vision Clinic*: visual impairment can be corrected or reduced by equipment such as a magnifying lens. The Hospital operates a Low Vision Clinic at which patients referred by their consultant can obtain access to such aids to help them cope with the consequences of their illness or disability.

Key observations

Given the focus of the research, our observations on how patients experienced the service are arranged under the following three broad headings:

- staff communications with patients

- wait-listing for surgery

- alternatives and choice in treatment

Two general comments are necessary before we describe these. We were struck by the absence of any formal Directorate consensus on the features of the various procedures and what a patient might expect to receive when referred for examination or treatment. The Directorate did not have any corporate policies or protocols covering referral and admission to hospital; on wait-listing; or on choice in relation to day/in-patient treatment or method of anaesthesia. To gain an accurate picture of the services offered by the Directorate one had to observe and analyse the practice of each of the four individual consultants' firms.

Unsurprisingly, we found significant variations in the ways in which individual consultants listed patients for elective surgery, informed patients of their listing and arranged their pre-operative assessment. For example, at the time of the interim report only two out of the four consultants called patients into hospital before the date for admission for pre-operative assessment.

Staff communications with patients
There was no systematic approach to planning and providing for the information needs of patients.[2] A person with an eye condition requiring examination and/or treatment would be faced with a confusing array of different professionals with varied roles, responsibilities and areas of expertise. Opticians (now termed optometrists), GPs, consultant ophthalmologists, junior medical staff, nurses, orthoptists and district nurses may all be encountered. After treatment the local social services department may have become involved in assessing and providing care services at home.

Although there were some standard information leaflets on treatments available from the Directorate, nothing was available which would reliably answer many specific questions for the patient with an enquiry, or even for the staff member new to the Directorate.

Sources of information
There were many potential and actual sources of information for the patient and it was not clear which should be the main point of contact, providing consistent and up to date details for a patient seeking them. We were told that former patients were a good source of information. However, we could not see how patients could obtain accurate and up to date information on their own initiative, for example, by listening to former patients of the department, or their friends and relatives. Two patients we interviewed

described how they received seriously inaccurate information from such sources.

Out-patient consultations and the anxious patient

A number of patients confirmed just how bewildering the out-patients' clinic can be to someone who is anxious. One patient was referred by an optician following a regular check-up, with suspected glaucoma. Her GP told her this could lead to blindness. She described herself as "in shock" due to these events. Despite wanting to ask a specific question of the doctor in the course of her out-patient appointment she did not do so, partly because she was "terrified of wasting the doctor's time", partly because of the frequent interruptions in the consultation. When this person attended the Eye Ward for laser treatment she said she had "butterflies as large as elephants". Good quality information supplied at the right time would have been useful to someone so anxious.

Correspondence with patients

At the time of our observations, many of the Hospital's personal communications with a patient at home were by letter. Most patients whom we interviewed said that such correspondence was difficult if not impossible to read because it was faint and in small print. Some could only do so with a magnifying glass and those who had difficulty stated that a large bold print letter would have been much easier to read. Staff were about to produce some standard large print information sheets, for general and day cases, to accompany admission letters. These would reduce some of the difficulties caused by the problematic correspondence.

Although the Admissions Office routinely sent patients the Hospital's general information leaflets when calling them for their operation, none of these were in large print. Furthermore none of the Directorate's four eye treatment information leaflets were available to the Admissions Office so none were routinely sent out to patients pre-operatively. Nor were patients informed in their appointment letter or in standard information of the existence of these leaflets.

Wait-listing for surgery

Most treatment in the Directorate was elective. The patient was therefore required to wait a period of time before being seen or treated. However, there was no agreed Directorate policy and procedure on the management of waiting lists and the calling of patients for admission for treatment. The result was that practice varied across the four different consultants for little or no apparent reason.

Most of the patients interviewed told us they left their initial consultation without any clear or accurate knowledge as to when to expect their treatment to occur. Sometimes when information had been given to them, it was extremely accurate; at other times it was not. One who was told the treatment would be in "two to three weeks" found he had to wait three months for the operation to happen.

Confirmation of listing and estimated date
The absence of clear and agreed policy on wait-listing meant that the Directorate did not have readily available a source of standards or targets which could form the basis of information for patients and help to ensure equity and consistency.

Unlike practice in some other hospitals, patients did not have confirmed to them in writing that they had been placed on a waiting list, nor were they given a firm estimate of the time when they might be called for treatment. Only in one consultant's case did patients obtain a firm date at an out-patient's appointment. With all consultants, the patient's GP received a letter from the consultant's secretary, but patients did not get a copy of this, nor any formal explanation of what they should do if the condition worsened and they felt they should be treated urgently. Nor was any information supplied as to whom to contact to discover their place on the list. Some patients who were interviewed clearly wanted more information as to the likely delay before treatment was to be provided.

Disability and prioritisation
Poor vision can disable. Its impact may be more or less serious depending upon the social circumstances or environment of the patient. A person's employment may be threatened by deteriorating eyesight, their mobility or ability to care for someone else may be threatened. Should that degree of disability affect the period a patient would be expected to wait before receiving treatment? If so, how far should decisions about priority depend on the patient's own choice, on the personal view of the consultant and/or the referring general practitioner, or on a set of principles agreed by all parties?

Without any clear and systematic policy or guidelines available to answer such questions, we had to doubt the capacity of the Directorate consistently to offer equitable access to its services to all those who might need them.

Alternatives and choice in treatment: anaesthesia
We were told that, unless clinical reasons precluded this, the patient could choose whether or not to have a local or a general anaesthetic. From what we gathered from our interviews we could not be sure that this principle was clearly reflected in practice at the time. After witnessing patients being seen in out-patients' clinics and in pre-operative clinics, we could not be sure precisely when the patient would be offered such a choice. Furthermore, after speaking to patients it was clear that choice had not been universally offered to all patients with the same treatment needs.

By the time the junior doctor sought formal consent from the patient to their proposed treatment and anaesthetic, complicated and costly steps had been taken to prepare the patient for a general anaesthetic, on an apparent assumption that this would be agreed to. The researcher saw one patient, when offered the choice of anaesthetic in this setting, initially ask for a local and then change her mind to a general. When another person was interviewed, she told us this had happened.

Some elderly patients may have been genuinely anxious about being "put to sleep" and did not understand that this could be avoided. We saw one 93 year old patient decline the offer of cataract surgery for reasons which neither she nor the relative with her articulated at all. It could have been this very anxiety which was on her mind.

We also came across examples of patients required to have a local anaesthetic who might have preferred a general anaesthetic, had the choice been clear to them. A patient referred for a small operation treated on a day case basis was given the impression that the operation would be done under local anaesthetic and that he did not have a choice. This suited the patient since he was happy with a local and would have one again if he had to. At the same time there was a patient also treated under local anaesthesia who was greatly distressed by the pain he felt. He might well have preferred a general anaesthetic if given the choice.

First stage: conclusions and outcomes
By the end of this first stage, we had sufficient impressions of how ophthalmic treatment was provided in the Hospital to propose some ideas we could develop as pilot projects. The key observations which had emerged from our early contacts with staff, patients and others in the area were the following:

- Although its services were subject to the Patient's Charter and to the Hospital's own charter, neither the Hospital's Board nor the Directorate had developed any systematic means of determining what were patients' rights and responsibilities and how they would be effectively informed of these.

- The Directorate had not conducted any independent consultation on patients' information needs or on their opinions of treatment.

- Hospital procedures were limited to a discharge planning protocol and a complaints procedure, though work was in progress on a Directorate protocol for use with the planned Day Case Unit. This restricted use of procedures rendered it very difficult to identify the standards which patients could currently expect from the Directorate's services, or to assess where an individual consultant's practice might differ from the rest.

- Unless variations in practice were recognised and altered or the differences discussed, justified and agreed, it would be difficult to envisage the Directorate being able to develop a rigorous approach to providing clear and specific rights to patients.

- The lack of any comprehensive approach to supplying information led to gaps in information and variations in the timing of information for patients.

- The environment in which patients were expected to seek information (eg during a rushed out-patient appointment, or just before their operation) often discouraged effective communication.

- Written communications with patients were sometimes ineffective due to presentation and content.

- We had little difficulty in applying the procedural rights analysis to this field of hospital medicine or in identifying a range of ideas for potential pilot projects.

- We nevertheless encountered a number of barriers at this preliminary stage. There was the difficulty of demonstrating how the theoretical concept of procedural rights could be relevant to busy practitioners. We also met some scepticism from the consultants, arising from the traditional freedom of doctors to determine their own procedures.

Second Stage: three pilot projects

Aims, methods, process

After meeting the Directorate's senior staff it was agreed that the study would continue and would focus on four of the proposals mentioned in the interim report. These were:

- the Patient Pathways Project

- the Prompt List Project

- the Wait-listing Project

- the review of written communications with patients

Our aim was to design, in consultation with staff and patients, some practical changes to the ways in which services were organised and run to enhance the rights of patients to information, to choice, and to fair treatment.

In view of the complexity and time-consuming nature of the work and IPPR's distance from the hospital, the Directorate and ourselves agreed that the assistance of a dedicated member of staff would be valuable. Accordingly, an application for the funding of a project nurse post was made to the Health Authority.

Unfortunately, this application was unsuccessful but the Hospital did not abandon its interest in the research and in piloting some changes. By early summer 1995, we had met with the Directorate's main management body and obtained its agreement to commence practical work on three of the projects. For technical reasons, due to the limitations of the Admissions Office printer, we could not work on the review of written communications.

Much of the credit for ensuring that we reached this far was due to the Medical Director's promptings and continued support for the project. He deputed the Hospital's Quality Facilitator (a member of his Directorate staff) to help facilitate the work and also chaired meetings of the Steering Group throughout the period of the practical work on the pilots. Without this close interest and commitment of time and support from the Medical Director's Office, prospects for the study would have been poor.

Methods and process
Central to our work on the pilots were the following elements:

● the Steering Group

● Multi-disciplinary pilot project working groups

● Patient consultation

The Steering Group comprised key Directorate staff, the Business Manager for Ophthalmology, the Medical Director and Quality Facilitator. In addition, a representative attended throughout from the local Community Health Council. We hoped to involve the junior medical staff in the project planning meetings but had no success in securing their regular attendance.

Although the Steering Group monitored each of the projects and offered views on detailed proposals as they were tabled for discussion and agreement, most of the detailed work needed was undertaken by smaller working groups of staff drawn from a range of different disciplines.

At its first meeting the Group decided that since there were, by this time, three consultants' firms it would be sensible and practicable for one each of the three project ideas to be developed by each consultant in conjunction with other colleagues. Although this limited the scope of some of our work to the practice of one consultant, rather than the whole Directorate, this was unavoidable in the circumstances.

IPPR and the Hospital always recognised the importance of establishing effective links with patients to ensure that their views and priorities influenced the work we were doing. We had hoped to establish some formal standing consultation panel or committee for this purpose but the failure to win additional resources for a project nurse prevented this from occurring. We still sought and obtained patients' views when the need arose, using an opinion survey, questionnaire and group consultation.

Changes to Directorate
Two major changes had occurred within the Directorate since our observations in the previous year and the completion of our interim report.

First, an Admissions Officer had been employed in the Eye Ward to be responsible for most aspects of the listing and admission for treatment of patients. This person was now available to inform patients of the likely time when they would have their operation and to answer many other queries which they might raise when telephoning. This post was unique in the Hospital. Its creation led to a practice of asking patients to telephone the Officer to discover the approximate time when they might be called for their operation. Also, patients were now receiving a copy letter from the consultant when they were listed confirming this.

Second, pre-operative assessment had been introduced for all patients receiving surgical treatment not just the patients of certain consultants. This change in practice was linked to new procedures designed to encourage day surgery. When attending the pre-operative assessment, the patient would now be seen by dedicated nursing staff (in addition to junior doctors) who would decide on their fitness for day surgery and give information about their proposed treatment. Only those patients who would be receiving a general anaesthetic would then undergo the full tests required to assess their fitness for this.

These developments superceded a number of our earlier findings and conclusions. The combined effect of the changes meant patients now had far better access to sources of information and advice about their intended treatment and the date when they would obtain this. It is impossible to say what impact, if any, IPPR's report of the previous year may have had in accelerating such changes or influencing how they were introduced.

Staff and management changes
No account of the pilot project work would be complete without some reference to personnel and managerial changes which took place during this stage of the research. Progress with the study and the Directorate's capacity to prioritise it was certainly affected by the disruption and discontinuity which these caused.

As practical work was about to commence, the Ophthalmology Business Manager took maternity leave. During her absence, her responsibilities were handled by a colleague from the Hospital's Planning Department, in addition to her other duties. By the time she returned to post, the Department of Health initiative to reduce Trust management costs had resulted in a review of management staffing. The temporary arrangement, and the reduced general management which it represented, was then formalised and the former Business Manager did not resume her responsibility for the Directorate.

Before work on the pilot projects was completed, the Care Manager in the

Directorate left to be employed elsewhere and at a crucial stage of our work the Clinical Director retired from this post and shortly thereafter from her employment in the Directorate. For some months the Clinical Directorship was undertaken by the Clinical Director for General Surgery who took no interest in the project, nor attended any of the meetings of the Steering Group. In due course, as we were concluding our work with the Directorate, another of its consultants – who had participated throughout the research – took over the role of Clinical Director.

Yet another change in staffing occurred during this period when one consultant, new to the Directorate but involved in one of the three pilot projects, left the Directorate to work elsewhere.

The Patient Pathways Project

The aim of this project was to attempt to agree a comprehensive and accurate account of what a patient could expect to receive by way of treatment and care. At various points in this description we intended to refer to details of the patients' rights and responsibilities. In many respects, the final document would comprise a form of treatment charter of the standards expected from all concerned – Hospital, Directorate and patient. We hoped this document might then be used as a source of consistent and reliable information to patients and, across the Directorate's different disciplines, would help to encourage acceptance of the patient's basic entitlements to information and to fair treatment.

The project was to be experimental and developmental and the limited time we had available might mean we would not develop the idea to its full potential. To prepare the pathway we did the following:

● investigated "clinical pathways" developed for common treatments, including cataract removal, in other hospitals

● in conjunction with staff, including one of the consultants, wrote a comprehensive pathway describing the treatment which she gave for a cataract

● obtained feedback on the draft pathway from patients recently treated by this consultant

Outcomes and evaluation
We contacted two hospitals which had introduced "pathways" as part of

centrally funded NHS pilot projects. Their experience was now extensive and provided useful background information. Some contrasts were immediately apparent between our approach and theirs.

The initiatives in Central Middlesex Hospital, London and in the Friarage Hospital, Northallerton were driven by a concern to increase the efficiency and reduce the cost of treatment activity by improving staff co-ordination, avoiding duplication and streamlining treatment process.[3] Once a treatment pathway was introduced, if clinicians or other staff decided to diverge from the pathway this variation would have to be recorded in writing with reasons given to justify it. The initiatives were not primarily driven by the need to ensure patients and others had better quality information though, if successful, this effect could result by encouraging a consensus view on the features of the service and what the patient could expect from it. Both of the written forms of pathway or protocol produced for cataract surgery were technical instruments for clinicians (medical and nursing) to use during the process of pre-operative assessment, admission for treatment and discharge from hospital. They were not written to be shown to the patient nor to inform patients of what to expect from the treatment.

Over a number of meetings, the working group responsible for this pilot agreed on the wording of a comprehensive pathway for cataract treatment provided by the consultant in the group. Two extracts from this document are reproduced in Appendix C; it is too long to include in full.

The first extract forms the introduction to the pathway. This explains its purpose and potential. The second part describes in words and in graphics the patient's route through the Out-patients' clinic. The complete document was surprisingly long (21 pages) and fairly complex. In addition to the Out-patients' clinic, there were sections on Referral to hospital; the Pre-operative clinic; Admission for surgery; and Discharge and After-care. Each written section concluded with a comprehensive description of patients' rights and responsibilities, before the basic treatment details were presented graphically.

Feedback from patients
At this stage, the document only reflected what staff themselves understood to be the experience which patients could expect when being treated. It was essential to test the pathway against the impressions of patients who had recently been treated to measure its accuracy and completeness. We convened two patient discussion groups to elicit the feedback needed.

Patients who had recently received treatment for cataracts from the consultant were invited to a meeting at the hospital. Taxi transport was offered to those without own transport. An average of eight patients attended each of the meetings, some accompanied by their spouse or another close relative.

The aim of the meetings was to listen to patients describe their experience of receiving treatment for a cataract relatively recently. It was not to trawl for complaints or for compliments, though these were voiced during both meetings. The purpose was to test the patients' descriptions against the staff pathways document, to examine whether there was divergence from this and, if so, where.

The groups did provide useful feedback on the treatment experience drawing attention to aspects of the "pathway" which were not being realised in practice. Some examples of these were the following:

- Although the pathway referred to a "short notice" list which patients could volunteer to go on if prepared to have treatment at very short notice, those in the groups were not universally aware of this system.

- The draft pathway included little reference to urgent treatment for those with post-operative problems following surgery. One patient had clearly been unfairly treated when she sought urgent treatment and attended the Ward when this was promised, only to find the doctor not prepared to wait to see her. To be complete and effective, the pathway would need to incorporate specific reference to this emergency service.

- The draft pathway unambiguously promised a patient choice of local or general anaesthesia, where this was clinically appropriate, and detailed when the choice could be exercised. However, the experience of patients in the groups suggested that only some patients were afforded any real opportunity to choose the method of anaesthesia. Furthermore, those who had been allowed to choose described how they felt this was mainly due to their persistence in asking.

- The pathway stated that all patients would be asked to contact the Admissions Officer to learn the approximate date for their operation. From the groups' accounts not all patients were being asked to do this.

- The pathway stated that all patients would be interviewed, following admission, by their named nurse. However, not all patients in the groups said they were aware of the named nurse system, nor of the role of the named nurse.

- The pathway made no mention of the District Nursing service, yet the groups reminded us of its role in helping to give eye-drops to a patient living alone and without assistance.

Pathways Project: conclusion

There were delays in convening these meetings and by the time they had been held, the consultant involved had left her employment in the Hospital. In view of this, it was agreed there was no point in adapting the draft pathway to reflect the points which the groups had raised, nor in using the graphics to produce some form of poster or flowchart. We reported to the Steering Group on the work undertaken to date proposing that the next logical stage would be to develop a Directorate wide cataract pathway, using the draft as a model. Although we understand this particular idea has not been actively pursued, there is interest in using written clinical pathways in the Directorate; development work on these is underway at the time of writing.

Evaluation of the Pathways Project

Our evaluation of the work which we undertook on the project concentrates on the following questions:

- Feasibility: was the procedure practicable?

- Impact: did the procedure affect the service?

- Rationale: did the procedure fulfil its aims?

Feasibility of the project

It is hard to reach firm conclusions in answer to any of these questions since the project was not completed within the time available and there were specific ideas which the planning group hoped could be tested but which could not be piloted in practice. Most of the difficulties which we experienced arose from the unique situation in which staff found themselves. None of them had ever been involved in a work project such as this and could have no clear perception of its possible benefit to patients or to the Directorate. In addition, the work was being undertaken by the consultant during the last months of her employment prior to her retirement from the NHS. Patient groups had never before been convened by the Directorate for consultation purposes to test the pathway and lack of experience caused some minor administrative difficulties when these had to be arranged.

Despite these disadvantages, the project demonstrated how a fairly technical description of the clinical stages of a commonly provided treatment could be allied with relevant information on rights and responsibilities. This could provide a useful focus for obtaining accounts of patients' experiences of the service and a benchmark against which these could be measured.

All involved in the research accepted that, in two respects, the project ended prematurely. We had hoped to produce a Directorate Pathway. From our experience in mapping one consultant's practice, it certainly appeared feasible to attempt this next logical stage but lack of time prevented this. The task would have been more challenging and valuable since all consultants would have to be firmly committed to disclosing and discussing variations in their practice and agreeing how these would, or would not, be incorporated into the consensus pathway. If the work had been extended across the practice of the whole Directorate, who is to say that we would not have encountered strong resistance to raising and discussing variations?

Secondly, the working group wanted to test out the graphical presentation of the pathway, or parts of this, in giving clear information to patients on what to expect. It should not have been too difficult to pilot such a flowchart poster or leaflet, once a Directorate document had been approved.

Impact of the project
The short term impact of the project seemed to be mainly educational. The pilot introduced Directorate staff to new ways of working together and relating to patients. It demonstrated the approach which would be needed if they wished to adopt a comprehensive approach to finding more uniform ways of working. Both the former and current Clinical Directors mentioned this effect. One observed that the approach could be applied across the Directorate "provided you make the consultants think that it is better to have uniformity. But, of course, that's an essential thing to improve any Directorate". The other stated: "It need not be controversial. The basic idea is very good. It is more important [than the other projects] and gives better results because it tells people what to expect and what to do when they come for an operation."

A staff nurse on the working group considered even the modest work on the project had been very useful. She had learned of aspects of the treatment pathway which she had not known about at all. She said: "If the patient needs to ask us about it we can tell them." The pathway would also help with training and the induction of junior medical staff who "didn't have a clue" when they first came to work on the ward. She speculated how much doctors might be prepared to discuss and agree a Directorate Pathway, given the clinical variations which she saw in their practice.

Rationale of the project

No-one involved in the project concluded that the work had had no point to it. Some were sceptical that it was able to produce concrete results of benefit to patients, but in view of its premature finish this was hard to assess. The aim of the project was to attempt to map out a standard specification of the core service a patient could expect to receive with the non-clinical dimension given as much prominence as the clinical one. When we ended, we had certainly made some headway in achieving just this and the potential of the concept was beginning to be realised and appreciated.

The Prompt List Project

The aim of this project was to improve the chances of anxious or inarticulate patients being able to ask questions of staff and receive accurate and comprehensive information. It would stress to patients their responsibility for seeking information and would strongly encourage them in the belief that it was right to do so. In consultation with patients who had been treated for cataracts, we planned to draw up a list of questions and supply these to patients before their consultation in the hope that this might prompt people to ask questions which they would otherwise have been reluctant to raise.

We undertook the work in the following stages:

- questionnaire survey of patients

- draft prompt list for cataract treatment

- pilot prompt list with patients attending pre-operative assessment

- telephone survey of patients to evaluate prompt list

Outcomes and evaluation

A sample of patients attending out-patients and pre-operative clinics were sent a simple questionnaire asking them to rate thirteen questions commonly raised with staff for their importance. They were also invited to add questions to the survey.

With the results obtained from this process, the working group drafted a Prompt List and had this approved by the Steering Group. We also sought the views of patients attending one of the pathways feedback discussions. The draft was unanimously welcomed by the latter group, who felt it would be helpful to patients. The Prompt List which we piloted is reproduced in Appendix C[4] and is largely self-explanatory. Covering one side of a yellow A4 sheet and in large print it was enclosed with the letters informing patients of arrangements for their pre-operative assessment.

Telephone survey

The early impressions of nursing staff running the pre-operative clinics was that the list was very rarely referred to by patients. To obtain an impression of its effectiveness a telephone questionnaire survey was conducted on a sample of patients who had responded to a request by letter. Ten of these patients had received the prompt list. Ten had not but, for the purposes of the interviews, were sent a copy of the prompt list so that we could obtain their reactions to it.

Of those who had been sent the list, all but one considered the document to have been useful in helping them to get the information they wanted. The remaining patient could not remember anything about the list. These respondents appeared to understand what was the purpose of the list and a number referred to specific questions which had been prompted as a result of reading it. Most felt it was supplied to them at the right time and confirmed that nursing staff volunteered significant amounts of information without the patient having to ask.

One very anxious patient had obtained great encouragement from receiving the list which he judged most helpful. He said that he was "frightened stiff" by the prospect of treatment and the fact that it had been sent to him encouraged him to trust the hospital and gave him "the courage to go through with it". He had even brought the list with him to hospital when he was admitted for his operation. He suggested that it be sent to all patients in his situation.

Of those who had not been sent the list before their pre-operative assessment, all but one considered it would have been useful to have received this before their appointment, although many observed that staff answered their questions without their having to ask, and they trusted them to do so. Again, one very anxious patient who described himself as "frightened to death not knowing what would happen" said it would have put his mind at rest to have obtained this list before coming into the hospital.

At this point IPPR's involvement in the Prompt List Project ended. However, it has continued to be used in the Directorate as part of its pre-operative assessment procedure.

Evaluation
Our evaluation concentrates on the following questions:

- Feasibility: was the prompt list practicable?

- Impact: what was the effect of the prompt list on practice?

- Rationale: did the prompt list appear to succeed in its aims?

Feasibility of Prompt List
Although it took longer than we expected to produce a final draft of the list, there was a general belief in the Hospital that the version which was piloted would be a useful aid to increasing patient confidence and ensuring good communication. We had no difficulty in arranging for the document to be sent out with letters to patients calling them to their pre-operative assessment. It might have made the list more effective if the invitation letter had been amended to refer specifically to the role and importance of the document.

Impact of Prompt List
If impact is measured by the extent to which patients referred to the document in the course of their consultation then this was slight. However, it may have had an impact without being apparent in this way. Certainly, patients who were sent it regarded it as useful. The anxious patient said he had been given great encouragement just by receiving the list. All but one of these patients recalled the list and told us that they understood its purpose. The Community Health Council representative confirmed the view that patients could be reluctant to ask questions unless specifically encouraged to do so. Of the Out-patient appointment she observed: "Patients expect to be in and out in a few minutes. They have this underlying feeling that the doctor is very busy and that they should not ask the doctor."

There were mixed views in the Hospital on the success of the pilot. The Clinical Director was not surprised at the limited results since he said he was sceptical about it, commenting: "Either [patients] are or are not bothered". However, he felt that it could be given out, but at Out-patients' with an invitation to phone the Ward to have the questions answered. The former Clinical Director said that she would feel more relaxed if patients had received the list before seeing her. The Medical Director thought that this project was going to be the most important because of the simple and practical impact it could have, and was surprised at the limited effects observed in practice.

The Quality Facilitator asserted that the list should be sent even if the number of patients who would use it would be small. This was because the document gave the message: "The Hospital says you can ask. It's OK to ask". The Staff Nurse who worked on the prompt list, and who saw patients who had been sent it, confirmed that she had never used anything like the list before in her practice. She believed it was a good idea since patients worried about asking doctors questions and some of the patients who came to her clinic had obtained little information from their out-patient consultation, perhaps because they had not been supplied with the standard cataract leaflet. She was sure that the list could be given a higher profile with patients by the invitation letter mentioning it or by using some method which would require the patient to write on the list in some way, for example by ticking it in places.

Rationale

The prompt list appeared to have achieved the purpose for which it was designed, even if only to stress to patients their responsibility for asking for information and that staff would respond if they did this. The main idea for a list had originated after we had seen the Out-patients' clinic in full swing. We had intended to pilot the list in that setting. However, we discovered that the wording of the list was inappropriate for distribution to patients attending their first appointment, since it assumed that they would be listed for surgery – an outcome which could not be predicted with any certainty at all.

The Wait-listing Project

The aim of this project was to try to improve the patient's experience of waiting for treatment.[5] Our earlier investigations had highlighted the unreliable information which patients received on wait-listing decisions and the absence of clear policy on the social factors which might be relevant to such decisions. We hoped to pilot changes which could actually improve decision-making on wait-listing and the information given to patients about this.

The working group given responsibility for this pilot project planned the following tasks:

- draft guidelines for wait-listing

- circulate draft to GPs and Opticians for comment

- conduct survey of patient's experience of waiting

- informed by survey results, produce a letter and information leaflet for patients to be given in Out-patients clinic immediately following the decision to list them for treatment

The Wait-listing guidelines
In the absence of any Directorate guidelines or protocol on wait-listing decision-making it was important to record clearly the principles upon which this was done by the consultant involved in the group and all the procedural aspects of wait-listing. Only when these had been drafted and agreed would it be possible to contemplate providing patients with better quality information. Without them there would be no reliable source from which to provide this.

The guidelines which the group produced were 8 pages long and included two appendices. They set out the purpose of the document (to ensure consistency and equity), its status and scope. Procedures governing listing on referral to out-patients were described with an appendix detailing the factors determining priority in listing. This page is reproduced in Appendix C below.[6] On the basis of these factors the referral would be classed as urgent, priority or routine. The rest of the document dealt with decisions on listing for treatment, describing the information which patients would be given on listing, and what they should do if needing to obtain earlier treatment or cancel their operation. Again, the guidelines outlined in an appendix, the factors influencing listing decisions. This is also found in Appendix C below.[7]

Each of these appendices drew attention to the clinical and social factors which could influence prioritisation of examination or treatment. Specifically, it highlighted the importance of an adult patient's caring responsibility; or the possibility of employment being affected or of the patient becoming virtually blind. Maximum waiting times were given in the guidelines in respect of each of the three categories described. We should stress that the guidelines described current practice. The process did not involve an evaluation of these criteria and a consideration of how fairer or better ones might be defined.[8]

Consultation with GPs and Opticians

We judged it was important to check the accuracy and usefulness of the guidelines with a sample of local GPs and Opticians and wrote to them inviting them to comment on the document. This produced no response whatsoever. We persisted with GPs and the document was circulated to the local Medical Audit Advisory Group. The response from its members was that there were no areas where the guidelines disagreed with GPs' understanding of the Hospital's current procedures.

Survey of patients

Having established the basis for current practice, it was then necessary to obtain a profile of the patient waiting for treatment. How many such patients would welcome more information? How many would find the experience made them anxious? We drafted a lengthy questionnaire to use in telephone interviews with a sample of 48 patients who had recently been treated and had agreed to be interviewed.

Selected data from the results of this survey showed what might be the priority concerns of patients waiting to be called for their operation:

● Over 31 per cent of patients felt that they waited too long for their treatment, whilst a larger percentage (37.5 per cent) felt the treatment was sooner than expected.

● Over 31 per cent of patients were anxious about waiting for treatment, the main cause of anxiety being uncertainty about when treatment would take place.

● 50 per cent of patients stated they had had problems coping with the practical effects of their condition while they were waiting (ranging from problems with mobility and reading to impact on employment tasks).

● 29 per cent of patients wanted more information about their condition and treatment when seen at outpatients.

- 37.5 per cent of patients wanted earlier knowledge of the date for their operation.

- 29 per cent of patients wanted information on the reason why they were having to wait.

- 19 per cent of patients felt that their circumstances justified greater priority in arranging their treatment.

- 23 per cent of patients stated that they would have agreed to another doctor undertaking the treatment if this had meant it would have happened sooner.

- Just under 50 per cent of patients seemed unaware of the Short Notice procedure.

- 54 per cent of patients said they were unaware of the Patient's Charter standards for waiting times.

- A few patients had experienced maladministration in the listing of their treatment, making enquiries after some delay only to discover that they had not been listed at all.

The Wait-listing letter and information leaflet
In the light of these results the working group agreed to pilot a new letter and information leaflet, to be given to patients during their Out-patients' appointment immediately after the doctor had decided to list them for an operation. The purpose of this new practice would be:

- to ensure that the patient knew precisely what was the maximum waiting time permitted under the Patient's Charter and of the Hospital's commitment to meeting this

- to ensure that the patient knew that listing takes account of factors giving priority to those with severe problems (clinical or social)

- to ensure that the Admissions Officer would inform each patient by phone shortly after their appointment of the likely date of their operation

- to ensure that the patient realised that their GP could contact the consultant if the patient's situation changed and their treatment required prioritisation

Outcomes and evaluation
IPPR produced a draft leaflet and in discussion with the consultant, and at his suggestion, a section was added which unambiguously confirmed the patient's right to choose both the mode of admission and the method of anaesthesia to be used in the operation, clinical considerations permitting.

Since time was running out for the research project, the finalised leaflet was introduced without further consultation with patients. The letter and the information leaflet are found in Appendix C below.[9] They stressed the need to contact the Admissions Officer to obtain the estimated date for treatment; the relevance of certain factors to priority listing and the choices which the patient would be permitted to exercise at their pre-operative assessment, if they were clinically appropriate.

The Steering Group envisaged that it would be desirable to evaluate the impact of the document after at least ten months had expired and the first patients who had received it had been treated and discharged. The Community Health Council might be asked to undertake this task.

From pilot to mainstream practice
Although the project envisaged the guidelines and the documents being piloted only in the practice of one of the consultants, within weeks they were adopted and were being used in the mainstream practice of the Directorate. The appendices included in the Wait-listing guidelines were supplied by the Admissions Officer to two new consultants when they joined the Directorate. These are now used by them when they decide on the listing category of patients.

In addition, the letter and leaflet were soon used by all consultants at Outpatients' when informing patients that they would be listed for surgical treatment. Shortly after its introduction, the Admissions Officer confirmed that the leaflet was having the effect of identifying patients whose circumstances had not become apparent and who should be given greater priority. Patients were telephoning her and mentioning social factors which they had not told to the doctor. This contact was prompted, in her view, by the contents of the letter and leaflet.

The letter and leaflet were introduced in July 1996 and have been continuously in use since that date. The Hospital is now adapting the practice to other specialities and a modified version of the documents is planned for use in the Ear, Nose and Throat Directorate and may also be employed in General Surgery.

Evaluation
Our evaluation concentrates on the following questions:

● Feasibility: were the Guidelines and Information Leaflet practicable?

● Impact: what has been their effect in practice?

● Rationale: did the project succeed in its aims?

Feasibility of the project
According to the Medical Director, who was very encouraged by the progress made with the project, the letter and leaflet produced for this project were unique within the Hospital. He knew of no other Directorate, which listed patients for treatment, providing them with the information which it contained. We encountered few practical problems in the drafting and agreement of the guidelines, surveying of patients and drafting and agreement of the letter and leaflet. The drafting of the guidelines involved a process similar to that adopted for the pathways project: asking a multi-disciplinary group to describe their practice in such a way that it could be written up formally. In a sense, we were defining a stage of the pathway for patients. GPs and opticians could not be persuaded to participate with the work. This was regrettable, given their importance throughout the process of referral for treatment and afterwards. We can only speculate as to their reasons for declining.

Importance of Admissions Officer post
It is important to stress that we would not have been able to make much progress on this project without the Admissions Officer being in post. After patients, she would gain most from the new policy and procedure initiative and her availability to patients as a source of information would be essential to the project's success. In August 1996, she was still the only Directorate based Admissions Officer found in the Hospital.

Impact and rationale
The Admissions Officer is sure that the Guidelines and Leaflet have affected practice and the patient's experience of being listed and waiting for treatment. She believes it has been an "enormous help", could be of general benefit in the Hospital and has empowered her in her role. When she started working in the Directorate she was told by the consultants how they wished to have patients listed. They did this "by word of mouth" and consultants differed in their approach. Now she reported that they seemed to have a universal approach and "… they all agree on the same thing. Through IPPR we've come

to the arrangement of certain things being urgent, certain things being priority, and the rest being routine." The framework set out in the appendices of the guidelines had become the common practice of the Directorate.

In her view the procedure was picking up those patients who had not told the doctor of necessary background information and who had been wrongly listed as routine when they should have been given priority listing instead. She concluded: "Prioritisation is happening in a more effective, more uniform and more consistent way. I think it is fairer".

These attitudes were echoed in the views of the Community Health Council representative on this pilot project:

> *I like the guidelines. It's the intention of it which I think is good and will have a good effect on patients. Because it is directed to giving the patient information, choice – its limited, we know – and an explanation of why they are waiting. So that it involves the patient more in what's happening to him and it also puts forward a pattern of fair treatment. I think it's the fair treatment and the information that's very important… It was the emphasis on it being open. Of there being a pattern of waiting list decision-making… with reference to other people's needs so they could see they were being handled in a fair way. That seemed to me to be the important thing about this project.*

In making these observations, she mentioned her concern that people feel others jump the waiting list for unacceptable reasons. She felt that being open and offering reasons for the decision on priority would help to remove any cause for complaint. She also injected a note of realism into our assessment of the importance of the changes. The procedure had not engaged GPs in any meaningful way, yet their choice of hospital and of consultant could be crucial to the patient's experience of waiting.

The consultant who had been involved in the working group admitted he had been sceptical about the project – in the same way as he was sceptical about any managerial initiatives which might draw him away from contact with patients. Despite this, he considered the aims of the project had been useful and it had produced a useful leaflet and letter. He was using both in his practice and consultant colleagues who had recently joined the Directorate had adopted his approach because they saw it was useful. There was a definite advantage in that the procedure was now taken up by the whole department and the information "goes a long way to answering the honest questions of the patient who couldn't ask them in the clinic due to shortage of time or the lack of facility or their worry to ask silly questions."

The staff nurse responsible for pre-operative assessment regarded the Wait-listing project as the most important of the three. In her view, the guidelines were very informative for patients and the leaflet would make a big difference. Before, patients did not know anything to do with the Waiting List. Now they could ring up and ask and were offered an important link with the Hospital. She confirmed that medical practice was definitely shifting towards respecting the right to choose that had been included in the leaflet. In her experience, patients were now given a genuine choice whether to be admitted overnight or as a day case. There was also a definite trend towards more patients being allowed the choice in anaesthesia promised in the leaflet. One consultant's clinical preference, however, still precluded patients under 60 years old from having a local anaesthetic for fear that they would move during the operation.

Conclusions

The Hospital

What are the implications of the project for the Hospital and for other hospitals? Are procedural rights relevant to these types of services and settings? The Medical Director was keen to undertake the work because he perceived it was linked to the Trust's quality strategy for which he was responsible, and because it developed ways of working with patients which reflected a "partnership" model rather than the conventional "medical" model. Furthermore, the Trust was beginning to feel some external pressures – for example, from the NHS Executive, which urged patient involvement in clinical audit. He wanted the Trust to be prepared for these changes when they were required.

The project interested him because he felt the need:

> ...to look at the whole way we provide a service in a much broader way than was traditional. The traditional medical model was very scientifically oriented. The quality of the service depended on the diagnosis, treatment, operation, the success of that and so on. The extreme caricature is where it does not matter how long the patient waits; it does not matter what the environment is. They should be jolly glad to see an expert like me at the end of the day and get their sight restored, or their hernia repaired or their appendix out.

If the project was to be effective at all he knew it was critical to "get the consultants on board". He expected there might be some resistance to it because it was not primarily a clinical research project. It concerned a

"… soft quality issue not a firm, scientific quality issue" and he feared that the enthusiastic participation critical to its success might not be forthcoming.

He regarded the project has having produced results which would be of benefit and which could be broadened into other specialities. The research pilots had produced a basis for taking the ideas forward into other areas of the Hospital's activity, and he undertook to ensure that development work would continue at least in the immediate future.

The Medical Director stressed the educational impact of the research. Within the Directorate, the project had "opened their eyes to some of the issues". He said it had given him new insights as well:

Equity did not concern me until this project. That was one of the things which really stimulated me because that was something I had not actually thought of, although I considered I was looking at service provision on a wider front than the merely technical.

The Hospital's Quality Facilitator also mentioned this important aim of the work and the potential which it might have to reduce inequality amongst those benefiting from the service. She observed:

The people getting the most from the service are the middle classes because they know how to go and ask. They can vocalise what they need. The upper classes will go privately anyway for most things. We have needed to work on allowing the others… to have a voice and to have a right. If the prompt list or whatever has helped in doing that I would think it has been a success.

Both the former and current Clinical Directors felt the project had been useful to the Directorate's work. The first summarised its effect as follows: "It has given the Directorate information about itself which it did not have. Clinicians did not do it and the managers did not do it." The current Clinical Director said he was sceptical of any managerial or administrative measures, mainly because they took up time which he felt should be utilised in seeing patients. However, he felt that the project had proved its point and was "worth the candle".

In summary, the research project appeared to have:

● reduced medical scepticism about enhancing patients' rights

- helped to encourage openness between staff and multi-disciplinary working

- demonstrated new ways of working, particularly in consulting patients

- offered new ways of tackling inequality due to social class or education

- enhanced the capacity of the Admissions Officer and the Pre-operative Clinic Nurse to provide information and enable patients to exercise their rights

- introduced practical ideas which might be used elsewhere in the Hospital

Despite these observations, there were a number of difficulties which were encountered during the work – barriers which could easily compromise further development of these ideas in the Hospital or elsewhere, if conditions are similar.

Changing the resistant culture

The methods of the research project – perhaps some of the principles underlying it – clashed with an organisational culture, particularly of medical practice. The ways in which doctors' services are organised and the independence which they have been traditionally allowed to enjoy do not fit easily with initiatives of this kind. The Hospital's Quality Facilitator commented on this situation:

> *I don't think its difficult for nursing staff to grasp and see the concept behind rights. I think its difficult for medical staff to do that because they have operated for such a long time in a culture where, subject to ethical obligations and professional guidance, they have been totally independent and, if they did not want to, they did not have to listen to anyone. If you give someone rights then you have to take into account what they say and if you cannot give them what they want you have to explain why.*

This can lead, in her view, to defensiveness and lack of co-operation from doctors. She referred to an underlying frustration that if managers cannot ask for guidance and support from doctors, processes put in place would not work and doctors would refuse to use them. Whilst she understood the stress which doctors worked under and the pressures which created this situation, she felt bound to comment – generally, not about the Eye Ward – "There's just something about doctors which says "I don't need to do this.

Why are you bothering me with this? I want to treat patients". However, she recognised that the project had led Directorate staff to face up to some of these issues and it had a positive effect because, for the first time, they had to sit down and discuss them.

The Medical Director was conscious of this when he admitted that when the pilot work was extended to other specialities, they would each need to go back to the same beginning. However, he hoped that the general climate was changing. The prominent role which the Medical Director himself adopted in promoting the research project probably helped to counter some of these discouraging features of organisational culture. Future initiatives will almost certainly need equivalent leadership at a Board level if they are to prosper.

Counter distracting pressures
The Directorate was an extremely busy department with all staff required to cope with armies of patients needing services. Such pressure of work has two effects. Firstly, the sheer weight of numbers can render it difficult or impossible to meet agreed minimum standards of practice, for example, the giving of clear and comprehensive information. Secondly, the compelling need to deal with the day's treatment activity can constantly distract staff at all levels from focusing on new initiatives.

We saw evidence of both during our work with the Directorate. Standards or rights which patients could reasonably expect were not being met with the consistency and reliability promised. Attendance at meetings or administration on the research sometimes also had to be sacrificed to pressures of competing commitments.

The lesson which this suggests, of course, is that leadership is essential to ensure focus and commitment. As the Quality Facilitator observed:

Unless you have someone to drive it and to push and to push them, it will disappear no matter how good it is.

It is also necessary to discover what are the incentives, if any, for staff to work on such projects which could encourage co-operation and commitment. Without these, enthusiasm is bound to be limited.

Recognise and limit impact of staff turnover
We have mentioned above the high turnover of personnel during the period of the research project. Undoubtedly, this added to the difficulties of

implementing the projects. Interruptions in the involvement of key staff weakened its impact on the whole Directorate.

Encourage new attitudes towards standards

The Quality Facilitator regarded some attitudes to standards in the NHS as ill-suited to the concept of rights. She believed it was still hard for the service to work to minimum standards and there was a "...general fuzziness of what is an absolute standard and what is something they will try and do". She accepted that there was a need for some absolute rights, but said it would be some time before rights, such as to be seen at any given time, could be guaranteed. It appears that, as with other services involved in this research, there may be a role for a new means of distinguishing between absolute and target standards, perhaps by introducing a new form of "public service guarantee" linked to the Health Service Ombudsman or a Regional Hospital Ombudsman system.[10]

Develop systematic patient consultation

A further barrier was the Hospital's general inexperience in systematically seeking patients' views about service development, and a lack of relevant expertise amongst key front-line staff. This perception was confirmed by the Community Health Council representative and acknowledged by the Medical Director. Furthermore, the narrow specialisation of professional roles in NHS service Directorates meant that it could be left to individual practitioners to decide on whether and how to seek patients' views. There was no perceivable demand for change from patients, but this was probably due to the fact that no-one had ever suggested to them that change was possible. Only when consultation with service users began as part of this research were patients' voices heard.

The Hospital will need to generalise the lessons from the research and experience gained in listening to patients if the effects of the project are to spread elsewhere in its services. It may be appropriate for the Board to set targets for patient involvement in planning, development and evaluation, and to identify who will be responsible for leading efforts to meet them. The recent NHS Executive paper *Patient Partnership: Building a Collaborative Strategy*[11] stresses the need for developments aimed at listening to patients and the need for a strategic approach to this.

Develop Board level policy on Patients' Rights

The Hospital, like any other, gives every appearance of being managed in a fairly hierarchical manner with key policy being set at Board level and implemented through the service directorates. It was therefore fascinating to discover from the Medical Director that the Board had not discussed issues such as the patient's right to choose (mode of admission or anaesthesia) and would not consider it within its role to determine hospital policy on such matters. It was expected that these decisions would be taken by individual clinicians or by the Directorate, to which more and more matters had in recent years been devolved.

The reluctance to establish minimum patients' rights across the Trust could be seen as a barrier to their further development. It will prove an obstacle to securing the collective acceptance of a set of core standards if some Directorates resist the idea. It may also produce an inequality of rights, if some Directorates agree to rights which others reject.

The research suggests that there may be a key role for the Board in defining and encouraging a set of core rights for patients which are not specific to any speciality. Information on wait-listing procedures and priorities[12] and choice in admission and anaesthesia (subject to clinical appropriateness) could be codified in this way throughout the Trust's hospitals, to give robust effect to the concept of "rights".

Impact on front line staff and lessons
None of those we interviewed complained that the project had been bureaucratic or that it had involved complicated procedures or documents. Even when the finished pathways document turned out far longer than expected, the working group hoped that extracts could be used with patients to convey information effectively. Doctors, the Staff Nurse and Admissions Officer all appeared to acknowledge that what had been produced would help them in their work and they saw the potential for these ideas to be adopted by colleagues in other parts of the Hospital. We heard no complaints about additional "paperwork".

Of course, neither the pilot prompt list nor the letter/leaflet on wait-listing required any member of staff to complete any new document or to record their decision in writing. It complemented the culture of mainly verbal communication, assisting it by encouraging it to work better. The Staff Nurse would still have to explain about a patient's operation but could believe that the patient would raise individual concerns which worried them. The Admissions Officer would still have to give information over the telephone but would know the patient had some standard information already broadly defining the parameters for the Directorate's approach.

One long term lesson may well be to have demonstrated to front-line staff how simple changes such as the Wait-listing letter and leaflet, costing very little, can have a significant impact on the patient's experience. This may encourage them to apply the same approach to other aspects of the service, such as the poor quality standard letters that were still routinely being sent to visually impaired patients when our work with the Directorate ended.

Another lesson is the importance of multi-disciplinary working and how this enabled staff to understand better the roles and responsibilities of each other and improve the links between them. Changes at the front-line required close co-operation among staff who would not usually meet together to discuss policy or procedure.

Patients: impact and lessons

The limits of the research project, and its timing, restricted our ability to assess the full impact of the changes on the patients' experience. We cannot, therefore, tell what has been the effect of the Wait-listing letter and leaflet and whether or not this has benefited patients and, if so, in what ways. Our telephone survey of patient attitudes to waiting revealed significant unmet need for information and a minority of patients dissatisfied with their experience. What effect has the new procedure had and has it led waiting patients to feel they have more power over their circumstances? The Hospital should conduct a follow-up survey since patients seen last year and given the documents will now have had their treatment. However, from what the Admissions Officer reported to us we would be surprised if the documents have not already improved patients' understanding of the wait-listing process and their rights under it.

Our survey of patients who did or did not receive the Prompt List revealed largely positive views on it, with those patients who described themselves as anxious strongly approving of the list. The aim of the list was to target the anxious patient, not the patient who could cope with asking questions or those who were not bothered. Furthermore, its rationale was to tell the patient they could ask if they wanted to. Whether or not patients refer to the document may not therefore be the test of its impact.

We piloted the list in a setting where the patient is already given extensive information by a nurse. It would be valuable to observe the impact of a suitably modified list on people attending Out-patients' for their first appointment, when anxiety may be higher and time more restricted, and where it is a doctor who has to respond to the patient's questions.

The Public: impact and lessons

None of our work with the Hospital concerned the public as distinct from those using the service and we did not attempt to measure the impact of our work on local people who had not been patients. However, it would be possible to discover public attitudes to the changes and how these would be interpreted. The Community Health Council representative asserted that the priority factors which had been disclosed in the course of the Wait-listing project probably reflected general public attitudes. Given the non-clinical nature of some of these factors there is an argument for wider public consultation on these factors to establish if there is a consensus about them.

As with other aspects of this developmental project, if the ideas and methods are to be extended further, it would be important to explore ways of involving the public in helping to define such principles.[13] It would strengthen the public's perception that services were being fairly distributed according to widely accepted notions of priority and entitlement.

Endnotes

1 Health Service Commissioner (1996) *Second Report for 1996-97, Selected Investigations completed April-September 1996*, Stationary Office.

2 For a comprehensive investigation of the causes of poor communication in hospital and how this may be improved, see Audit Commission (1993) *What seems to be the matter: communication between hospitals and patients*, HMSO.

3 Morgan G and Layton A (1996) "Clear winners", *Health Service Journal*, 30 May; Brown J and Simpson L (1994) *Co-ordinating Patient Care: Putting principles into practice*, Department of Health.

4 See p.217.

5 Martin M (1995) "Life in the Slow Lane", *The Health Service Journal*, 25 May.

6 See p.218.

7 See p.219.

8 New approaches to Wait-listing prioritisation have been piloted at Salisbury Health Care NHS Trust and in hospitals abroad. For recent developments in New Zealand, see Ham C (1997) "Cue to end queues", *The Guardian*, 9 April.

9 See pp.220–221.

10 See p.175.

11 Quality and Consumers Branch, NHS Executive (1996) *Patient Partnership: Building a Collaborative Strategy*, NHS Executive

12 For a call for more fairness and sophistication in prioritisation, see Edwards R T (1997) "Showing how to make a drama out of the waiting list crisis", *Health Service Journal*, 20 February.

13 For full treatment of public participation in setting health policy and local priorities see Cooper L *et al* (1995) *Voices Off: Tackling the democratic deficit in health*, IPPR.

5 The Co-op: fair treatment rights and general medical services

What the Chapter contains

In this chapter, we describe the work we undertook with an Association of NHS GPs providing "out-of-hours" deputising services to a mixed rural/urban area (total registered patients: 308,780). The project concerned the Co-op's intended use of its legal power to decide when a patient would be asked to visit its base to be seen there rather than at home. The pilot aimed to protect the rights of patients to continue to be seen in their home in certain defined circumstances.

The chapter is in three main sections which follow an outline of the project's aims. First, we describe the nature and scope of the service which the Co-op offered and what we learned when investigating opportunities for the development of procedural rights. In the second section we report on our planning for the pilot project, and explore reasons why it was not ultimately adopted. In the third section we set out some general observations obtained from those closely involved with the project; we discuss its importance and the lessons which our experience offers for future policy in this field, and for procedural rights.

Project aims

GPs' services form a crucial component in any comprehensive primary health care system. Patients' rights to obtain such services from their registered doctor, within a reasonable time and, if necessary, out of normal hours, have long been recognised. Furthermore, the legal framework and organisation of general medical services has always been strikingly different from that governing the provision of hospital medicine.

During initial discussions with the Family Health Services Authority (FHSA), IPPR anticipated working with individual general practice partnerships, not with an association of doctors. One practice which we approached, however, had been closely involved in setting up the Co-op in 1989. Its senior partner felt there was little scope for piloting procedural rights within his practice.

Instead, he believed there was an opportunity to develop and pilot a project within the Co-op. His suggestion was to formulate written criteria designed to influence the way that doctors' decided whether or not to visit patients at home. This would offer the researcher considerable scope and require a high degree of practical innovation. As an idea for a pilot on patients' rights it was impossible to resist.

The GP's responsibility for out-of-hours cover was alive with discussion and controversy. As we started our work, in early 1994, the British Medical Association was pressing the Department of Health for changes to the GP's Terms and Conditions to provide greater flexibility when doctors determined how they fulfilled their legal obligation. Some GPs condemned patients for "abusing" their right to a medical service out-of-hours by making trivial and unnecessary demands upon it.[1] Others regarded the rise in patient consumerism to be responsible, fuelled by initiatives such as the Patient's Charter.

The growth of GP out-of-hours co-operatives, in some districts subsidised by the local FHSA, resulted from their members' increasing concerns about their contractual responsibility to provide a 24 hour service to patients. To them, co-operative arrangements helped to meet rising levels of demand for out-of-hours contacts, reduced the disruption this caused to their working and home lives and brought tangible improvements in the quality of medical care provided to patients.

The controversy surrounding the future of out-of-hours services raised issues which were highly contentious but of great practical importance to patients as well as to doctors. Later we discovered the risks attached to working so near to controversy. This may have been the very dimension to have contributed to the project's premature end.

Why should procedural rights be important to out-of-hours services? There are few if any standard procedures governing the provision of such services by GPs.[2] To the outside observer, this can encourage the belief that the extent of services offered by a GP will differ significantly from doctor to doctor and partly this is true. Determining whether or not it is necessary to see a patient out-of-hours involves the exercise of a clinical judgement and a calculation of risk – each influenced to an extent by the experience, competence and temperament of the doctor.

However, other factors, such as the patient's social circumstances, may dictate how or whether a patient obtains a service particularly if the doctor insists on the patient travelling elsewhere to be seen. Here there may be less, if any, justification for doctors to have different views on when it is reasonable to require a patient to use a taxi in the early hours, or leave their children with neighbours or travel ten miles to be seen at the doctor's surgery.[3]

The procedural rights approach can encourage fair and unbiased decision making, and at the same time help the public to see the reasons why they have been treated in a particular manner and the sense and justice of it happening. This was the focus for our work with the Co-op.

First Stage: investigating options

Aims and methods
The aim of this first stage was to examine how the Co-op provided its services to patients so that we could formulate a viable proposal for a pilot project. The methods we employed were the following:

- background research into the legal framework for provision of emergency general medical services

- observations and interviews

- interim report to the Co-op's directors

Observations and interviews
In order to discover the nature of services provided by the Co-op, the routes which patients took to obtain these and assess options, IPPR's researcher spent five rota sessions at the association observing work in practice, including overnight and at weekends. This entailed watching the receptionists receive and pass telephone calls and joining rota doctors when they were advising by phone and seeing patients in person at the Co-op's surgery. We also spent time accompanying rota GPs as they were driven around the district attending patients for consultations in their homes. At the same time we sought views on current practice and on our research project from the FHSA through its Director of Primary Care Development and from the Community Health Council through its Chief Officer.

The Interim Report
After completing our observations and background research, we delivered an interim report to the directors of the Co-op, setting out our findings and proposal for a research pilot project and the tasks involved in setting it up.

Both the contents of the report and its suggestions met with the approval of the directors and formed the basis for much of our later work on the project.

Findings: the legal framework
Patients obtain general medical services through a legal contract made between the Health Authority for the area where they are resident and the general practitioner with whom they are registered. Since the research was completed, Family Health Services Authorities, which formerly held the contract, have merged with District Health Authorities. A practitioner who fails to comply with the terms of this contract can be held to be in breach by the Authority's Service Committee and can suffer financial penalties as a result or have his or her conduct reported to the General Medical Council. GPs, however, are only obliged to provide services to those people registered with them and may ask the authority to remove a patient from that list without having to give any reason for doing so.

Under the contract, the GP must render to his or her patients "all necessary and appropriate personal medical services of the type usually provided by general medical practitioners".[4] Doctors have to offer consultations to patients and, where appropriate, physical examinations. However, the duty is qualified since no GP is required to show a higher degree of skill, knowledge and care than that which GPs "as a class may reasonably be expected to exercise".

When we started the research, doctors were required to provide services at their practice, or if the patient's condition required this, at the patient's home, or elsewhere if approved by the Authority.

The duty is a 24 hour one but a GP can delegate his or her responsibility to another doctor, such as a partner in their practice, or to a deputising service such as the Co-op or a commercial deputising service. At the start of our research, deputising services – whether co-operative or commercial had limited powers to ask patients to attend the co-operative surgery for a consultation since the contract required them specifically to have regard to the convenience of patients.

Early into the research, we learned that aspects of the GP's contract (the "Terms of Service") were being renegotiated between the British Medical Association and the Department of Health. One of the BMA's aims was to strengthen the GP's power to decide where out-of-hours consultations would take place – to help to reduce the occasions when doctors carried out unnecessary home visits. Agreement was reached during the first stage of our research, but the legal changes which resulted did not come into force until February 1995. We describe the changes and their significance in the next section of this chapter.[5]

Findings: the Co-op's origins

Co-operative arrangements between GPs are still fairly novel. How the service is organised varies from place to place. Until 1989, many GPs in the Co-op's area used the services of a commercial deputising agency when they wished to arrange cover for their out-of-hours obligation. This was considered by the Community Health Council amongst others to provide a poor service to patients with frequent long delays in visits and limited, if any, telephone advice to patients.

As a result of a Regional Health Authority supported initiative, the Co-op was formed, offering its services to those local GPs wishing to join.[6] From the outset the service attracted widespread support from local GPs. It now provides the vast majority of deputising services within the local district.

The FHSA supported and assisted the development of the Co-op making substantial payments for ancillary staffing and accommodation costs, providing an attractive subsidy for participating practices.

Key characteristics of the Co-op: facilities and staffing

The Co-op's base comprises a suite of comfortable ground floor offices together with a consulting room and waiting room. Commonly used drugs and other medical supplies are stored at the premises and basic resuscitation equipment is also available.

Doctors who are on call and attending patients at home are transported there in cars driven by drivers employed by the Co-op. Base staff comprise an administrator, reception staff who work on rota, and drivers, also working on rota.

The Co-op is incorporated as a company under the Companies Acts not as a true co-operative under the Industrial and Provident Societies Acts. Limited by guarantee – and therefore not profit sharing – it has three Directors, who are GP members, who meet regularly with the Administrator to undertake the day to day running of the organisation. A larger Council of participating GPs meets on a quarterly basis. Nearly all of the general practitioners who work in the area (158 in number) are members of and use the services of the Co-op. At the time of our investigation about ninety of these were undertaking rota work, some doing many more sessions than others.

Receiving and processing calls

Callers to the service complain of symptoms such as pains in the chest; shortness of breath or difficulty breathing; severe coughs or colds in young children; vomiting and diarrhoea; rashes; food poisoning; abdominal pains; dizziness or blackouts; earache; severe anxiety or depression; or internal bleeding. These are just examples of only the commonest problems reported.

The Co-op provides a range of services to its member practices. Demand fluctuates from time to time and the number of staff on duty and the organisation of medical rotas is adjusted accordingly to meet these demands as they occur. There are always "back up" staff and doctors available to come in to assist should workload exceed normal levels. At the time of our observations services were provided in the following way:

Answering service: the reception staff can act as a limited answering service for a GP or partnership wishing to have their calls answered for them. Some calls are automatically intercepted, being routed directly to the Co-op's base. Alternatively, the caller obtains the Co-op's phone number from a taped message on the surgery phone. A call will be received, details taken and the practice doctor on duty will be telephoned or bleeped. When contact is established the doctor may deal with the call personally or ask the Co-op to handle it.

Deputising service: if a call is received from a patient for whose doctor the Co-op is providing not just an answering but a fully deputising service then the response will be different. The caller will be asked by the receptionist if s/he wants to have a visit from the doctor or advice on the telephone. If the caller requests a visit from the doctor then this will be recorded on the database. Very brief details of the person's reported complaint or condition are taken by the reception staff and recorded.

If the person is mobile and can come or be brought to the base surgery, which is in operation from 8pm until midnight on weekday nights and for periods over weekends and bank holidays, then the receptionist will encourage them to use this facility though she will never insist upon it. If the person requests a visit and the reception staff have no doubt as to the need for this then it will be promised and the call passed to the doctor who will attend.

If the receptionist has some doubt as to the appropriateness of a doctor attending and there is either a doctor based at the surgery who can telephone or a doctor "on the road" who can do so, then the receptionist may insist that the doctor calls the patient and discusses the problem before a visit takes place.

A receptionist should never refuse to pass a call to the doctor since a clinical judgement is needed to support every decision not to visit. The GPs' contract makes this clear and the changes made to them in 1995 did not modify this rule.

Services to patients: advice by telephone

Often someone will ask for a visit but it is suggested to them that the matter can be dealt with by advice. When this happens, many callers will be content for the doctor to telephone them to give advice and satisfied with this when it happens.

The Co-op's doctors told us that often patients had little awareness of the limited effect a GP's intervention can have on some conditions, such as self-limiting infections with flu-like symptoms. There were therefore many calls for advice and help for children with viral infections for whom the doctor can only give advice including the taking of medication obtainable without prescription. Any patient receiving telephone advice is told to phone again if the problem worsens or changes in a way not predicted by the doctor.

Whether or not a patient gets advice on the phone may be influenced by who is on duty when they call. We learned that not all the Co-op's doctors are willing to give advice to patients by phone and often prefer to visit them at home. A number of factors, not just relating to their level of experience or confidence, may cause this. With the patients of one hundred and fifty eight different GPs using the service it is most unlikely that an on-call doctor will know a patient who makes contact with the service and may need advice. In these circumstances, the doctor's judgement will depend on what they are told by the patient on the telephone. Some prefer to trust what they can discover from a face to face consultation rather than over the telephone.

Furthermore, at the time of our initial investigation, GPs believed that the Terms and Conditions of Service then in force created an expectation that patients requesting a visit would be entitled to one. As we have noted, the regulations required doctors to have regard to the "convenience" of the patient. In view of this, some practitioners' preference for face-to-face consultations, many in the patient's home, resulted from fears of possible complaints or litigation if unpredicted consequences occurred following limited telephone contact.

Services to patients: base surgery

Patients who need to see a doctor and who are willing to attend the base for the consultation will be able to do so on weekday evenings and during the day at the weekend or on bank holidays. The Co-op does not provide transport for patients (unlike at least one other co-operative) and attending the surgery will only be attractive to someone for whom it will be practicable and convenient. Although Co-op staff and doctors try to encourage base attendances, at the time of our initial observations they did not insist on patients visiting the base when this is appropriate.

Services to patients: home visiting

If the doctor does visit the patient then this will be no different from any other domiciliary visit save that a more detailed history may need to be taken since it is unlikely the person will be known to the doctor. Medication or other supplies may be provided or a prescription given. Patients are advised to contact their own doctor as soon as possible and are supplied with a copy of the Co-op form to pass to their GP.

Findings: documentation

The service uses a minimum of paperwork. In addition to basic details recorded on the database, if a visit is to take place then a simple form is completed by the receptionist giving brief details and the number of the call. This is passed to the doctor who will provide the consultation, or the details are radioed through if the doctor is already "on the road".

If only advice is sought then a different form will be completed and will be passed to the doctor on duty in the surgery who will telephone the caller and provide information and advice over the phone, recording brief details of the problem and the advice given on the form. A copy will be forwarded to the GP whose patient has been advised.

Findings: quality standards and monitoring

At the time of our initial investigation there were no explicit criteria used by the Co-op to rank calls for medical priority, or to distinguish between those calls requiring a home visit and those where a base surgery consultation would be appropriate.

A time target was in force for visiting which required doctors in 98 per cent of calls to attend on the patient within two hours. Additionally, the Co-op's service, like others in the district, had its quality and adequacy monitored on behalf of the FHSA by an independent GP liaison officer. The Co-op monitored levels of patient satisfaction by sending to every thirtieth patient visited a brief feedback questionnaire seeking views on their experience of the service. Later on during the research, the FHSA revised the quality audit system to require explicit ranking of priority of calls and target times for dealing with defined proportions of each of three priority categories.

From our observations, the Co-op was busy and getting busier by the month. Demand for visits obviously fluctuates over the year but, at the time, the Co-op was making in excess of one thousand home visits per month. It passed on roughly the same number of calls to the patients' own doctors. A proportion of the latter figure returned to the Co-op if it was asked to make the visit. At the same time it was providing over seventeen thousand advice calls per annum, but seeing only four thousand four hundred patients at the base surgery.[7]

The Co-op was well regarded by both the FHSA and by the Community Health Council. The latter, particularly, had noted the enormous improvement in the quality and availability of out-of-hours services since the creation of the Co-op.

Findings: the future

Co-op practitioners told us of a huge increase in demand for out of hours services. There was every indication that this would continue to rise. We were told that the year on year growth rate in contacts was 8–10 per cent.

To meet rising demand, the Co-op's Directors were keen to encourage more calls to be dealt with by advice only and greater use of the base surgery for medical consultations. The proposed changes to the GP's contractual Terms and Conditions created an opportunity for doing so since these were expected to clarify the GP's right to decide when a consultation was needed and, if so, where it should take place.

The directors justified these changes on the following grounds:

- many calls could be appropriately handled solely with telephone advice

- the Base premises offered a far more suitable environment for the personal examination of an ambulant patient

- a doctor could deal with at least ten cases per hour at the Base, whilst it could take one hour just to travel to a patient's home, deal with their problem and return to base

● achieving such changes might be expected to reduce the costs of the service to the participating GPs and to the FHSA, enabling the redeployment of savings to other initiatives, eg the employment of a Co-op nurse or higher FHSA subsidies to smaller co-ops, or the reduction of GPs' subscriptions

The need for criteria
When announcing its agreement with the BMA in May 1994, the Department of Health reiterated the significance of certain social rather than clinical factors in determining where the patient should be seen. Thus Dr Brian Mawhinney MP, then Minister of State reported "...a sensible clarification and modernisation of the GP's terms of service which... clarify the GP's responsibility for deciding whether an individual needs to be seen immediately at home and, if not, when and where treatment can most appropriately be given".[8] Annexed to this statement was a list of "illustrative examples... where a doctor, subject to the precise clinical circumstances, might reasonably judge a home visit to be necessary". These included social circumstances such as:

a single mother with two children, one sick, one asleep, where the patient is the sick child and the mother does not wish to leave the sleeping child in the care of a neighbour; ... a carer who is sick, but does not wish to leave their dependent relative [child or adult]; a frail person or person with learning disability living in the community; a person in genuine and justified fear of going out at night.

The BMA, on the other hand, summarised the changes rather differently,[9] excluding any reference whatsoever to social factors as a justification for continuing to visit a patient at home:

*GP's terms and conditions for service are to be amended to make clearer the scope GPs have to decide the most appropriate location for providing general medical services to their patients when treatment is required. **In effect, this scope means that GPs are only obliged to visit a patient at home during the night if travel by car or taxi could endanger that patient's health.** [Author's emphasis] This is intended to ensure that care is provided in a clinically appropriate and secure setting, that doctors' time is used more efficiently and that the rising demands for Out of Hours care is constrained.*

In our interim report, we drew attention to these contrasting perceptions and the possible consequences for the Co-op if its doctors were to use their new powers to require patients to attend the surgery wherever possible. The area had a strong tradition of home visiting and any general drive to reduce this would be noticed immediately. Patients could be confused; some might be annoyed at what they perceived to be a reduction in the service which they had until then been able to use. Vulnerable and isolated patients who truly needed domiciliary emergency care may become reluctant to seek it believing it was no longer on offer. As a relatively simple service became more complex so misinformation might abound and the Co-op's ability to discharge its legal duty to all who needed its service might be compromised by these difficulties.

We felt the prospect of this change in practice offered an opportunity for a pilot project on procedural rights and proposed this to the directors. The project would not concern itself with clinical criteria since it would be hard, if not impossible, to achieve a workable consensus across a large number of practitioners on appropriate approaches to clinical management. What we suggested was the formulation of a set of criteria which would define those circumstances when social, rather than clinical, factors would still entitle a patient contacting the Co-op to a visit in their home. The directors agreed to our working further on this proposal – the detailed planning of which we describe in the next section.

Second Stage: the pilot procedure

Aims and methods

Our aim was to draft and pilot a new procedure incorporating guidance on home visiting. In order to do so we needed to establish whether or not a variety of potential social factors were relevant or not to the doctor's decision to visit at home. Furthermore, we needed to examine the circumstances of a sample of patients whose right to a home visit might be put in jeopardy by the new rule. We also needed to secure, where possible, the agreement of the FHSA and of the Community Health Council to the pilot project. Our full set of tasks were as follows:

- survey of medical opinions on reasons for visiting

- survey of patient opinions and investigation of circumstances

- drafting of decision guidelines document

● discussions with the FHSA and Community Health Council

Survey of doctors' opinions on visits
We drafted a written questionnaire survey form in consultation with the Co-op's directors and after piloting it with two doctors when they visited patients at home. One aim of the survey was to identify a number of patients who could then be contacted and interviewed about their circumstances. These could be compared with the doctor's recorded views about them, providing "snapshot" case studies to assist in drafting and implementing the guidelines for decision-making.

The survey took place in January 1995. Every doctor was personally asked to participate, but not all did so since only 380 survey forms were completed, while some 500 home visits were undertaken during this period.

The Survey Results
After each completed home visit, doctors had to state whether or not they considered the visit had taken place at home largely for clinical or for social reasons: 60 per cent of visits were judged to have been clinically justified; 40 per cent were for social reasons. In the latter cases, respondents were asked to specify the reason from a range of options given on the survey form. The data which emerged is shown in Table 4.1 below.

Doctors were asked two more essential questions concerning the home visits they had undertaken. The first asked them if the patient could have been seen at the base surgery. We set out the results in Table 4.2 overleaf.

Table 4.1: Social Reasons for Home Visits

Reason	No	% of total*
Age of patient	53	34.6
Patient alone	15	9.8
Physical mobility	18	11.7
Access to transport	66	43.1
Distance from Base	40	26.1
Responsibility for others	22	14.4
Mental or emotional state	15	9.8
Communication Difficulties	8	5.0
Time of Visit	20	13.0
Weather conditions	19	12.4
Other reason	40	26.1

* Note: Total exceeds 100 since some doctors gave more than one social reason for visit.

Table 4.2: Location for consultation

	Could see at Base	Could not see at Base
Total	218 (57%)	163 (43%)
Where reason for visit clinical	86 (38%)	142 (62%)
Where reason for visit social	132 (86%)	21 (14%)

The second question sought to gauge their general view of the need to see the patient. To the question "Was it reasonably necessary for the patient to be seen at all out-of-hours?" the doctors' replies are analysed in Table 4.3 below.

Table 4.3: Need for patient to be seen

	Definitely	Probably	Probably not	Definitely not
Total	128 (34%)	134 (35%)	79 (21%)	40 (10%)
Clinical reason for visit	117 (51%)	73 (32%)	27 (12%)	11 (5%)
Social reason for visit	11 (7%)	61 (40%)	52 (34%)	29 (19%)

Despite the survey's limitations, these results established a number of clear findings relevant to our intended pilot procedure:

- only one in ten visits made by doctors were regarded as definitely unnecessary consultations

- nearly half of all home visits, in the opinion of the doctors, were made mainly for social reasons

- no access to transport, the patient's age and distance to the base were the three most common reasons given for such visits

- visiting doctors believed that 57 per cent of the patients they visited at home could have been seen at the base surgery

● but the same doctors felt that about 14 per cent of patients seen at home largely for social reasons should continue to be seen there in similar circumstances

Conclusions from the survey
The results strongly suggested that, were doctors to be encouraged to require patients to attend at the base surgery, many callers would find themselves asked to do so. However, the data supported the view that there was a group of patients for whom social reasons might justify a visit at home. It also appeared to confirm the relevance of the social factors which we had included on the survey form.

The purpose of this survey was to enable us to estimate the impact of the planned changes, assist in the accurate drafting of guidelines, help us to contact patients and for use in discussions with the FHSA. The authority was highly interested in our findings and the pilot project we were planning. It proposed a county wide initiative to take forward the lessons learned from IPPR's research.

Discussions with the FHSA: the Para 13 Guidelines Working Party
Early in 1995, the authority's Director of Primary Care Development had been approached by one co-op in the area. It sought assurances from the FHSA that it would not be acting improperly or illegally if, in the future, the co-op required patients to attend its base surgery instead of being seen at home.

By this time Paragraph 13 of the GPs' Terms and Conditions had been revised.[10] Deputising doctors were no longer obliged to have regard to the convenience of the patient when deciding where to see the patient. Patients calling the co-op and needing a consultation could be required to attend the base surgery for this purpose, once it had been approved by the FHSA. However, the wording of the new paragraph was ambiguous. In deciding whether or not the patient should be seen for a consultation out-of-hours the doctor had to have regard to the person's "medical condition" but in deciding where the consultation should take place the person's "condition" had to be considered. The legal effect of this choice of different terms was uncertain.

The co-op wanted the authority's support if it started to use its new powers rigorously. The authority could not give such an indemnity but offered to work with the co-op to develop guidelines. By the early summer, other co-ops were expressing interest in working with the authority on a set of guidelines to assist in using the new version of Paragraph 13.

First Working Party meeting: a rebuff

A meeting was convened by the FHSA in August 1995 to discuss the proposal. Present were representatives of two co-ops (including the co-op described in this study), the Local Medical Committee (BMA), Chief Officers of two Community Health Councils, a Health Authority Non-Executive member and a GP who is not a member of an out-of-hours co-operative.

We outlined the purpose of our research, the findings from our survey and our plans for piloting decision making criteria in the Co-op. Participants had been circulated in advance with a note summarising the main survey results and a preliminary set of draft guidelines.

To our surprise, there was no support at all for the development of an agreed guideline document. It was unanimously rejected by the doctors present, but for a variety of different reasons. The local BMA representatives were against the use of guidelines and criticised the Co-op for embarking on the research without first discussing it with the Local Medical Committee. It was argued that guidelines became rules and then were used against doctors.

Another GP felt that the envisaged document would make the doctor's contact with the patient confrontational. A third that "there were no absolutes in general practice". Overall there was a sense that the guidelines would not help to manage rising demand for services. It was said that this was for the government to solve (BMA) or that the solution lay with better public awareness (others) – it was the patients who needed guidelines! The meeting concluded with a request that the FHSA come up with proposals aimed at altering the attitude of patients before they called the doctor. Some public education proposals were needed. A further meeting was arranged to discuss these.

We left this meeting with some vivid impressions. There was a sense that general practice is far too varied for central guidance – from on high – to be accepted and therefore effective. Local co-ops and doctors would have to develop their own guidance – and needed incentives for doing so. Amongst GPs there was a strong belief that the pursuit of "fairness" or what is "reasonable" might invite wholly different responses. However, we were certain that there were still problems to resolve concerning the boundary between clinical and social factors and their respective relevance to the decision to visit at home. Furthermore, all present appeared to agree that rising demand created severe problems for practices and for the co-ops. The majority view seemed to be, however, that these difficulties were for others to solve, not the doctors.

The Co-op's principal director was disappointed at the outcome of the meeting though still wanted IPPR to work on a document for use with their doctors. He had read the draft guidelines and agreed that, subject to some changes, these could be piloted. We were permitted to ask doctors if they were willing to use them in their practice. For those who volunteered we could do some work evaluating them. However, he envisaged the following difficulty. The guidelines were not law and therefore the doctors would feel that they could not rely upon them in practice. Furthermore, it would be necessary for the Co-op's Council to approve the next stage of the work.

Second Working Party meeting: a proposal

The FHSA reconvened its working party in October 1995 and, after further discussion, this reached an unexpected conclusion. Participants, some of whom were not at the previous meeting, felt that there might be a place for some sort of pro forma which could aid doctors in deciding how to implement Paragraph 13. All, including the BMA representative, were agreed that any strict application of the new power to require attendance at a surgery could be contentious especially if the patient was refused a home visit. It was said that it would be helpful to introduce some means of recording the doctor's decision.

We proposed and it was agreed that a pro forma would be piloted with the Co-op and afterwards the working party would reconvene to assess the results and its usefulness elsewhere in the county.

The pro forma and explanatory notes

We returned to our first draft guidelines for the use of the amended Paragraph 13 and substantially rewrote them. The Working Party had suggested the need was for a pro forma rather than guidelines.[11] This would be the focus of the project but doctors using the form would also need explanatory notes. We recast the draft guidelines as these notes, providing practical advice to a doctor when completing the pro forma, not prescriptive guidelines defining desired outcomes.

As will be seen from the draft,[12] the pro forma was built up from the three stages of decision-making envisaged by the new Paragraph 13. We were assisted in this process by interviews with a number of patients who had received visits during the survey earlier in the year. We wrote short "snapshot" case studies of their circumstances for use in discussing our draft with the Co-op's doctors. From the small sample whom we interviewed it was clear that a number of patients who had been seen at home were in fact able and willing to attend the base surgery if required to do so.

The pro forma covered a single A4 sheet. Intended for rapid completion it was designed to take the doctor through a process which would structure the exercise of their discretion and ensure that all relevant factors were brought into consideration. The stages were as follows:

- Firstly, it prompted the doctor to consider if she or he had all the information required to decide if the patient needed a consultation out of hours.

- If all necessary information was to hand, the doctor would then have to decide if the patient needed such a consultation or whether another option, such as seeing their own doctor the next day or going to hospital immediately, should be advised.

- In the latter circumstances, the doctor was asked to confirm that he or she had told the patient the reason why no consultation would be offered.

- If the doctor had decided that the patient needed a consultation out-of-hours, the third part of the form asked if this should be at the base surgery.

- If the doctor determined it should, then he or she was to confirm this on the form and also confirm that relevant clinical and social factors had been considered. The doctor was asked to confirm that the patient was given the reason for being asked to attend the surgery, and that they stated they understood this explanation.

- Lastly, there was space for the doctor to record the patient's reaction to the request and any reason which the patient gave if refusing to come to the surgery.

The explanatory notes described the legal responsibilities of the Co-op doctor and the status of the pro forma and notes.[13] In line with our earlier work with the Co-op and the results of the survey, we outlined and illustrated in these notes the many factors which might be relevant to the doctor's decision on the location of the consultation.

These were not meant to be prescriptive. As the notes said: "The list is intended to trigger a consideration of the issues. Furthermore, confirmation that it has been used may reassure patients that the decision was fairly and properly made". Copies of the draft documents were sent to the FHSA and to the Community Health Council in readiness for consultations with them.

The pilot project: sudden death

The draft documents were discussed at a meeting of the Co-op's Council in January 1996. One member present was the doctor representative to the FHSA working party and who had been at the recent meeting which resolved to pilot a pro forma. Surprisingly, the Council decided not to support any further work on the project. Thus, the pro forma and explanatory notes were not approved for piloting by any of the Co-op's doctors even on an entirely voluntary basis.

What was the reason for this sudden withdrawal of approval? In the view of its members, we were informed, the changes to Paragraph 13 had given an explicit discretion to the doctor. Only clinical grounds were relevant to the exercise of that discretion since the paragraph contained no reference at all to any social factors. Accordingly, the pro forma and explanatory notes were of no use to the Co-op. At this point, and finally, our work on this project therefore ended.

Postscript

On 22 March 1996, the *General Practitioner* magazine carried the bold banner headline "Out-of-hours visit rules need rewriting".[14] The Vice-chairman of the National Association of GP Co-operatives, and a director of the Co-op, stated that the new Paragraph 13 had done nothing to control patient demand. The Co-op had recently been visited by the BMA's General Medical Services Committee Deputy Chairman whose view was that the new paragraph "...did not rule out a GP's obligation to take into account social factors, such as a patient lacking their own transport, when deciding whether to make a home visit." The Co-op's doctors were, apparently, "stunned" to hear this.

The interpretation, it was said, was necessary because the new rule used the term "condition" in two different ways. GPs had to decide whether and when a consultation was needed solely on the basis of a patient's "medical condition". However, where that consultation is to take place should be decided by the doctor on the basis of the patient's "condition". It was reported that the significant omission of the word "medical" was demanded by health ministers, the implication being that a GP must take into account social factors when deciding whether to require the patient's attendance at a base surgery.

The edition of the same magazine for 5 April developed the story further under the headline, "GPs demand clarity on refusal to visit".[15] It was reported that the Chairman of the General Medical Services Committee had asserted the view that the new Paragraph 13 was clear and that only the patient's medical condition should determine whether, when and where a consultation should take place. This was contradicted by representatives of the Medical Protection Society and Medical Defence Union who both accepted that social factors could be relevant in some circumstances and that to ignore them might leave GPs vulnerable to complaints. GP representatives, including the Co-op's Director, were quoted as calling for clarification from the Department of Health. One said, "If the DoH was to say… patients could demand a home visit because they did not wish to attend a centre for personal, social or other reasons, the whole development of co-ops would be threatened".

Feedback on the project: Community Health Council
After the project ended, we interviewed the Community Health Council's Chief officer about our proposal and the pilot documents. He had also served on the FHSA working party and was aware of how it had been received there, firstly rejected and then revived. He was sure that patients' growing demand for out-of-hours contact with GPs required new measures, such as could be seen with the development of the Co-operative movement. Before the Co-op was set up, deputising services were poor with patients experiencing long delays. The Co-op had resulted in improved quality of service, guaranteeing patients they would be seen not only by a practising GP but one who was also local to the area. In his view, response time was very good and quality control was also good. The Co-op also provided telephone advice which was an improvement on the previous system. However, the Council knew of a patient's recent experience which suggested that excessive demand was affecting the Co-op's ability to meet all of its patients needs:

If people are frivolously asking for home visits when they are not required this is clearly not in the interests of the community. At Christmas a patient had a medical emergency and she spent the whole day trying to get through to the [Co-op] service and their lines were continuously engaged. That was over a time of high demand and in the end she had to drive herself to the local Accident department in order to get a service… and at great risk to herself and she has suffered a disability as a result of her condition.

For this reason he was not opposed to a more sophisticated system which ranked patients' needs against accepted criteria in order to ensure that the service could respond most effectively to those in greatest need. As far as the CHC was concerned, this could include the provision of advice on the phone or consultations at the base, in circumstances where this would be justified. He felt that what was important was to communicate to the public that their medical problem was being dealt with in an appropriate and satisfactory way, not dismissed as a non-problem.

Some social factors, in his view, were unavoidably relevant to the medical decision as to where the consultation should take place. He believed, for example, that doctors currently have regard to the age of the patient – where the person is elderly – and would continue to do so. The factors which had been identified by the research and which appeared in the draft documentation were those which would help to contribute to a fair system. There would certainly be a need for guidelines if poor practitioners sought to use their new powers under Paragraph 13 in a rigorous way:

> *I am concerned about those doctors who would take a very literal or legalistic view of their responsibilities and not use common sense. It is those we have to be concerned about. The little pockets of poor practice where the standard of general practice is variable… We have to watch for those people who might be stuck with a GP who takes a very literal line on Paragraph 13 as I think some still will. There is no point in saying, "Well a complaint can arise and this may be upheld or not". I am concerned about avoiding such situations because a lot of people won't complain. The number of people who complain to us about failing to visit is quite small in relation to our total population and I just worry there is bad practice going on that we just don't hear about – we just see a tip of the iceberg… In some areas where you have got a higher standard of general practice, I think that things will carry on much as they always have done. But where doctors retreat behind regulations and rules, I think it is a recipe for discontent.*

In his view, guidelines could offer an opportunity for improving patients' understanding of the doctors' role and of their own responsibilities, by suggesting what would be reasonable and what would be unreasonable. It would help to reinforce the idea that there was a range of different, but appropriate, responses to a person's need for medical care. Guidance would therefore be as important for patients as it would be for doctors:

> *What we are faced with at the moment, of course, is a refusal by the doctor to give any guidance whatsoever about what Paragraph 13 means. So not only are they apparently in the dark. They are leaving patients very much in the dark. The problems will just perpetuate until that is done… [Patients] will demand their rights but come up against a system they cannot cope with and they do not understand. Hostility comes into it and complaints will arise from it. Complaints that are needless, really.*

He acknowledged that doctors may worry that a pro forma and guidance notes could "be framed and used to beat them over the head" in disciplinary hearings. He thought compliance would be poor: dentists had been required in law to complete a pro forma providing a patient with details of their dental health and they had proved highly reluctant to do so. The Co-op's doctors simply did not accept that Paragraph 13 could include any consideration of social factors. Like their colleagues, they were a group of very independent professionals, despite their organising within a co-operative. He was disappointed that the idea would not be piloted and with it would be lost the opportunity to investigate further the "rationale" for medical decision-making on this question. He implied it was unreasonable to expect patients to change their behaviour if the trust needed between patient and doctor was being ignored and was breaking down – trust dependent on the doctor behaving consistently and fairly.

> *All [patients] are used to is a home visit or go to the surgery the following day. There has not been much given to the public about Paragraph 13... It needs something a bit more sophisticated than saying it's clinical or nothing, really.*

Feedback: Family Health Services Authority
The views of the Director of Primary Care Development, a former General Practitioner, echoed a number of these observations. He believed that the GP co-operative movement was particularly effective in providing a high quality out-of-hours service for the patient with a high quality relief service for the doctors with that responsibility. They are also cheaper and their costs are lower.

They provided an alternative way of managing the provision of medical care out-of-hours. The FHSA provided nearly £2m per annum towards the costs of co-operatives in its area. With this came a responsibility to monitor the quality and adequacy of the arrangements they made for responding to patients' calls. Various methods could be used and recently the liaison officer system had been replaced by one requiring each co-op to prioritise calls according to their clinical priority in three categories – urgent, important and other. The FHSA had set targets in consultation with the co-ops for dealing with each of these allowing each co-op to decide how to categorise common conditions.

He agreed that demand for out-of-hours contacts was increasing and that it was now necessary to develop new means of coping with this. He identified two distinct approaches amongst GPs. One sought to create mechanisms in order to handle the increase in a way which was good for the patients and best for them. This meant ranking priority, involving other professional help such as from nurses etc. Another group believed that the problem of demand should be dealt with by making the contact between doctor and patient "as difficult as possible". He preferred to encourage an approach which enabled greater patient education, acknowledging that there is a greater demand probably for legitimate reasons and which has to be handled in a way that is beneficial and appropriate. Methods could include the Co-op's plans for requiring patients to attend the base surgery for a consultation:

It is entirely reasonable for a large number of people to request a visit – could actually need a face to face consultation out-of-hours... [these] could quite reasonably see the doctor rather than the other way around.

He believed that social factors – he termed them "soft factors" – were relevant to practice out-of-hours. In his view, many GPs would recognise and act on these and he had done so when in practice. He understood the wording of the new Paragraph 13 still to require the consideration of such circumstances – where they were relevant to arriving at a reasonable judgement – and said that the FHSA would wish to see GPs acknowledging the importance of social factors to assessing the patient's "condition", where these were inescapable. The advice which the Co-op's doctors had received from the Local Medical Committee was, in his view, "misguided".

He anticipated that a rigorous use by GPs of their new power under Paragraph 13 could lead to confrontation with patients and greater clarity of the position would be very beneficial:

I think it is likely there would be some degree of conflict between doctors and patients where doctors try and insist that the patient comes to them and the patient feels for whatever reason that that is not appropriate. When a conflict occurs in those circumstances it is prejudicial to the doctor/patient relationship for the purposes of that consultation. If the doctor does visit then the doctor does so in a bad mood. That can create problems when you actually arrive, thinking about the complaints process. I can think of examples where an argument has ensued at the patient's house. The end result being that the consultation has not occurred. The doctor has attended but because there has been a verbal fight, the doctor and patient did not get together. It is in nobody's interests.

He was disappointed with the outcome of the Working Party's discussions and the Co-op's discontinuing further work on the pro forma. He did not believe it was a "tall order", observing that "...it was likely to provide support and protection for the doctor and, if anything, more protection and benefit for the doctor than for the patient". A pro forma might help in the education process of both doctor and patient and help both to understand better what issues had to be considered. He added:

> *Some doctors are reluctant to give telephone advice and some are reluctant to ask patients to come to them. This can change. They fear that what they are doing is going to get them into trouble. They are not sure of the ground on which they are standing. They are not sure whether they have the authority to do it. They do not like to debate with patients because they do not think they have the authority to tell the patient to come to them. If they have guidelines which are accepted by the membership of the Co-op – all the GPs who belong to the Co-op say that in these circumstances the patient should be asked to come to the Co-op   that provides that doctor with that much more authority to say to the patient, "Well, all the doctors who work in the... area consider that in these circumstances it is reasonable for you to come".*

However, he recognised some of the reasons why the Co-op may have abandoned the proposal. There was a suspicion in the area about the use of guidelines and a fear that these would become regulatory and a basis for complaints against doctors. There had been very few examples of FHSA guidelines and none similar to that proposed by IPPR. The co-ops were still relatively new at trying to get their doctors to behave in a particular way and he sensed they were therefore reluctant to confront their membership and say, "Thou shalt do this". It would be inappropriate for the FHSA to issue such advice. That was the responsibility of the profession and had to be agreed within the Co-op and by its members.

He predicted that this resistance to collective working would reduce over time and that GPs in the future would become more willing to establish standards for practice in guidelines and protocols and would appreciate the benefits of doing so. He believed that amending the law would not provide the answer, doubting that it would be possible to produce legal or contractual guidelines which could be sufficiently flexible to cover all the circumstances necessary.

Reactions from the Co-op's Principal Director
In interview afterwards, the Co-op's principal director elaborated on the reasons why our approach may not have been acceptable to his colleagues on the Council. In his and their view, the changes to Paragraph 13 had created clear and unambiguous law. It was the doctor who had to decide

where the consultation should take place. In doing so he or she should be concerned with clinical factors alone and doctors were entitled to refuse a home visit where this was not clinically necessary. He explained the Council's decision in this way:

The barrier you hit was the conservatism of GPs when asked to change. That is what you met. But it was actually based on a fair and reasonable argument. Before we change, why do we need to evolve a paper based system which appears to be diluting that law back to where it was before. We struggled for so long to try and get the law to be clear enough so that we can say to patients, "No, you do not need to be seen medically. There is no reason why you should be seen at home". Now you are trying to make that clear legal distinction fuzzy, going back to the bad old days. There is nothing in it for them. It was not taking us forward. It was taking us back to where we were... It had no role to play. I could not see that at the end of the day and certainly our representative on the Working Party could not see that it had any role to play. Because the legal definition of our rights and obligations under Paragraph 13 is now quite clearly defined. All this pro forma did was blur that boundary.

The director had evidently changed his mind about the aims and intended methods of the research project. He was now highly sceptical about its practicability and relevance. He doubted it was possible to draft any useful guidelines which would not fail in their objectives. In any event, he now regarded a paper based method as inappropriate for dealing realistically with the problems faced by the Co-op. If transport to the base surgery was a problem for some patients then this should be provided to them. One co-op in the Newcastle area provided a transport service which produced a high rate of base attendances.[16] If responsibility for others made attendance difficult, then a professional carer might have to be provided whilst the person was visiting the doctor at the base surgery. He summarised the approach which he now preferred thus:

I do not think you could ever produce a pro forma which would identify a group of people with non-clinical conditions who for social reasons need a home visit. I do not think it is possible. There will be patients who abuse that system. Some patients will suffer because they will not complain enough. A lot more would amplify their problems in order to get a visit. We will not say no social grounds whatsoever but we will try to provide a sociological answer to those problems either to put a carer in short term, a neighbour or friend, or a paid carer moved around, or you have a transport system.

These were the preferred methods the director felt that the Co-op should employ when seeking to influence the behaviour of patients and their expectations of the service, in combination with the new Paragraph 13 power. He believed that this was the best way to preserve and enhance the patient's right to medical care.

> *What is the patient's right? The patient's right is to have access to good quality medical care. If that is their right then we are providing that. I do not see it is the patient's right to have a home visit... to have care brought to him because of vague social factors when clinically that patient could be seen at the base. The right to access medical care is still there. No-one is interfering with that. The place of that care is being decided by the doctor. The right to have that care is not being removed.*

Conclusions and lessons

Resistance to paperwork
Many causes, not any single one, meant IPPR was in the end unable to pilot the pro forma and notes which it had drafted. Professional attitudes, the way the Co-op is organised and the legal framework for General Medical Services: all contributed to the rejection of our idea. At a purely pragmatic level, general practice is not a professional service which tends to reach for a paper based solution unless there is a compelling case for it. What we saw of the Co-op in action demonstrated this and the difficulty which it might have in persuading doctors to use the proposed pro forma. Only a proportion of doctors had been prepared to participate in the opinion survey. This was an indication of the likely reaction to any procedure demanding a thorough and accurate completion of standard documentation.

Clinical freedom and fairness
At a more fundamental level, the project was compromised by the resilience of ideas about clinical freedom and the limited capacity – and willingness – of the Co-op to direct individual doctors in the manner in which they should practice. This approach is reinforced by the legal framework within which services are arranged, with individual doctors under their individual contracts being held personally responsible for their decision making, not the practice or co-op to whom they are engaged to provide the service.

In stark contrast to the Social Services Authorities we worked with, there was no source of central authority which could determine and direct what was to be "the line" on the subject of Paragraph 13. Neither the Co-op directors nor its Council felt itself able or willing to do this. Nor did the FHSA consider it proper for it to offer such a view. Indeed, we identified a general reluctance amongst doctors within the profession to determine for their peers what it might be fair or reasonable for them to do in particular circumstances. The advantage therefore in providing a transport service or carers for dependants left at home would be that it would remove the need for practitioners to have to make such decisions. A consistency of approach could be achieved regardless of individual medical views of fairness and merit. Co-op's director may, indeed, have hit on the most desirable solution, given the variations which would occur if doctors had to decide whether or not patients were deserving of a home visit.

No incentive to change

As the principal director informed us, doctors did not perceive any incentives for them to pilot the new procedure. Clearly, for measures like this to be developed voluntarily there will usually need to be some expected benefit. We could not persuade them that fairness alone was a reason to introduce the procedure, nor that it would help to remove their fear that, in insisting on attendance at the base, they would be opening themselves to criticism. If individual doctors had made a mistake in their decision making under Paragraph 13, perhaps they may have been more inclined to adopt a publicly discussed and supported procedure which would offer them, as well as patients, protection when there was an argument about what was or was not a reasonable decision.[17] Our intervention came too early for that.

Could there be any financial incentive in using a pro forma system to aid decision-making? GPs are paid when they, or the Co-op on their behalf, attend on a patient at home. At present the form which they use upon which to claim for the night consultation (GMS4) asks for no details at all concerning the reason for the visit. If doctors had to justify, even briefly, on their claim form the reason why the Co-op visited the patient at home they might have an incentive for introducing a procedure which would help to identify that reason.[18]

Reluctance to say no

As with some care managers in London Borough, we encountered some reluctance to work with these types of procedures within a professional relationship which is largely discretionary and personal. It should not be regretted that there are doctors who would resist using the procedure where it would lead them into confrontations with their patients. These same doctors may recognise the limits of their personal authority as individual practitioners to restrict the home visiting service. However, if the service does have to change in the public interest and if measures are to be used to alter patients' perceptions of the service and how to use it, it is hard to see such practitioners taking on these tasks.

Failures of public policy and law

Many of our problems resulted from ambiguities in public policy and in legal amendments designed to implement it. The changes made to the wording of Paragraph 13 in February 1995 clearly do not adequately explain either the rights and responsibilities of the doctor or those of the patient. As a policy designed to encourage the greater use of out-of-hours centres, it was not at all clear. It will be recalled that the Department of Health's view on the meaning of Paragraph 13 had to be found in the notes attached to a Departmental Press Release.

No wonder our draft appeared less than appealing to the Co-op's GPs. The argument for such a procedure will only prove compelling when these uncertainties are removed; and when the case is clearly demonstrated for a consistent and fair approach to assessing the importance of social factors to the patient's right to see their doctor out-of-hours.

Fair treatment or consumer rights

For doctors to be persuaded of the merits of this approach, it may be important to stress, not the rights of patients, but the obligations of doctors to act fairly. As with the other pilot projects, we can see the origin for these duties arising not in consumerism but in something more fundamental, citizenship. This means that the obligation can exist and be effective without the public being aware of it or claiming it as their right. Only in this way can the principle be relevant where the public is refused a service or refused the one which they want. This emphasises the crucial role which the Community Health Council can perform in giving to any procedure such as this one collective approval and legitimacy.

Lessons for patients and the public

There are lessons from the study not only for individual patients but also for their representative body, the Community Health Council. Councils need to monitor the use by practices and co-ops of their new powers under Paragraph 13 to assess the extent to which access to services may be unfairly denied to certain groups of patients and why. Although the Co-op conducted satisfaction surveying with patients, it had established no formal means of consulting with a range of patients using the service. There must be scope for Councils and for Health Authorities to encourage co-ops to improve their methods of participation and consultation. Given the controversy still surrounding the future of home visiting and the pressure for changes in the service it is essential for the patients' voice to be influential if future plans are to be responsive as well as fair.

Endnotes

1 In 1994, some GPs called for patients to be fined for making "trivial" calls. "GPs support fines for trivial call-outs", *The Guardian*, 17 February 1994.

2 Hallam L (1994) "Primary medical care outside normal working hours: review of published work", *British Medical Journal*, Vol. 308, 249–253.

3 Cragg D K *et al* (1994) "Out of hours primary care centres: characteristics of those attending and declining to attend", *British Medical Journal*, Vol. 309, 1627–1629.

4 Paragraph 12, *The National Health Service (General Medical Services) Regulations 1992*.

5 See p.151.

6 The first co-op started in Bolton in 1977. In mid July 1994 it was reported that there were 30 co-ops in the UK providing cover for 2,500 doctors. They ranged in size from just 15 GPs (Cambridgeshire Doctors Deputising Service) to 180 GPs (Leeds Doctors Cooperative).

7 *Doctors' Availability to Patients*, Unpublished FHSA paper, June 1995.

8 Department of Health Press Release 94\252, 19 May 1994.

9 BMA Background Brief for the Media, 19 May 1994.

10 The National Health Service (General Medical Services) Amendment Regulations 1995, S.I. 1195 No. 80.

11 For attitudes to use of clinical guidelines in primary health care, see Siriwardena A N, (1995) "Clinical guidelines in primary care: a survey of general practitioners' attitudes and behaviour", *British Journal of General Practice*, 643–647. For NHS Executive Good Practice Guidance see, NHS Executive (1996), *Clinical Guidelines*, Department of Health.

12 See pp.222, 223.

13 See pp. 224–230.

14 *General Practitioner*, 22 March 1996 p.3.

15 *General Practitioner*, 5 April 1996 p.1.

16 Newcastle and North Tyneside CHCs (1996) Newcastle Emergency Doctor Service (NEDS) Patients' views of a GP Out-of-Hours Scheme in the Inner and Outer West Locality of Newcastle upon Tyne, Unpublished Report.

17 "Patient backlash at GP night care units", *Doctor*, 10 October 1996.

18 When a duty solicitor providing a call-out service to suspects detained in police custody claims a legal aid payment for advice given over the telephone without seeing their client they must give written reasons on their claim form to explain why their was no attendance at the police station (Legal Aid Board Duty Solicitor Arrangements, 1994).

6 Conclusions and recommendations

What the Chapter contains

First, we summarise what the research tells us about the purpose and importance of fair treatment rights from the perspective both of the public and also of those running services. The next section deals with practicalities: what were the opportunities for developing rights and the barriers we encountered when introducing them? Then we compare the various provider organisations, noting the contrasts shown in the research. Lastly, we set out some recommendations for public policy and for practice.

Rationale

The challenge facing public services

Expectations that reliable, good quality services will be available to meet needs for health or social care are high and continuing to rise. We see this in the reactions there have been to restrictions on community care services, to waiting lists in the health service or in demands for new medical treatments to be provided by the NHS as soon as they are technically available. As consumerist generations age, replacing their more deferential elders, these attitudes will increase not diminish. They will exert growing pressures on those having to assess spending priorities and to determine the fair distribution of services. Fair treatment rights may become especially significant in such circumstances.

Social inequality presents a further challenge to public services, which should be instruments for reducing disadvantage not reinforcing it. Yet unequal consumption of services, due not to greater need but to the impact of social, educational or income advantage, continues. For rights to public services to be enjoyed by all citizens, policies must be sensitive to the reasons for unfairness and consciously seek to overcome them. Some of the approaches we tested in this research – such as the provision of advocacy – may be suited to this task.

The third challenge concerns public attitudes to the political system. Services depend upon this system yet, increasingly, it fails to win widespread public trust. Individual politicians are regarded as unreliable or have lost the confidence of a more sceptical society. Decision-making institutions themselves no longer command the respect once accorded to them. They can be perceived as distant, secret and impersonal; out of touch with the public and often unresponsive to its needs. Legitimacy for the political choices needed for the fair allocation of public resources now has to be earned the hard way. This has implications for the ways in which social rights are defined and delivered.

Citizenship not consumerism

The origins of fair treatment rights derive, not from some narrow concept of consumerism, but from citizenship and the pursuit, by publicly accountable organisations, of just dealing between citizens. This means there may be more reason to promote such rights within services than the need just to respond to consumers. The research has identified a variety of useful purposes which procedural rights can serve beyond the guarantee to service users of fair treatment and openness.

Information on eligibility

To possess effective rights depends on possessing power, which is often derived from information. During this research, we have discovered how new practices can provide information on eligibility to services. This may serve two purposes. First, it will advertise what the service offers. Unknown rights are no use at all. Next, it will enable someone who has sought a service to check a provider's response against its declared policy and priorities and make them accountable for any failure to do so.

The Personal Care eligibility criteria and leaflet in London Borough and the Wait-listing leaflet in the Hospital - each of these demonstrates how fairly straightforward measures can dramatically increase the information available to the public.

Participation in decision-making

A number of our projects showed the potential for increasing participation in decision-making with the help of procedural rights. The Care Plan project in London Borough drew service users into a process of recording needs and specifying services in a far more explicit way than had been practised to date. The 15+ procedure in City Council contained elements to encourage participation and may have had this effect, at least to a limited extent. The Prompt List we piloted in the Hospital was similar, introducing a practice designed to raise patient participation in acquiring information about treatment for cataracts.

Encouraging fair decisions

Fair decisions are those which are only based on relevant factors and which are unbiased. Procedural rights could help to encourage such decisions. In a number of the projects, we attempted such a task by defining what were proper considerations for the decision-maker to have regard to. In this way, immaterial factors could be excluded.

This role was seen at work in each of the four projects: with the Personal Care criteria in London Borough; the "issues list" and matrix accompanying City Council's 15+ procedure; the wait-listing categories written with the Hospital and the decision pro-forma drafted but not used with the Co-op.

Increasing accountability

Ensuring those controlling health or social services are accountable for their decisions to those affected by them is crucial if these are to operate fairly and be seen to be doing so. Whether or not this is effective will depend upon two factors. First, the person or persons affected by a decision will need to know the reason for it. Second, the means must be available to hold that person, or the organisation they represent, to account. In the course of this research we developed a number of ideas addressing the first of these requirements.

In London Borough, both the Criteria and Care Plan projects were designed to increase accountability by encouraging reasons for decisions to be given. This was also the aim of the projects in City Council and the Pathways and Wait-listing work in the Hospital.

Building public trust: improving legitimacy

For those with political or managerial responsibility for services, we have seen the potential for procedural rights initiatives to help build up public trust and confidence in the way those services are run. Some public organisations can appear distant, secret and impersonal, out of touch with those needing their help and incapable of responding to their needs. Procedural rights help to show where responsibility for decisions should rest: with an individual professional, with their organisation or with both of them.

A number of pilot projects illustrated how this might be tackled in practice. All three projects in London Borough promised more open and personal contact between the organisation – in addition to the care manager – and someone assessed for care. The Care Plan project was welcomed by staff there for the way it highlighted the borough's responsibility for the scope and level of service. If the pro forma had been used in the Co-op this could have added legitimacy to controversial changes in out-of-hours visiting. The Wait-listing leaflet told anyone listed for surgery in the Hospital why they might have to wait longer than other patients. In this way, those having to wait "...could see they were being handled in a fair way", as the Community Health Council representative observed.

Focusing public service delivery
Public resources should be devoted to meeting real needs not those which have been inaccurately assessed or wrongly assumed to exist. With some of the projects we saw managers wishing to use the initiative better to target their organisation's resources on those they perceived to be needing them. This role was particularly prominent in London Borough's projects on personal care and disability and with the draft procedure developed with the Co-op. Indeed, in the latter case the idea for the project was suggested to us because the directors wished to restrict home visits only to those who really needed them.

Promoting equity
Public service providers will wish to ensure that their services are delivered according to a principle of equity so those with the same needs receive a response from the organisation which is largely the same. Assessing for personal care in London Borough, or financial assistance for a care leaver in City Council, deciding on wait-listing priority in the Hospital or the response of the Co-op to a housebound caller: all these situations raise the potential for inequity. The research tells us that procedural rights, where practicable, may help to prevent this.

Practicalities

Opportunities
Our work needed the agreement and full collaboration of each of the provider organisations. Of the nine pilots which were developed, seven were introduced in practice. For the remaining two, one could not proceed due to its bad timing - financial assistance in City Council. Only the Co-op project failed to win support on principle.

Such a level of co-operation from the providers suggests there are many opportunities for developing feasible projects in similar settings. Measures can be straightforward, relatively simple and cheap to introduce. They can fit the priorities of providers as well as meeting the expectations of the public.

We found that procedures do not have to be excessively bureaucratic or unwieldy, though they may attract criticism for being "paper based". The research shows us that a paper based approach will be essential at least in part and that this may have a limited effect unless administrative burdens are recognised and properly managed. The poor use of paperwork may be counterproductive since it can confuse and alienate the public not give them any greater power. It may also alienate staff in the service. The research demonstrates the need for high standards of administration if procedural rights are to be effective for all.

Barriers

What barriers did we encounter during this research which may face others planning or introducing new rights? Our findings show that for all the recent focus on standard setting and performance measurement, the characteristics of many specific public services are still largely undefined, particularly where professional services are provided. Reliable information on those standards of service which the public can expect to receive still remains elusive, if it exists at all.

Though each of the organisations we worked with defined and worked to a number of explicit and accepted standards, these disciplines were still fairly new ones affecting only some aspects of service delivery. The organisations were prepared to work with us as though to develop good or best practice. What if the obligations which we wrote into procedures were mandatory? The research suggests that the notion of standards, even procedural ones, having to be met in each and every case could prove difficult for providers to accept and work with. Rights are not just targets but represent absolute or guaranteed standards and, on the evidence of the research, public service culture may need to develop further before it can accommodate these demanding expectations.

A further barrier was the persistence of professional cultures tending to reinforce independent, autonomous decision-making and to discourage collective working and accountability. The research suggests that introducing fair treatment rights for the public in the types of organisation we worked with will demand a collective approach if it is to be viable. Procedural rights are concerned with accurate information, with equity and with freedom from bias. All of these highlight the importance of agreement amongst those providing a service on its key features and how they will respond to the public. Developing fair treatment rights will be hard if not impossible in any organisation which does not yet work in this way.

The research produced mixed results on the public's interest in having these rights. Consumer organisations, particularly those used to representing individual service users, supported the projects once they saw their potential. Some users were keen on these new opportunities. Others were indifferent. We have already asserted that fair treatment should not depend upon consumer demand – it is a right not a privilege. Nevertheless, gauging the public's reactions to their treatment is essential when it comes to developing new rights. If an organisation has no experience of doing so or is unwilling to listen to what it may hear from the public, this will present a major barrier to the successful development of new rights.

Contrasts

Rationale
To determine basic eligibility for service, inform people of this and be accountable for the choices made seemed far higher priorities for the social care bodies, London Borough and City Council, than for those who deliver health care. A number of factors may explain this. Social care is highly rationed and financial resources influence definitions of need employed by social services. It is therefore a relative concept, not an absolute one. Frontline staff, as much as members of the public, need to know who qualifies for services and who does not. Managers, therefore, have an incentive for working with criteria and procedures.

Health care professionals usually apply definitions of need and of eligibility not affected by the availability of resources. Lack of resources might, for example, delay the provision of medical treatment but would not in general affect how a doctor judged whether or not someone needed it. Furthermore, in the Hospital, the GP's referral mechanism may already have fairly accurately identified who should be in the service and who should not. With the Co-op it would be beneficial to be clear about a patient's eligibility for a home visit or for a base attendance. However, due to the clinical autonomy of GPs and their long tradition of independent decision-making the organisation was not used to working with the sort of rigorous and standardised criteria that this would require. The Co-op doctors preferred – being permitted by law and professional guidance – to cope without them.

In other respects, the research suggests that procedural rights are no less important in health care services, than in social services. Health service providers could have as much interest in measures which provide information on entitlements and choice, encourage participation, and increase the accountability of those who make decisions. The organisational aims, also, could be as relevant to a health care provider as to a social care body. Both will need to ensure that services reach only those who really need them, are equitably distributed and in ways which win public trust in the service.

Practicalities

Contrasts between social service and health care providers when assessing practical considerations were quite striking. In theory at least, each social services department is a single body, capable of setting standards for the whole organisation. Social workers are more familiar with procedural working and with working to policies. These characteristics were more pronounced in London Borough than in City Council, where there was a tradition of practitioner autonomy and absent policy and procedure. Compared with the health service organisations they offered opportunities for more complex and demanding projects. It may be said this was because the need for them in these organisations was greater.

The continuing influence of ideas about clinical freedom, less use of paper based practices and a more diffuse management culture posed practical difficulties when working with the health service bodies. Although we made significant progress in introducing new rights-based practices in the Hospital, our objectives were only partly fulfilled. With the Co-op, our pilot was not tested at all.

A further explanation for these differences may be found in the context within which each organisation had to operate. The social services providers seemed exposed to greater external monitoring than the health care providers. Such oversight can lead an organisation to prioritise new policy and overcome the barriers to change. Furthermore, in Community Care and Children's Services, recent law and guidance has required a new priority to be given to the development of policy, procedures and individual practice. Pressure from Government could be applied through the Social Services Inspectorate and there were signs of this occurring. For the health service providers, such monitoring was not evident. Where the Department of Health had produced new policy on service users' rights, in the Patient's Charter, this was not framed in law nor was it accompanied by detailed practical guidance. As a result, the new expectations and standards introduced – particularly those giving rights to information – were still regarded as permissive if they were acknowledged at all.

Recommendations

Public policy: a higher priority for fair treatment

Fair treatment needs a higher priority in public policy on health and social care. When new initiatives are introduced or existing ones reviewed, consideration should be given to the principles of fair treatment and their potential impact.

Changes can be expected relatively shortly in three of the four policy areas within which we worked. Introducing new fair treatment rights may be necessary when these occur. The Labour Party's manifesto promised a new Patients' Charter, a "Long-term Care Charter" and proposals to reduce waiting lists.[1] Other commitments made prior to the election may include reforms to the planning of after-care support for care leavers, including a requirement that a local authority provides each of its care leavers with a formal written care plan.[2] How will any such new rights be introduced and enforced? Will care leavers find they must wait years before legislative intentions bring tangible benefits?

There will be further policy challenges for the new Government to face in the future. Are health authorities to continue to be free to ration or deny treatments to their residents, and, if so, will new policy be used to prescribe how this should be done so that fairness and equity are preserved?[3] How will emergency general medical services be developed to meet patients' ever growing expectations? Any changes restricting access to traditional services will be controversial with the public. They could have unfair effects if social factors affecting access are not acknowledged and continue to remain unrecognised in the law.

As well as giving fair treatment a higher profile, the overall aims of policy should be to improve the competence of providers in introducing and maintaining high standards of fair treatment and to find fresh possibilities for guaranteeing it. A strategy for furthering these aims should have the following elements:

- new approaches to guaranteeing procedural rights

- using public views to audit practice and develop policy

- an effective and creative use of policy and procedure

- independent advice and assistance, available when it is needed

- adapting the culture of professionalism to a model of partnership

- monitoring enforcement and impact

Guaranteeing fair treatment

If fair treatment is to be a right not simply a privilege it will be necessary to find ways of giving it higher status in the policy and administration of health and social services bodies. Sometimes the only acceptable way to achieve this will be by introducing new rights by law. We have seen this recently with the new rights for carers to a community care assessment. The problems we found in the Co-op can only be resolved by using the law to clarify the doctor's and the patient's rights and responsibilities.

However, not all rights will have to be created in law. It should be possible to develop further a hybrid approach, peculiar to public administration, which means that service providers can make firm commitments and have to deliver on them but without failure resulting in costly and wasteful litigation.

Building on the concepts of maladministration and failure of service, both applying in the health service, the former only to local authorities, IPPR has proposed the creation of a new means of guaranteeing standards.[4] If such a new power to guarantee were to be created then procedural rights could be designated as guaranteed. Any failure to comply with the standard specified could give grounds for complaint and, in certain circumstances, redress. The advantages of this approach are that, subject to any guidance from Government, service providers would have the freedom to define the standards which they promised to meet. Furthermore, enforcement would not, in the routine case, be in the courts but would be through a new local ombudsman system, linked where necessary to the existing national ombudsmen.

Combined with this proposal or as a separate initiative there is scope for giving fair treatment a higher profile by issuing a statutory code or codes.[5] These could incorporate many of the principles we have explored during this research, applying them to the particular policy area in question and providing explicit guidance to providers and practitioners on how they should treat the public. New Zealand has recently introduced a national Code of Patient's Rights which may offer a useful model.[6] In the United Kingdom, we see a precedent in the detailed Code of Practice issued under the Mental Health Act 1983 or the statutory Code dealing with special education. Such codes do not have the force of law but have high status as guidance setting practice standards which stress the duties of professional staff as much as the rights of patients. Their potential has only just begun to be realised in health and social services. In these types of services, they could prove far more effective in encouraging professional development and ensuring compliance than the current Citizen's Charter.

A new role for the public's views

The public's views about their treatment must be sought out and acted upon. Service providers in health and social services need to become more skilled at listening to service users and incorporating their perceptions in policy and practice development and in audit and evaluation. So long as provider bodies ignore the need to resource such consultation methods and develop their competency at undertaking it, their ethos will continue to be one modelled on their staff's view of what is fair, not that of the public they exist to serve.

Effective and creative policy

The research has shown the need for effective and creative policy and administrative procedures, especially where the law or national guidance is silent on the detail of new initiatives. If local policy is to be the means by which new rights are introduced it must be clear and comprehensive, accurately reflecting the new commitments being made to the public. It needs to fit the administrative resources available to the organisation, otherwise it will raise expectations that cannot be met. An information strategy will be required to ensure that the public benefit from the rights given to them and are informed of any responsibilities which are expected of them. Indeed, for all but the simplest of changes, there is a role for a service Action Plan to tell staff what they have to do. This should also require the regular review of practice to check that procedures are working as intended and their impact.

Independent advice and assistance

Throughout the research, support for the pilot projects has been strongest from voluntary organisations which provide advice, assistance and representation for service users and patients. If, from their perspective, the case for rights appears compelling then this suggests a further element is needed in our strategy - to ensure that those given new rights have access to independent advice and advocacy to assist in enforcing them. Without such help, the research suggests the fair treatment rights we propose may have little impact in organisations unwilling to acknowledge their new obligations.

For local authority service providers, this means that voluntary sector advocacy projects should be developed where they do not exist and preserved where they do. Those incapable of representing themselves will need to have advocates appointed for this purpose. The 1986 Disabled Persons Act provides a means of doing this and should be brought fully into force. For the health service, any changes to the structure, role or powers of Community Health Councils must recognise the continuing need for local NHS advocacy resources. Future policy should encourage the funding of advocacy services located within hospitals and services themselves to encourage better access and the provision of timely advice and support.

From professionalism to partnership

Most of the rights which we have tested in this research are to be used within a relationship between someone needing a service and a professional – a care manager, social worker, consultant, nurse or general practitioner. Professionals who are used to exercising personal discretion and autonomy can still find it hard to respond to a rights-based approach and the new demands of accountability and consistency which it places upon them. Changes will be needed which transform such attitudes and adapt them to a new model of partnership between provider and service user. This does not mean that the professional's skills and judgement are to be ignored or underestimated, only that new ways of using them are acknowledged and employed. In three respects this will create new demands for change and development. Many procedural rights concern giving and receiving information: professionals will have to become skilled and responsive communicators. Fairness in decision-making will require a new acceptance of consistency in approach and a willingness to work collectively to achieve this aim. Lastly, new rights to information may cause frontline staff to disclose their reasons for refusing or limiting services. If this happens, then their personal responsibility *vis-à-vis* the organisation must be clearly acknowledged. The public must be able to discover if the decision results from the policy of the organisation, which they may not be able to complain about, or the exercise of an individual's professional judgement which may be mistaken and open to challenge.

Monitoring enforcement and impact

Respect for new rights and their enforcement will need vigilant monitoring. This will check that the aims of policy are met; that power truly passes to those given new entitlements, such as to information, to choice or to participation. A range of methods can be employed for this purpose. Enforcement in individual cases could be assisted by the development of service specific ombudsmen systems – with a high local profile, independent status and influence with the organisation providing the service.

Many possessing rights are reluctant to complain, even if these are ignored. Compliance may then have to be monitored by independent inspection or investigation. Inspectorial bodies, such as the Social Services Inspectorate and the Audit Commission, could monitor and report upon compliance with fair treatment obligations when conducting their joint inspections of social services authorities developing with service users, where necessary, standard measures of fair treatment to assist them in this task. The role and responsibility of the local ombudsman and of the Health Service Commissioner might also be extended to include a new power to investigate and report on systemic unfairness or maladministration and propose measures to reduce or eliminate it. At least each of these bodies should propose standards for policy and practice, with positive advice about implementation and further development.

Endnotes

1 Labour Party (1997) *New Labour: because Britain deserves better*, Labour Party, London.

2 "Labour scheme to appoint guardian angels for all young people in care to end abuse in homes", *The Guardian*, 17 March 1997.

3 Lenaghan J (1996) *Rationing and Rights in Health Care*, IPPR.

4 Bynoe I (1996) *Beyond the Citizen's Charter*, IPPR, pp.121–127.

5 See Bynoe I (1996) *op cit* p.111 and following for description of the role of a Fair Treatment Code.

6 New Zealand Code of Patient's Rights. This came into force in July 1996 and sets out the rights of health consumers. Complaints alleging a breach of the Code can be made to the Health and Disability Commissioner and, if unresolved, can be taken to a tribunal.

Appendices
Documents used in the pilot projects

Appendix D   222

Appendix A
Documents used in London Borough

The Personal Care Project

ELIGIBILITY CRITERIA FOR PERSONAL CARE

1. WHO IS "IN NEED" OF PERSONAL CARE?

A person shall be regarded as "in need" of assistance known as PERSONAL CARE if, following an assessment, a Care Manager or other officer undertaking an assessment is satisfied that:

(a)　the person has some physical or mental ill health or disability (whether or not long lasting); and

(b)　this affects her or his ability to undertake or complete, without significant difficulty, those tasks needed for their usual personal care, and/or for their daily living and/or for the management of their home; and

(c)　taking account of their own wishes and preferences, their cultural background and previous lifestyle and circumstances, unless appropriate assistance is given to them s/he will be hindered or prevented (or will be in the foreseeable future) from recovering, sustaining or preserving their personal independence and freedom to determine how they wish to live.

2. WHAT IS MEANT BY "PERSONAL CARE"?

(a)　personal care tasks include: washing, dressing, using the toilet, shaving and haircare.

(b)　daily living tasks include: getting up and preparing for bed, preparing food and hot drinks, apart from the main meal, ensuring a warm and safe home environment.

...cont'd

(c)   home management tasks include: domestic cleaning to maintain safe and hygienic standards, washing small items of clothing

3. WHO WILL BE ELIGIBLE FOR A "PERSONAL CARE" SERVICE FROM [LONDON BOROUGH]?

A person who is assessed to be "in need" shall be eligible to receive a personal care service suited to their individual circumstances and provided or arranged by [LONDON BOROUGH] if, following assessment, the Care Manager or other officer undertaking the assessment is satisfied that:

(a)   this accords with the person's expressed wishes and preferences; and

(b)   the person's main carer, or any other relative or friend will not or cannot (without unreasonable inconvenience, difficulty, or stress) provide the assistance needed; and

(c)   no assistance which is more appropriate is available from any other statutory authority or from any voluntary organisation or body; and

(d)   there would be an unacceptable risk of physical or emotional stress, discomfort, inconvenience or harm to the person assessed, to anyone living with them or to any other person if assistance was not provided; and

(e)   without the provision of assistance, the person's circumstances will deteriorate; and

(f)   to provide or arrange a personal care service would be otherwise appropriate to meeting some or all of the needs of the person.

4. OTHER CONDITIONS

The person must have been advised by the Care Manager of their need to contribute to the cost of the service and of the likely cost of so doing, if, following an assessment of their resources, they are judged to have the means to do so.

PERSONAL CARE INFORMATION SHEET

Introduction

This information sheet is being supplied to you because you (or someone on your behalf) have asked us for help in the home and we are looking into your request. It will tell you who has a right to personal care and assistance in the home. It will also answer some of the questions we are commonly asked about how we decide if someone needs help from the Council. Personal care is only one of a number of possible services which could be arranged for you. If you want details about other services then please ask.

Who makes the decisions and how do they do this?

We can only provide a Personal Care Service to you after a member of our staff has looked into your situation, discussed your needs with you, and sometimes others who may be affected, and decided if you are entitled to a service. This person will be called a "CARE MANAGER" or "SOCIAL WORKER" and the procedure is termed an "ASSESSMENT".

When this person meets you, she or he will explain what they need to know and why. You can, if you wish, have someone with you when you are being interviewed by the Care Manager. In some situations, this will be the person who decides if you are to get any service and, if so, what it should be. In other circumstances, where the cost of the service is higher, then the Care Manager must ask a more senior colleague to approve it.

Who has a right to a PERSONAL CARE SERVICE?

The Care Manager or Social Worker will use a clear and agreed set of rules which set out the circumstances in which [LONDON BOROUGH] has accepted a person has a right to its service. The Care Manager may refer to these rules when talking to you. You will find a copy of these rules attached to this sheet. Broadly speaking, the rules say that a service will be offered to someone who:-

● is ill or who is disabled; and

● needs help in order to care for themselves and their home;

...cont'd

- where there is noone else able and willing to provide this help; and

- if help is not provided, then that person, or someone living with them, will be at risk of unacceptable stress or harm.

When – and how – will I find out if I will get a service?

When the Care Manager has gathered all the information which s/he needs in order to make a decision, including your views and the views of anyone who may already be helping you, s/he will decide if you are entitled to a service from the Council and, if so, what this should amount to. Some assessments have to be done very quickly indeed, for example, if you are about to leave hospital. Others may take longer. Make sure that you ask the Care Manager how long it is likely to take, if you are not told this. If you later think of something important which you feel you should have told the Care Manager, just phone them with this information.

Will I have to pay for the service?

If a service is arranged for you then we will assess your financial circumstances to work out if you must pay a weekly contribution towards its cost. You will not have to pay for any of the time which the Care Manager spends assessing your need for a service nor in advising and supporting you and providing you with any necessary information.

What can I do if I disagree with the Care Manager?

The Care Manager's decision is not final. If you disagree with the decision or you are dissatisfied with it in any way then you can complain, though it would be sensible to tell the Care Manager your opinion first, since an explanation may resolve the problem. If you need to take your complaint further then ask for the Council's leaflet "GETTING IT RIGHT" which explains how to do this.

The Disabled Persons Project: *LETTER TO CUSTOMER*

Social Services and Housing Department
[London Borough Council]

Dear ....

YOUR RIGHT TO AN ASSESSMENT FOR COUNCIL SERVICES

You recently applied to the Council for a Concessionary Travel Pass/ Disabled Person's Orange Badge and I understand that you have now received this service.

You will recall that, when you completed the application form, you told us that you had a disability. The Council has accepted this, and that the disability is one which could lead to your registration on the disability register kept by the Authority.Anyone who has a disability also has a right to ask the Council for a range of other services and for the Council to assess which of these he or she may need and be entitled to receive. The type of services I mean could include the following:

* Practical help in the home * Help in getting a radio, TV or library facilities * Lectures, games, outings, and other recreational facilities * Transport * Home adaptations for greater comfort, safety or convenience * Holidays * Meals at home or elsewhere * A telephone or help in getting one and any special equipment needed to use it *

My reason for writing is to inform you of this and to tell you how you might apply for such an assessment. I have enclosed with this letter an application form which you can use if you decide to request this. If you do, I will arrange to meet with you to discuss how we might be able to help. The Council has agreed basic rules to determine who is entitled to services and I can explain these to you if you apply for an assessment.

The assessment will not cost you anything, but if we decide that you need and are entitled to a service, it will be necessary to make a financial assessment of your means since you may have to contribute towards its cost.

If you have any query concerning this letter or wish to discuss its contents with me then please get in touch, by writing or telephoning me at the extension given above. If you wish to receive independent advice about this letter then you may wish to contact your local Citizens' Advice Bureau (see Phone Book for details) or the national disability organisation, RADAR (Phone: 0171 250 3222) for advice.

If I do not hear from you within 28 days I shall assume that you do not wish to request this assessment at the present time.

Yours sincerely

Care Manager/Social Services Officer

APPLICATION FORM FOR AN ASSESSMENT

FULL NAME OF PERSON COMPLETING FORM

. . . .

FULL NAME OF APPLICANT, IF DIFFERENT FROM THE ABOVE

. . . .

FULL ADDRESS AND TELEPHONE NUMBER OF APPLICANT

. . . .

. . . .

. . . .

POSTCODE . . . .

TEL: . . . .

I acknowledge receiving your letter concerning an assessment for Council services for disabled persons.

I confirm that I have a disability. I understand that I have the right to request such an assessment and I would like you to assess my needs for the services mentioned in your letter.

I look forward to hearing from you so that this can be arranged.

(Delete if not applicable) I have a difficulty with communicating because . . . .

SIGNED . . . .
APPLICANT

SIGNED . . . .
ON BEHALF OF APPLICANT (if unable to sign)

DATE . . . .

The Care Plan Project: *LETTER TO CUSTOMER REFUSED SERVICE*

Social Services and Housing Department
[London Borough]

Dear............

YOUR ASSESSMENT FOR COMMUNITY CARE SERVICES

[opening para. personal]

I am writing to tell you what I have decided having now looked into your request for help from the Council. As I explained to you, this Authority is responsible for social services, not for the medical or nursing which comes from the NHS. I am sorry to have to tell you that we shall not be able to help you at the moment. This letter tells you more about the results of the assessment and our reasons for this decision. We expect that you will want to have a record of these.

If you find this letter difficult to understand or you want more information or I need to explain to you further how I made my decision, then please get in touch with me straight away.

[OPTIONAL PARAGRAPHS – ONE SET MUST BE COMPLETED AND INSERTED]

[Option I]

You asked us for help because [CM/SSO to summarise reason here]. However, I am sorry that this does not usually qualify you for a service from the Council. When deciding if I should arrange some assistance, I have to work to guidelines which Council members and senior managers have set to ensure that our limited resources are fairly spent and we meet our legal obligations.

Unfortunately this means that not everyone who wants help or believes that they need it can be helped by us. I do not expect this situation to change in the near future and so as long as your circumstances remain the same and do not get worse, I will not be able to do more than give you advice.

[Option II]

You asked us for help because [CM to summarise reason here]. Having listened to

...cont'd

---

you and looked into your situation I am sure that you require some help with [CM to summarise needs here]. However, I believe that you have an alternative source of help and, for the time being, I have decided that it is more appropriate for you to get the help which you need from [CM to summarise alternative here] instead of from the Council.

When deciding if I should arrange some assistance, I have to work to guidelines which Council members and senior managers have set to ensure that our limited resources are fairly spent and we meet our legal obligations. Unfortunately, not everyone who wants or needs a service can receive one. The Council has decided that people who have no alternative source of help must be given priority.

[Option III]

You asked us for help because [CM to summarise reason here]. I accept that you have a number of needs which would be helped if a service was provided to you. These are [CM to summarise position here]. However, when deciding if I should arrange some assistance, I have to work to guidelines which Council members and senior managers have set to ensure that our limited resources are fairly spent and we meet our legal obligations.

Unfortunately, this means that not everyone who wants or needs a service can receive one. For the foreseeable future, the Council has decided that people in your situation do not have sufficient priority to get a service and none is therefore available.

I have based this assessment partly on what I have been told and partly on written information, for example, from your doctor. In normal circumstances, if you want to see any written information which we hold about you then the Council must allow you to see it, but there is a formal procedure for doing this. Please tell me if you want to see any of the written information and my record of your assessment.

You may disagree with this decision. If so, then you have a legal right to complain under a formal procedure agreed by the Council. You will find that the enclosed leaflet can be used to start off this procedure.

There are a number of organisations in the Borough able to advise and assist people who are seeking help from the Council, who may be unhappy with its decision. Your local Citizens' Advice Bureau (see Phone Book for details) will be able to give you information on them.

Yours sincerely
Care Manager/Social Services Officer

LETTER TO CUSTOMER OFFERED SERVICE

Social Services and Housing Department
[London Borough]

Dear............

YOUR ASSESSMENT FOR COMMUNITY CARE SERVICES

I have now looked into your needs for community care services and investigated the ways in which [LONDON BOROUGH] may be able to help you with your present difficulties. I am writing with details of the results of this assessment since it is important that you have a record of these. Most of these details are found in the "Care Plan" document which is enclosed with this letter. *If you find this letter or the Care Plan difficult to understand and you want more information or I need to explain to you why I made these decisions, then please get in touch with me straight away.*

Taking all your circumstances into account and bearing in mind what you, and others, have told me about your situation I have now assessed what your needs are for community care services. I have summarised my assessment in section 12 of the Care Plan.

I have based this assessment partly on what I have been told and partly on written information, for example, from your doctor. In normal circumstances, if you want to see any written information which we hold about you then the Council must allow you to see it, though there is a formal procedure for doing this. Please tell me if you want to see any of the written information on which this assessment and Plan are based.

Council members and managers in the Social Services and Housing Department have decided that the claims of some people needing its services must be given priority, subject to the Council's legal obligations and to its available resources. I have had to assess your entitlement to services in the light of these priorities. Bearing them in mind and taking full regard of your needs, I have decided that you are eligible to receive from [LONDON BOROUGH] the services described in the Plan.

Where this is applicable, I have now ordered the necessary services. Because so many people need our services, you may have to wait some

...cont'd

time before a particular type of assistance or facility can be arranged for you.

The Care Plan gives details of the person who you should contact if there are any problems with the service. For some services, the Council is expected to require a financial contribution towards their cost from those who are considered able to afford this. After an assessment of your financial circumstances, I have worked out that you are liable to pay the charges shown on the Care Plan.

It may be that you disagree either with my assessment of your needs or with the plan of services which I have devised to meet them. If this is the case then you have a legal right to complain about either decision under a formal procedure agreed by the Council. You can use the enclosed leaflet for this purpose if you decide to do so.

Customers have a right to tell the Council what they think about the service which they are getting at any time. **This rule applies even though the service may in practice come from an independent agency. You can make a comment or suggestion or a complaint about a service.** If you want to complain then, again, the leaflet can be used, or you can contact the person mentioned on the Care Plan.

There are a number of organisations in the Borough able to advise and assist people who are needing to seek some service from the Council or are dissatisfied with any service which they are receiving. Your local Citizen's Advice Bureau (see Phone Book for number) will be able to give you their details.

Yours sincerely

Care Manager/Social Services Officer

CONFIDENTIAL

[LONDON BOROUGH] SOCIAL SERVICES AND HOUSING
DEPARTMENT CARE PLAN

This is the record of a Plan for care and assistance which has been arranged
for the Customer following an assessment under the NHS and Community
Care Act 1990. It is an important document which we hope Customers will
find useful and may want to refer to when contacting the Council about the
services they receive.

1. COMPUTER NO: ....

2. DATE PLAN COMPLETED: 199

3. NAME OF CUSTOMER: ....

4. ADDRESS: ....

   ....

   ....

5. TELEPHONE: ....

6. NAME OF NEXT OF KIN: ....

7. ADDRESS: ....

   ....

   ....

8. CARER (if not next of kin); ....

9. ADDRESS: ....

   ....

   ....

10. TELEPHONE: ....

THIS CAREPLAN CONTINUES OVERLEAF

11. SUMMARY OF CUSTOMER'S CONCERNS AND WISHES:

. . . .

. . . .

. . . .

12. SUMMARY OF NEEDS FOR COMMUNITY CARE:

. . . .

. . . .

. . . .

13. DOES CUSTOMER AGREE WITH THIS ASSESSMENT?

YES / NO

14. IF NO, WHAT ARE THE AREAS OF DISAGREEMENT?

. . . .

. . . .

. . . .

15. DOES CARER (IF ANY) AGREE WITH THIS ASSESSMENT?

YES / NO

16. IF NO, WHAT IS THE AREA OF DISAGREEMENT?

. . . .

. . . .

. . . .

17. SUMMARY OF AIMS AND OBJECTIVES FOR
    PLANNED CARE:

    . . . .

    . . . .

    . . . .

18. DETAILS OF NEEDS WHICH CANNOT CURRENTLY
    BE MET BY SERVICES:

    . . . .

    . . . .

    . . . .

19. CONTACT POINTS(S) FOR SERVICES

(i) FOR PROBLEMS WITH SERVICE QUALITY/RELIABILITY:

     SEE DETAILS ON ACCOMPANYING SHEET

(ii) FOR URGENT/TEMPORARY CHANGES TO SERVICES:
     NAME: . . . . .POSITION . . . .
     TEL: . . . .

20. THIS CARE PLAN WILL BE FORMALLY
    REVIEWED ON 199

    HOWEVER, IF THE CUSTOMER'S CIRCUMSTANCES
    CHANGE BEFORE THIS DATE THEN AN EARLIER
    REVIEW WILL OCCUR.

    TO ASK ABOUT THIS, PLEASE CONTACT:

    NAME: . . . . .POSITION: . . . .
    TEL: . . . .

(TO BE COMPLETED BY PERSON UNDERTAKING ASSESSMENT)

I CONFIRM:

- THAT THIS CARE PLAN RECORDS THE RESULTS OF MY ASSESSMENT OF THE CUSTOMER'S NEED FOR COMMUNITY CARE

- THAT I HAVE EXPLAINED ITS CONTENTS AND IMPORTANCE TO THE CUSTOMER

- THAT I HAVE SUPPLIED A COPY OF THE CARE PLAN TO THE CUSTOMER

SIGNED: . . . . .POSITION: . . . .

DATE: 199

(TO BE COMPLETED BY CUSTOMER AND CARER (IF ANY))

I CONFIRM:

- THAT A COPY OF THIS CARE PLAN HAS BEEN GIVEN TO ME

- THAT ITS CONTENTS AND IMPORTANCE HAVE BEEN EXPLAINED TO ME

SIGNED: . . . . .CUSTOMER: . . . .
DATE: 199

SIGNED: . . . . .CARER (if any): . . . .
DATE: 199

[LONDON BOROUGH]

NAME OF CUSTOMER: . . . .

. . . .   DATE COMPLETED

COMMUNITY CARE DIVISION   TIMETABLE OF CURRENT COMMUNITY CARE SERVICES

DUE TO BE REVIEWED   . . . .

	MONDAY	TUESDAY	WEDNESDAY	THURSDAY	FRIDAY	SATURDAY	SUNDAY
MORNING							
MIDDAY							
AFTERNOON							
EVENING							

CONTINUING SERVICES (eg laundry); NIGHT TIME SERVICES OR
NON-[LONDON BOROUGH] SERVICES

NOTES

THIS CARE PLAN HAS, WITH THE CUSTOMER'S CONSENT, BEEN COPIED TO THE FOLLOWING:

CARER/FAMILY   YES/NO

GP   YES/NO

OTHERS (LIST, IF ANY)

CONTACT AND EMERGENCY NUMBERS

[LONDON BOROUGH]
COUNCIL'S OUT OF HOURS NO:

DETAILS OF CHARGES PAYABLE TO [LONDON BOROUGH] COUNCIL FOR COMMUNITY CARE SERVICES PROVIDED TO CUSTOMER:

SERVICE	COST £	CHARGE TO CUSTOMER (£)
......	......	......
......	......	......
......	......	......
......	......	......
	TOTAL £	......

Appendix B
Documents used in City Council

The Care Leavers' Project: *Extract from Guidelines to Staff on 15+ Reviews*

After-care issues to be considered by 15+ Review

I. The time when it is likely that the young person will cease to be "looked after" or "accommodated" by the City Council

II. On this happening, the young person's expected needs (bearing in mind their expressed wishes and preferences) in relation to each of the following matters:

- accommodation
- education
- employment and/or training
- income
- any other financial assistance
- practical advice and assistance
- emotional development/relationships
- culture, language, religion & race
- health
- disability
- other

III. For each matter identified under II, the steps required to be undertaken to plan and/or prepare the young person and other Review participants, where appropriate, for the time when the young person leaves care and thereafter.

IV. The timescale for such planning and preparation.

V. The person(s) who will undertake and/or will coordinate such planning and preparation work.

VI. The resource implications, if any, for the Department in meeting the anticipated after-care needs of the young person.

Information Leaflet for Young Person

Your future starts here. READ ON...

You have been given this pack because your social worker is arranging a REVIEW of the plans for your future in the Council's care - and afterwards if you are about to leave care.

So that you can fully take part in this meeting and be able to get your views across, you will need to know some essential things about how a review works. This leaflet explains about it. Young people have found that unless you get yourself prepared for the meeting, you might find it confusing, difficult and sometimes overpowering.

A group of young people who know what it is like to be in care joined in with writing this pack. It is to help YOU to get READY, **SO PLEASE READ ON.**

You will probably want to tell the review about your thoughts and plans. The leaflet comes with another sheet on which you should write down what you want those coming to the review meeting to know in advance about your current situation and plans. **THIS IS YOUR *CONTRIBUTION SHEET*.** You don't have to answer all the questions if you do not want to.

What happens in the review and what it will decide is important, so you may want to get ADVICE about it and how you should handle it. The Childrens' Rights Service, an organisation completely independent of the Council and Social Services, can give you advice about your review. Someone from the Service can even attend the review if you want. A letter to you from the Service is also enclosed explaining who they are and where you can find them if you want to.

What is a review?

A review is a meeting which Social Services must hold to discuss how its plans for looking after you are working out. They have to consider whether the plans need to be changed at all and the meeting is the way of finding this out. A written procedure tells Social Services staff how the review should be run.

...cont'd

What happens before the review?

Before the date for the review, your social worker must discuss it with you in advance and get written contributions from you, from your parent or parents and any carer(s). The social worker must also write a report on the current situation, plans for the future and any suggestions for changes in those plans. If you can do this, it is better for you if you make a contribution. You can use the sheet with this pack on which to do so and you can always ask for help in filling this in if you find it hard work. Also, you can always add to what it says at the meeting if you need to.

Who will be – and won't be – there?

Usually, the Social Services will ask your parent or parents to attend the review. Other people like your foster carers, teacher, doctor or residential home worker may also be asked to come to the meeting. If you want someone to be there then ask your social worker if he or she can be invited. If you feel that the presence of any of these people will upset or frighten you then you should tell your social worker, or write this on the *Contribution Sheet*. The person in charge of the review (the Chairperson) may then decide that this person cannot come to the meeting or only to a part of it when you are not there. If you want someone from the Childrens' Rights Service to go with you, then this person should be allowed to attend the meeting.

What happens at the review?

The Chairperson (who is a senior social worker) will introduce everyone; will ensure that all the written contributions and reports have been read and understood and then lead a discussion. There is no fixed time for the meeting. It could last anything from one hour to three hours.

What will be discussed?

The discussion will centre on the Social Services' plans for your future, your reactions to these, and the views of others present on the plans. If anything needs to be planned for when you are expected to leave care then this has to be carefully discussed. The discussion might cover any of the following topics: accommodation, education, employment or training, income, financial help, practical advice, relationships, cultural, racial or religious issues, health services, disability issues.

...cont'd

What if there are disagreements?

If you disagree with the plans or arrangements decided at the review, then you have a right to make formal "representations" or a complaint to the Social Services Department. Make sure that you tell those present at the meeting what your views are and obtain independent advice on your rights if you need to.

What happens next?

You, and all others who came to the meeting, will receive a note which records the conclusions which were reached. If the review decided that planning or preparation for the time when you leave care should be started or continued then a summary of the decisions about this will also be distributed which will show who is responsible for putting the plans into action.

Where can I get further advice?

The Childrens' Rights Service is at [address]. Its phone number is [tel. no.] You can get independent advice about your review from this service. **CALL IT IF YOU WANT A CONFIDENTIAL CHAT...**

Now have a look at the next document in the pack, your CONTRIBUTION SHEET...

Contribution Sheet for Young Person

YOUR CONTRIBUTION SHEET

You should use this sheet to tell your social worker and others who attend the review your thoughts and feelings about your present situation and what are your plans. You should get the sheet to your social worker in good time before the meeting. Then it can be distributed to others beforehand. An extra copy of the sheet is enclosed so you can keep your own copy of what you write.

If you need help with understanding any of the questions or filling it in then, please ask your social worker, foster carer or residential care worker. If there is not enough space for your contribution then continue on a separate piece of paper and attach it to the sheet.

Remember that you do not have to answer all the questions if you would prefer not to.

1. Where are you currently living and how long have you been there?

2. If you are still at school then give details of the school and say how long you have been going to it. When will you be leaving the school?

3. If you are in college, then give details of the college and of your course and say how long you have been doing it. How long it will last?

4. If you are doing youth employment training, then give details and say how long you have been doing it, and how long it will last.

...cont'd

5. If you are in work, then give details and say how long you have had this job. Is it permanent or temporary? If temporary, when will it end?

6. If none of the above apply, how do you spend your time?

7. For the activity(ies) you have mentioned, what do you like most about what you do?

8. And what don't you like about what you do?

9. What do you think is Social Services' plan for your future in the next six months? If you expect to leave care soon then what plans have been made for this?

10. Do you agree with their plan for you? If not, then what would YOU like the plan to be?

...cont'd

11. At what age would you like to leave care?

12. Are you currently being helped to develop the skills you will need when living independently? If so, in what ways?

13. What help ("aftercare") would you like to have from the Social Services when you have left its care? Are you aware of what are the responsibilities of the Social Services after you have left its care?

14. Over the next six months, what are you most looking forward to?

15. Over the next six months, what are you least looking forward to?

16. If you are already in touch with your family, then describe this contact. Do you want this to continue?

17. If you are not in contact with a family member then do you want to make contact? If so who and how – letter, phone or visit?

...cont'd

18. Is there anything else which you want to tell the review in addition to
what you have already written?

I confirm that this is the contribution which I wish to make to my review.

I agree that other participants in the review can be sent or given a copy of
this contribution. Apart from these people, I ask that its contents be treated
as confidential.

I would like . . . .
to attend the review and I would like them to be requested to do so.

I would prefer it if . . . .
was not present at the review.

Signed . . . . .Date. . . . .

Summary Action Plan for use with 15+ procedure

What are the needs and how will they be met?	What is the timescale?	Who should do this?	Resource implications for council	Notes
ACCOMMODATION				
EDUCATION				
EMPLOYMENT/ TRAINING				
INCOME				
OTHER FINANCIAL ASSISTANCE				
PRACTICAL ADVICE/ ASSISTANCE				
EMOTIONAL DEVELOPMENT				
CULTURE, LANGUAGE, RELIGION AND RACE				
HEALTH				
DISABILITY				
OTHER				

Extract from Preliminary Draft Policy/Procedure on Financial Assistance

---

3.00 *Eligibility: who is entitled to assistance from the Authority?*

As stated above, it is for the Authority to determine who is in need of assistance and what type or level of assistance should be given having regard to the resources which are available to it and the needs of all those who may require assistance. [City Council] has decided that the following criteria will generally apply when decisions are taken as to whether or not to provide assistance:

(A) A young person shall be regarded as in need of assistance from the Authority if the Authority is satisfied that:

    (a) the person is qualified to receive assistance from the Authority; and

    (b) taking account of their own wishes and preferences, their cultural background, lifestyle and other circumstances, unless assistance is provided:

        (i) he or she will be at risk of becoming or remaining homeless or otherwise without appropriate accommodation; or

        (ii) he or she will be or become at risk of physical or emotional stress, discomfort, exceptional inconvenience, hardship or harm; or

        (iii) he or she will be unable to secure, preserve or recover their personal independence and freedom to develop; or

        (iv) he or she will be unable to benefit from an educational opportunity, training place or offer of employment which s/he has or will obtain; or

        (v) he or she will be unable to contact or remain in contact with a family member or former foster or residential carer; and

...cont'd

(c) no appropriate assistance is available from any other statutory authority (in particular the Department of Social Security) or from any relevant voluntary organisation or body; and

(d) the Authority is satisfied that any assistance offered will be used for the purpose for which it is to be provided.

(B) A young person shall be entitled to assistance when the Authority is satisfied that s/he needs it and there are resources available to provide for it.

4.00 Eligibility: what sorts of financial assistance can be provided?

4.01 Assistance may be given in cash or in kind to meet the following needs. This list is not exhaustive and, in exceptional circumstances, other assistance can be given if this is necessary:

(a) *weekly daily living expenses*: Young people of 16 or 17 yrs may be unable to claim income support or housing benefit or may be paid at a reduced rate of benefit which will seriously weaken their ability to live independently. Payments may be made by the Authority on a weekly basis to top-up benefits which are received or substitute for them if none are received. Such payments will last as long as the need for them lasts and/or until the young person reaches 18 years and is able to claim benefits at higher and more adequate levels.

(b) *housing or accommodation expenses*: A young person may require a deposit as a down-payment for a tenancy, may need assistance with the payment of rent, or may fall into rent arrears which situation renders their accommodation at risk. The same might apply in relation to liability for council tax and, perhaps more rarely, the cost of household insurance.

(c) *cost of furniture and household equipment*: When a young person moves into new accommodation the cost of furnishing and equipping this will be substantial and may not be met by a grant

...cont'd

or loan from the DSS. Such expenses are commonly met from the Authority's "leaving care grant" paid when a young person first establishes their own home. However, the Authority is not limited to making payments of this type only in these situations.

(d) initial or recurring fuel expenses: In new accommodation, a young person may be required to make a down-payment or deposit to obtain gas or electricity connection or may incur expenses for fuel consumption for which a payment may have to be made.

(e) cost of food: There may be circumstances when a payment should be made to enable a young person to purchase essential food or drink.

(f) cost of clothing: There may be circumstances when a payment should be made to enable a young person to purchase essential new clothing or footwear.

(g) recreation expenses: There may be circumstances when a payment should be made to enable a young person to participate in some recreational activity, hobby or interest.

(h) educational or training expenses: The Authority may make a financial contribution towards the expenses incurred by a young person in living near the place where he or she is or will be receiving education or training. In addition, the Authority may make a grant to enable a young person to meet expenses connected with their education or training. The Authority may continue to make such payment although the young person reaches the age of 21 years before the end of the course in question, and may disregard any interruption in his/her attendance on the course if s/he resumes it as soon as is reasonably practicable. (s. 24 (8) and (9))

(i) employment expenses: The Authority may make a financial contribution towards the expenses incurred by a young person in living near the place where he or she is or will be employed or seeking employment.

...cont'd

(j)   transport expenses: There may be circumstances when the Authority should make a payment to a young person to enable him or her to make a specific journey or series of journeys.

(k)   expenses of former foster carer(s): Where a young person has left foster care but wishes to remain in touch with their former foster parents, then the Authority may make a payment to them to defray or reimburse them any additional costs of providing that young person with accommodation, food or recreation.

4.02 The expenses described in (a) to (k) above do not constitute a fixed or exhaustive list. There may be other expenses for which assistance should be given in order to meet the criteria set out in section 3.00 above.

Appendix C
Documents used in the Hospital

The Patient Pathways Project: *Extracts from Patient Pathway for Diagnosis and Treatment of Cataract*

1.00 INTRODUCTION AND PURPOSE OF PATHWAYS DOCUMENT

1.01 What experiences will a patient have when he or she passes through a routine service, such as for cataract surgery? Will their experience roughly equate with that of a person in similar circumstances who receives the same diagnosis and treatment? Will a patient be able to choose between alternatives or will the patient have choices in the management of their treatment? What are the patient's responsibilities towards those who are treating or caring for them and their own healthcare?

1.02 Agreeing and defining the central features of a particular hospital service is an essential process if these questions are to be faced and answered for patients, their carers, and for professional staff. Not only in this way can the core expectations of the service become clear but the operation can also help to reveal necessary differences in treatment or alternatives which patients can choose between.

1.03 As part of its work with IPPR, the Ophthalmology Directorate has developed the following document to provide – in narrative and visual formats – a framework for describing how a patient referred with a cataract condition will receive treatment from one consultant. Although the project is limited in this way, if its results are effective and of value then the process can be repeated for other treatments and the practice of other consultants. Ultimately, Directorate pathway documents could be produced which reflect agreed approaches towards the treatment of all consultants' patients.

1.04 One aim of the document is to enable multi-disciplinary staff to recognise the occasions when information and explanation for patients

...cont'd

is desirable if not essential, how this should be provided and who should be responsible for doing so. It will therefore be a practical application of the right to information found in the Patient's Charter. Furthermore, it may give staff more confidence in appreciating that for some aspects of the service, clearly defined for the first time in this document, all patients will have clear "rights" which should be respected. Patients have responsibilities towards those who have to diagnose or treat their condition but should be enabled to understand and undertake these. The document will also be able to highlight where the patient has to provide information, make decisions or cooperate with plans made for their care.

1.05 In practice, the pathways approach may better enable the directorate to produce clearer and better quality written information – possibly in a wall chart format – to enable more effective communication of complex details concerning the patient's expectations of the service.

1.06 The document has been produced by a working group including staff from the Ophthalmology Directorate, Medical Directorate and Corporate Planning Department. The group also included a representative of the local Community Health Council. It has been circulated to staff in the Directorate, Admissions Office and Out-patient's Department staff, the Health Authority and GPs who refer patients to the Trust.

1.07 The document will be kept under review and will be formally reviewed after four months in use. All hospital staff and any other individuals who have suggestions or comments to make about the document and its use are requested to use the sheet at the back of this document for this purpose and forward this to [Name], Clinical Director, who is in charge of monitoring this project.

.../...

3.00 OUT PATIENTS CLINIC: DESCRIPTION

3.01 The patient attending the appointment will check in at the reception desk and be asked to wait until his/her name is called. When the nurse is ready she will call the patient into an examination room where she

...cont'd

will ask the patient a few simple questions about his/her sight, administer a short distance sight test, take the patient's blood pressure and take a sample of the person's urine and complete a routine test of urinanalysis.

3.02 The patient will then return to the waiting area to await their consultation with [Consultant]. When this happens [Consultant] will obtain an adequate history of the patient's general health and eye health and conduct a basic examination of the eyes.

3.03 The clinic nurse will then administer drops to the patient's eyes and [Consultant] will measure the intra-ocular pressure in the eyeball.

3.04 After this, the nurse will administer further drops to the patient's eyes to cause the pupils to dilate after approximately 30 minutes. The patient will wait during this time in the waiting area. When the pupils are fully dilated, the patient will again see [Consultant] for the consultation to continue.

3.05 [Consultant] will examine the back of the eye. After this, she will assess the patient's condition and what treatment, if any, should be offered for it. Where the patient has a cataract which can be treated then s/he will be offered treatment. [Consultant] will explain the nature of the operation and will discuss with the patient whether or not s/he agrees to it. If the patient agrees, then [Consultant] will consider with the patient whether the operation should be undertaken as a day or overnight case and whether under local or general anaesthetic. The patient will be asked to state their preference at this stage for day or overnight admission or for local or general anaesthesia. If the patient wishes to have time to think about their decision, is anxious about it or wishes to talk it over with relatives then [Consultant] will permit him/her time to do so, asking the patient to contact her secretary to inform her of the decision. The patient will be normally be given a copy of the Directorate's "cataracts" leaflet. [Consultant] will obtain from the patient details of their social circumstances sufficient to judge whether or not the treatment should be prioritised. Treatment will be listed either as "Urgent" or as "Routine".

...cont'd

3.06 For both [Names of Out-patient Departments] patients, the details of the patient will be passed by [Consultant] to her secretary for entering on the list. In either case, the patient will be asked to telephone the Admissions Officer after seven days to be informed of the likely period when s/he will be called for their operation.

3.07 If the patient's condition is not amenable to treatment, or if the patient declines the offer of treatment, s/he will be discharged. In rare situations, if the position is unclear but may become so in the foreseeable future, the patient will be offered another appointment when their condition will be reviewed.

PATIENTS' RIGHTS AND RESPONSIBILITIES

INFORMATION

3.08 A patient who has been listed for surgery will be given a copy of the Directorate's leaflet on cataracts on leaving the Out-patient clinic together with letter confirming the listing. S/he will be asked to telephone the Admissions Officer in order to learn of the likely date of their admission.

EQUITY

3.09 Patients who are referred for examination and/or treatment may have very different circumstances. [Consultant] will endeavour to ensure:

(i) that all patients in the same or similar circumstances are treated equally; and

(ii) that patients requiring priority in listing for clinical or social reasons are accorded this.

In order to do so, it will be essential for patients to provide [Consultant] will all relevant information and to ensure that any change in their circumstances is reported to their GP and/or to [Consultant].

...cont'd

3.10 Because the administration of eye-drops affects eyes differently, there may be occasions when patients are seen out of order in Out-patients because of delay in the dilatation of the pupil. This practice is to ensure that the time of staff is not wasted and patients who are fit to be examined are not caused unnecessary delay.

CHOICE

3.11 Unless choice has to be restricted by [Consultant] for clinical reasons, a patient is entitled to choose between having surgery under local anaesthetic or under general anaesthetic. In addition, if the patient meets the criteria for day case admission then s/he may choose to be admitted in this way or for an overnight admission.

RESPONSIBILITY

3.12 The patient is responsible for bringing to the clinic appointment details from their GP of the medication which they are taking and will also need to bring with them any spectacles which s/he is using. The patient is responsible for informing the Out-patient's clinic if, for any reason, s/he will not be able to attend their appointment.

3.13 The patient is expected to behave responsibly and appropriately when visiting hospital for his/her appointment.

PATIENT'S CHARTER

3.14 The National Patient's Charter provides the following relevant "rights":

(i) to be given a clear explanation of any treatment proposed, including any risks and any alternatives, before the patient decides whether or not to agree to the treatment;

(ii) to be guaranteed admission for treatment by a specific date no later than 18 months from the day when the consultant places the patient on the waiting list;

...cont'd

And the following relevant National Charter standards:

(i) arrangements to ensure everyone, including people with special needs, can use services;

(ii) patients will be given a specific appointment time and be seen within 30 minutes of that time;

And the following relevant Local Charter standard:

> ...to be guaranteed admission for treatment by a specific date no later than 12 months from the day the consultant places the patient on the waiting list.

...cont'd

3.15 OUTPATIENTS CLINIC: PLAN

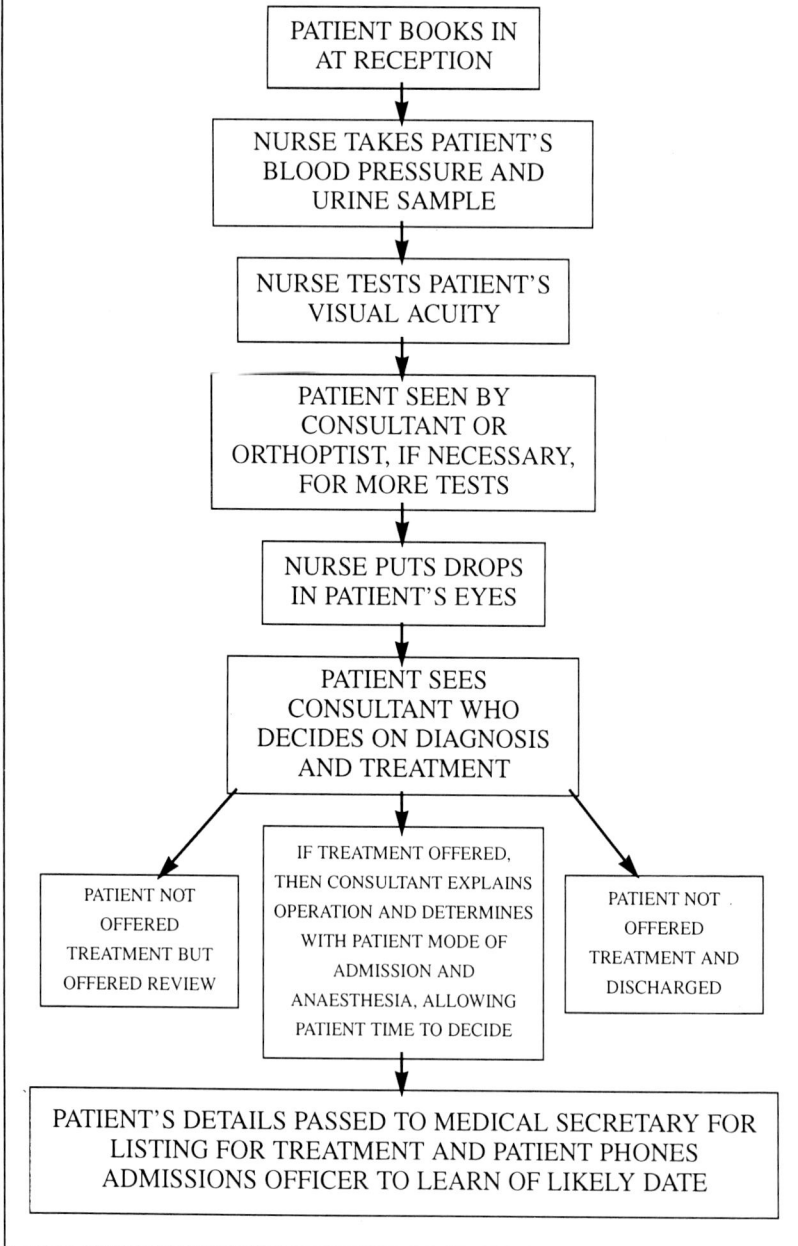

```
            PATIENT BOOKS IN
             AT RECEPTION
                   │
                   ▼
           NURSE TAKES PATIENT'S
           BLOOD PRESSURE AND
              URINE SAMPLE
                   │
                   ▼
           NURSE TESTS PATIENT'S
             VISUAL ACUITY
                   │
                   ▼
             PATIENT SEEN BY
             CONSULTANT OR
        ORTHOPTIST, IF NECESSARY,
             FOR MORE TESTS
                   │
                   ▼
            NURSE PUTS DROPS
            IN PATIENT'S EYES
                   │
                   ▼
              PATIENT SEES
             CONSULTANT WHO
          DECIDES ON DIAGNOSIS
             AND TREATMENT
```

| PATIENT NOT OFFERED TREATMENT BUT OFFERED REVIEW | IF TREATMENT OFFERED, THEN CONSULTANT EXPLAINS OPERATION AND DETERMINES WITH PATIENT MODE OF ADMISSION AND ANAESTHESIA, ALLOWING PATIENT TIME TO DECIDE | PATIENT NOT OFFERED TREATMENT AND DISCHARGED |

PATIENT'S DETAILS PASSED TO MEDICAL SECRETARY FOR LISTING FOR TREATMENT AND PATIENT PHONES ADMISSIONS OFFICER TO LEARN OF LIKELY DATE

The Prompt List Project: *The Prompt List*

"WHAT DO YOU WANT TO ASK THE DOCTOR?"

We want to help **you** to get the best information from us when you need it. Please read these before your appointment. Feel free to raise them – *and any other queries which you may have* – with the doctor or nurse who you see when you visit the hospital.

What is a cataract?

How long will I be in hospital?

How long will my operation last?

Will I be asleep during the operation?

How likely is the operation to be effective?

I am currently on medication. Do I continue this when I have my operation?

Will I need to change my glasses afterwards?

Following the operation, what activities (for example, driving a car or washing hair) can I do and what can I not do?

Do I have to wear dark glasses after the operation?

After the operation will I have to come back to the hospital again?

Use this space to write down any other question which you want to ask

. . . .

. . . .

The Wait-listing Project   Extract from "Wait-listing Guidelines"

WAIT-LISTING FOR OUT-PATIENTS CLINIC APPOINTMENTS

Listing category	Clinical factors	Social factors	Maximum waiting time
"URGENT"	Patient under 1 year old Eye injury Acute glaucoma Condition requires urgent assessment due to its sudden deterioration or instability		One week of decision to list
"PRIORITY"	All other glaucoma All other patients below 14 years of age Consultant has agreed to expedite patient's appointment following GP's request Patient has been referred by other Consultant	Patient responsible for minor children or adult relative Patient's employment affected by condition Patient virtually blind ie v. poor sight in both eyes	Six weeks of decision to list
"ROUTINE"	Not as above	Not as above	Up to 14 weeks

WAIT-LISTING FOR TREATMENT

Listing category	Clinical factors	Social factors	Maximum waiting time
"URGENT"	Patient under 1 year old Eye injury Acute glaucoma Condition requires urgent treatment since it is sight threatening		List and call within week of request or next op list whichever is sooner
"PRIORITY"	All other glaucoma All other patients below 14 years of age Patient's consultant agrees to expedite after request from GP	Patient responsible for minor children or adult dependant Patient's employment affected by condition Patient virtually blind ie v. poor sight in both eyes	Within 6 weeks to two months
"ROUTINE"	Not as above and condition treatable and patient him/herself agrees	Not as above and condition impairs lifestyle of patient to degree patient cannot cope with	Up to 12 months (Trust max)

The Wait-listing Leaflet

[The Hospital]
NHS TRUST etc.

Dear Patient

This confirms that I will now arrange for you to have an operation for . . . . .I will be the consultant responsible for your treatment and I will tell your GP about the operation.

Shortly before your operation, the Eye Ward Admissions Officer will write to you giving details of all the necessary arrangements. In the meantime, please read or have read to you the essential information for patients provided on the inside of this leaflet.

Yours sincerely

[Name of Consultant]

Consultant Ophthalmic Surgeon

...cont'd

ESSENTIAL INFORMATION FOR PATIENTS

THE DATE FOR YOUR OPERATION

To find out the likely date when we call you for your operation, please phone Mrs [Name of officer] (Eye Ward Admissions Officer) on [tel. no.] after fourteen days. Mrs [Name] will also explain to you how we might be able to treat you earlier, if you are willing to come into hospital at short notice.

THE PATIENT'S CHARTER GUARANTEE

In line with the Patient's Charter, the [The Hospital] NHS Trust guarantees that no patient will have to wait longer than 12 months from the date s/he is listed before having their operation.

PRIORITY LISTING

Some patients' operations must be given priority. This is because their *condition* is serious or causing difficulties in other ways, for example affecting their job or their ability to care for other family members.

We will arrange the date of your operation in the light of what we presently know of your condition and your circumstances. Unless I tell you, your operation will not be given special priority. If your condition worsens or your circumstances change, then I may need to bring forward your operation. Please see your GP if you feel that this ought to happen. If your doctor agrees, then s/he will contact me to arrange this.

FURTHER INFORMATION ABOUT YOUR OPERATION

We ask you to come into hospital for an assessment shortly before your operation takes place. On this occasion, we will decide if you will need to be admitted as an inpatient and whether you should have a local or general anaesthetic. In each case, *unless medical reasons prevent this* you will have the right to choose.

If you have any questions concerning your condition or the planned operation then you should ask these at this appointment.

Appendix D
Documents used in the Co-op

Pro Forma for Medical Decision-making under Paragraph 13

1. Do you have enough information to decide if the patient needs a consultation out-of-hours?

   No: seek more information.
   Yes: go to Q.2

2. Does the patient need a consultation out-of hours?

   Yes: go to Q. 3.
   No: indicate reason below:

   ✓ here

   ☐ Clinical condition not requiring a medical consultation

   ☐ Condition can wait to be seen by own doctor on . . . .
   at . . . .

   ☐ Patient referred urgently to Hospital

   ☐ Other(specify) . . . .

   Where applicable, please confirm patient told the reason why no consultation to be offered.

   Patient told at . . . . .am/pm on . . . .

3. Should the patient's out-of-hours consultation be at the BASE SURGERY?

   No: arrange for patient to be seen at home.

   ...cont'd

Yes: please confirm by ticking box that in your judgement the patient should be required to attend the Base Surgery for their consultation:

☐ ✓ here

Please also confirm that in making this decision you considered the relevance of each of the following factors:

✓ here

☐   Nature or degree of patient's condition

☐   Patient's physical immobility or frailty

☐   Patient's mental or emotional state

☐   Patient's responsibility for dependants

☐   Patient's access to reasonable means of transport

☐   Prevailing weather conditions

Please confirm that when you asked the patient to attend the Base Surgery, you gave the reason for this and patient stated s/he understood your explanation.

Patient told at . . . . .am/pm on . . . .

Does patient agree to attend Base Surgery for consultation?

Yes / No (Please circle)

If no, what reason (if any) does patient give you for not agreeing to attend Base Surgery? . . . .

Explanatory Notes for use by [THE CO-OP] Doctors when using
Paragraph 13 Pro Forma

1.00 Introduction

1.01 The Paragraph 13 Pro forma has been prepared to assist individual
Doctors, and [THE CO-OP] staff supporting them, to decide how to
respond to a call to the service from or on behalf of a patient seeking
assistance. These explanatory notes accompany the form. They should
be read in conjunction with the relevant terms of service (paragraph 13,
National Health Service (General Medical Services) Regulations, as
amended). Anyone using these notes should be particularly aware of
the recent changes made to those terms. These permit Deputising
Doctors (ie [THE CO-OP] On-Call doctors) to reasonably require the
attendance of a patient at an approved Out-of-Hours Centre (such as
[THE CO-OP]'s Base Surgery at [NAME]).

1.02 Doctors undertaking [THE CO-OP] sessions may welcome advice on
how they should approach the task of responding to calls in the light of
those changes. This may be so in view of the impact which their
decisions may have on patients and the possibility that when Doctors
seek to encourage greater use of the Base Surgery, patients may not
understand the reason why no visit at home is to be arranged unless
specific steps are taken to encourage this. The pro forma is being
piloted in [THE CO-OP] and after evaluation may be recommended for
use in other out-of-hours cooperatives in [AREA].

1.03 The notes attempt to provide such advice and explain how a doctor
may use the pro forma in his or her practice. They have been produced
as part of a research project on "procedural rights" and may help both
doctors and patients to be clear as to the reason or reasons for the
doctor's decision. This may also encourage all those affected to believe
that such decisions have been made fairly and appropriately, taking
account of all relevant considerations.

...cont'd

2.00 Status of Pro forma and notes

2.01 The pro forma and these notes offer guidance only. Neither are required by law and they cannot have the force of law. Nor can they replace the need for an individual doctor both to make his/her own judgement on the application of Paragraph 13, and also to remain personally accountable for any such judgement. However, they have been discussed with the Family Health Services Authority and with the local Community Health Council. [here refer to views of each of these, if available and helpful]

2.02 General Practitioners who undertake [THE CO-OP] sessions and wish to use the pro forma and notes in their practice may find that there are circumstances when there may be good reasons for ignoring them. Their use is entirely voluntary and if a doctor judges that, in order to comply with his/her legal and/or professional obligations, it is necessary to disregard them, then s/he must be at liberty to do so.

3.00 Responsibility of the Doctor

3.01 After a call has been referred to a Doctor for action then it is the personal [and sole?] responsibility of that Doctor ("the Doctor") to determine whether or not the patient should be seen, and if so, whether s/he should be seen at home, at the Base Surgery or elsewhere.

3.02 Under the Terms and Conditions of Service the Doctor on Call is responsible in law for their acts or omissions. It is not the responsibility of [THE CO-OP]. [This needs to be clarified with the Directors]

4.00 Using the pro forma

4.01 In determining whether the patient should be seen, and if so where, the Doctor has to have regard to the wording of Paragraph 13. When applying this in practice, a series of questions have to be addressed. The pro forma identifies the main questions and, in addition, suggests a number of common factors which a doctor may wish to have in mind when making a decision.

...cont'd

SHOULD THE PATIENT HAVE A CONSULTATION OUT-OF-HOURS?

4.02 Firstly, the Doctor must discover as much information about the patient's medical condition as will enable him/her to decide whether or not it is necessary for the patient to have a consultation at all. To comply with the Terms of Service, the Doctor must form a reasonable opinion on the facts as known, bearing in mind:

- the next time when the patient could be seen during working hours and

- the need, if any, for the patient to be referred to hospital.

In practice, the Doctor will usually decide this after interviewing the patient (or the patient's parent or other relative or carer) on the telephone, and after offering all necessary and appropriate verbal advice. In urgent circumstances, the Doctor may decide to rely on information obtained from reception staff rather than directly from the patient, for example, where s/he decides, in the light of it, that the patient should have a consultation/examination at home or should be urgently advised to attend hospital. The pro forma is not for use in such circumstances.

4.03 If the Doctor decides that the patient does not need an out-of-hours consultation then the pro forma should show the reason for this decision. This could be because the person's medical condition does not require any consultation, or the person could wait to be seen by their own doctor, or the person has been referred to hospital. If there is another reason then this should be specified and, where applicable, the Doctor should confirm that the patient has been informed of the decision and the reason for it.

...cont'd

> ### IF THE PATIENT NEEDS AN OUT-OF-HOURS CONSULTATION, WHERE SHOULD IT BE?

4.04 If the Doctor decides that it is necessary for the patient to have a consultation out-of-hours then s/he will have to decide where this should take place. The patient may have to be told to come to the Base Surgery, and, if so, of the reason(s) for this.

> ### SHOULD IT BE AT THE BASE SURGERY OR SHOULD IT BE AT THE PATIENT'S HOME?

4.05 The Base Surgery has been approved by the FHSA in accordance with paragraph 29A of the Regulations and therefore *patients can be required to attend it if the Doctor decides that this is necessary.*

4.06 If the Doctor decides that a home visit should be arranged then nothing more need be written on the pro forma. On the other hand, if the Doctor decides that it is appropriate for the patient to be seen at the Base Surgery and it is reasonable to require the patient to attend it for a consultation, then the Doctor can use the pro forma to confirm the reason. In effect, the Doctor is asked to indicate that in his/her judgement there are no factors which are present which make a home visit necessary or advisable.

> ### WHAT FACTORS COULD BE RELEVANT TO THE CHOICE OF LOCATION?

4.07 Many different factors may be relevant to the Doctor's choice of location and some may weigh more heavily with some doctors than with others. Although Paragraph 13 stresses the importance of clinical factors and makes no mention of social factors, it is self-evident that patients' social circumstances vary significantly. As a result, some patients will be far better able (and may be more willing) to use the Base Surgery than others. The pro forma and these notes offer a number of commonly encountered factors that a survey of [THE CO-OP] visits suggested might be relevant from time to time. These notes

...cont'd

do not prescribe how the Doctor should treat any of these factors nor the weight which should be given to them. The list is intended to trigger a consideration of the issues. Furthermore, confirmation that it has been used may reassure patients that the decision was fairly and properly made.

FACTORS WHICH MAY AFFECT DOCTOR'S CHOICE OF LOCATION:

- NATURE OR DEGREE OF PATIENT'S CONDITION

- PATIENT'S PHYSICAL MOBILITY OR FRAILTY

- PATIENT'S MENTAL OR EMOTIONAL STATE

- PATIENT'S RESPONSIBILITY FOR DEPENDANTS

- PATIENT'S ACCESS TO REASONABLE MEANS OF TRANSPORT

- PREVAILING WEATHER CONDITIONS

4.08 **The nature or degree of the patient's clinical condition** and the risk of its further deterioration, caused by his/her having to attend the Base Surgery. This is clearly the main factor. Examples might include the breathless patient; or one who suffers from a condition which will be affected by exertion or exposure to cold air. It may not be reasonable to expect a patient to attend the Base Surgery whose clinical condition might be harmed or put at risk by their having to do so, and the Doctor may decide that such a patient should be seen at home.

4.09 **The physical mobility or frailty of the patient.** A patient whose physical mobility is significantly affected by age, illness or disability such that being required to attend the Base Surgery would be impossible or difficult may need to be seen at home. This could include a patient whose condition impairs their mobility (eg by making them dizzy or disorientated) although it would not be made any worse by travelling. Whilst a Doctor may decide that a frail elderly patient should be seen at home, s/he may consider that an accompanied child

...cont'd

patient clinically fit to travel and who can be transported without difficulty, may be expected to attend the Base Surgery unless other considerations rule this out.

4.10 **The patient's mental or emotional state.** There may be occasions when it would be unreasonable to expect a confused or very distressed patient to attend the Base Surgery and such a patient should be seen at home. It would also be unreasonable to expect a patient to travel whose condition (eg diarrhoea; vomiting) could cause them serious embarrassment if required to be in the company of others (eg on a bus). A child patient who is distressed but who is clinically fit to travel, may nevertheless be required to attend the Base Surgery with a parent or carer.

4.11 **The responsibility, if any, which the patient has for any dependants.** Patients' circumstances vary greatly and so will their ability to arrange or summon assistance to care for a dependant or dependants whilst a visit is made to the Base Surgery. A Doctor may decide that it is inadvisable to require a patient who has sole responsibility for a dependant or dependants to arrange at short notice their care or supervision.

4.12 **The ability of the patient, or their relative, friend or carer, to use private transport** (eg own car) to travel to the Base Surgery. A Doctor may decide that a patient with access to such transport and who is fit to travel should normally be required to attend the Base Surgery for a consultation.

4.13 **The affordability and availability of any alternative means of transport** (eg taxi), and the patient's stated ability to pay for this. Some patients will not have their own means of transport. Where other means of transport are unavailable or unreasonably costly then a Doctor may decide that it would be proper to visit him/her at home.

4.14 **The weather conditions prevailing at the time the call is made.** When severe weather conditions (eg snowstorm, torrential rainstorm, severe ice or fog) make it difficult or impossible for a patient to travel to the Base Surgery then a Doctor may decide that the patient should be seen at home.

...cont'd

4.15 **Any other factor.** No list of factors can attempt to be comprehensive and this one is not. If a Doctor considers a factor is relevant to deciding a fair, lawful and professional response to the patient's request then s/he is at liberty to do so.

5.00 Recording the Decision and informing the patient

5.01 Where a Doctor decides that the patient should be required to attend the Base Surgery and will not be entitled to a consultation in their home, then s/he shall ensure that the reasons for this decision are recorded and that the patient is clearly informed of them. The pro forma which accompanies these notes may be used for this purpose.

5.02 When a pro forma is used then the completed form should be attached to [THE CO-OP]'s copy of the numerical record sheet.